W9-DEX-969

The Techniques of Writing

THIRD EDITION

The Techniques of Writing

THIRD EDITION

Paul Kinsella

JEFFERSON COMMUNITY COLLEGE

HARCOURT BRACE JOVANOVICH, INC.

NEW YORK   SAN DIEGO   CHICAGO   SAN FRANCISCO   ATLANTA
LONDON   SYDNEY   TORONTO

To My Students

(. . . with gratitude for their kindness and encouragement in the writing and revising of this book)

Copyright © 1981, 1975, 1969, 1968, 1967 by Harcourt Brace Jovanovich, Inc.

All rights reserved. No part of this publication, including removable pages, may be reproduced or transmitted in any form or by any means, electronic or mechanical, including photocopy, recording, or any information storage and retrieval system, without permission in writing from the publisher. Although for mechanical reasons all pages of this publication are perforated, only those pages imprinted with an HBJ copyright notice are intended for removal.

Requests for permission to make copies of any part of the work should be mailed to: Permissions, Harcourt Brace Jovanovich, Inc., 757 Third Avenue, New York, N.Y. 10017.

ISBN: 0-15-589728-4

Library of Congress Catalog Card Number: 80-83211

Printed in the United States of America

A NOTE TO THE INSTRUCTOR

The Techniques of Writing stresses basic principles that students need to know if they are to write acceptably on the college level. It gives priority to the problems that seem to occur most frequently in the writing of undergraduates, as indicated by errors and deficiencies in the themes I have graded over the years. And, for the most part, the presentation of topics follows my strong conviction that it is better to teach a few principles thoroughly than many superficially.

I have tried throughout to emphasize writing as a branch of language closely related to speaking rather than as a highly technical and special form of communication. I am convinced that many college students, especially the ones who find writing most difficult, have developed a psychological block. They are often confused by grammatical terms and definitions and tend to believe that writing is almost totally unrelated to speaking. Thus their compositions are often pretentious, imprecise, and nearly incomprehensible. Like its predecessors, this new edition of the book urges students to take advantage of their innate language abilities in overcoming the fear of writing. And toward this end, it offers a new opening chapter devoted to the problems involved in getting started on a writing task.

If you face the usual constraints of an academic setting, the following observations on presenting the book's material to students may prove helpful to you. First, given the number of students I teach each semester, it is impractical for me to assign a composition more often than every other week. Thus, in a fifteen-week period, I usually ask my students to write about six or seven compositions, most of them under one thousand words. However, by assigning the exercises in this book, I am also able to give my students a considerable amount of practice at writing that does not require subjective grading.

Each of the exercises in the book—there are now ninety-nine—can be given as classwork or as homework. But, however an exercise has been assigned, after it is handed in I always discuss the answers in class so that the students can benefit from the answers of their classmates. While some of the exercises require more time than others, none of them should take more than fifteen minutes; most students should be able to complete and discuss several exercises in one session. Over the years, I have found that the mixing of lecture, practice, and discussion has a number of advantages. Among the most important is the fact that this technique holds the student's attention much better than the traditional lecture approach usually does.

I have also found that I obtain better results when I spread the exercises in a chapter over the entire semester, rather than assigning all or most of them with the reading of the chapter. For the most part, the exercises on any given topic in the book have the same degree of difficulty. Only the exercises in the chapters on sentence structure vary in this regard, becoming progressively more difficult.

In the chapter on punctuation, along with the usual exercises there are several lengthy ones that review all the fundamentals explained in the text. Each of these exercises is headed "General Review of Punctuation" and can either be assigned toward the end of the semester as intensive study or given as a final exam.

One of my basic assumptions in revising this book has been that students in the 1980s are more visually oriented than students of even the recent past. They learn more by seeing and doing than by listening to oral instructions. I have found that many of my students (perhaps most of them) need to go over a grammatical principle by themselves a number of times before it "sinks in." Consequently, in this new edition I have increased both the number of sample sentences for many principles and the number of exercises at the end of most chapters.

Whatever your approach to the material, I wish you and your students great success in using *The Techniques of Writing*. If reading it generates comments or questions that you would like to bring to my attention, please do not hesitate to write to me. I will be pleased to hear from you.

I would like to take this opportunity to acknowledge the suggestions of the following instructors: Sister Mary Cyrilla Kendra, Mount Aloysius Junior College; Leo Rockas, University of Hartford; and Victor B. Watson, College of the Southwest. In addition, I would like to express my gratitude to all those who assisted me at Harcourt Brace Jovanovich—especially Carolyn Johnson and Marguerite L. Egan.

PAUL KINSELLA

CONTENTS

3: Organizing the Composition   37

4: Introduction and Conclusion   65

5: Logic for Composition   81

16: Spelling   353

The Techniques of Writing

THIRD EDITION

1: Getting Started

USING KEY THOUGHT WORDS

For most people, the most difficult step in writing is the first one: getting started. For example, your English teacher may walk into the classroom on a Monday morning and assign a 500-word composition that is due the following Monday. You may be given a topic or allowed to pick your own; but unless you have a good background in writing, you may not know where to begin. So you put off the ordeal until the last minute and finally dash off something that is far below your capabilities.

If you think carefully about how you think, you may discover that you use just a few key words in organizing your thoughts and that you frequently use these words to ask questions. For the most part this mental process is unconscious. However, for the sake of improving your writing (especially to help you get started), we intend to make you very much aware of this mental activity. What you learn about it should help you in constructing sentences, in organizing paragraphs, and in completing all types of writing—from a short composition to a lengthy book.

The seven key thought words are as follows:

HOW   IF   WHAT   WHEN   WHERE   WHO   WHY

(We could have included the word *whom;* however, most people use *who* in place of *whom.* So to simplify matters, we shall use *who* to denote the subject as well as the object of a sentence.)

These words are listed in alphabetical order to help you memorize them. You should be able to recall them as readily as your name and address, for we shall be using them over and over in this and succeeding chapters.

The use of key thought words is a great help in solving two of the most difficult problems in writing: (1) getting started and (2) limiting your topic. Getting started is difficult for a number of reasons. For most people, writing is an unpleasant task; for some it is downright torture.

When we finally sit down to write, unless we have written the same thoughts before, we usually have just a vague idea of what we want to say. Our thoughts are in a state of flux. We don't know where to begin or exactly how to introduce our ideas and support them with details. Anxiety and false starts result. The second problem can be equally frustrating.

Most textbooks on writing advise students to limit their topics. This is indeed an important writing principle—and one that is frequently violated. In such instances, the piece of writing produced is likely to lack logical order and coherence. In other words, it is likely to be nothing more than nonsense; and seldom is nonsense a writer's goal. Using one or more of the key thought words as a starting point is an easy way to limit your topic in writing a paragraph or a composition.

Before explaining why the use of key thought words is the best means of solving both problems, let us see how these words can be related to the basic unit of most compositions—the sentence. Most English sentences can be diagramed in terms of the key thought words.

Who or What Subject	Predicate	Whom (Who) or What Object
what kind / adjective	how / adverb when / adverb where / adverb why / adverb	what kind / adjective

THE ABILITY TO GENERALIZE

The ability to generalize is probably one of the most important functions of the human mind, and without doubt it is a crucial ability in writing. For unless you can generalize you will not be able to formulate an adequate topic sentence for a paragraph or a main idea (or thesis) statement for a whole composition.

ASKING QUESTIONS

Relating one or more of the key thought words to your topic and asking a question is an easy way to get started on a writing task. After you have asked your question, answer it with a generalization; this generalization can become the topic sentence for your paragraph or the main idea (or thesis) statement for your composition. We will explain this concept further in the chapters that follow. For now, let us consider some examples of what you should *not* do if this technique is to help you solve the frustrating problems of getting started and limiting your topic.

WHAT NOT TO DO

If possible, use only one thought word in asking the topic or main idea question.

Poor	*Where* did we visit and *how* did we spend our time?
Better	*How* did we spend our time on our visit to New York?
Poor	*What* is my favorite sport and *why?*
Better	*Why* is football my favorite sport?
Poor	*Who* is my best friend and *why?*
Better	*Why* is Leora my best friend?

The topic sentence or the main idea (or thesis) statement must be understandable without the topic or main idea question.

Question:	How can we parents help to motivate our children to do well in school?
Statement:	
Poor	By encouraging our children to do their best at all times.
Better	As parents we can motivate our children to do well in school by encouraging them to do their best at all times.

Be sure that what is used as a topic question or main idea (thesis) question is really a question.

Poor	What I did when I spent a day in San Francisco?
Better	What did I do when I spent a day in San Francisco?
Poor	How to raise African violets?
Better	How do you raise African violets?

Be sure that the main idea statement or topic sentence provides a direct answer to the question.

Question:	How do you make yeast bread?
Statement:	
Poor	Although the making of delicious yeast bread is an art, it is one that can be readily acquired.
Better	In making yeast bread, you must first of all acquire the necessary ingredients and then follow a time-tested recipe with care and precision.
Question:	How do you give a baby a bath?
Statement:	
Poor	Bathing a baby is not as complicated as it may seem.
Better	In giving a baby a bath, a person must have the right materials and follow the correct procedures.

Question:	How do you change the oil in an automobile?
Statement:	
Poor	Changing the oil in your automobile on a regular basis can extend the life of your engine.
Better	Anyone changing the oil in an automobile should be sure to follow a few simple steps.

USING A TAPE RECORDER

Another technique that sometimes helps the "stuck" writer get started is the use of a tape recorder. Although it is best not to depend on this "crutch," it may be employed as a rescue when the more conventional approach has proven unsuccessful. Thinking out loud (with or without a recorder) often helps a writer crystallize ideas that have remained vague despite periods of prolonged silent thinking. You may find that freeing yourself (temporarily) from the mechanics of writing allows you to concentrate more on the formulation of your thoughts. Indeed, closing your eyes as you think and/or speak may also add to your concentration.

When you do use a tape recorder, you may be able to dictate the first draft of your composition in a matter of minutes. But then, of course, you will have to listen to the playback and transcribe what you have dictated. Moreover, in all likelihood you will have to do considerable rewriting, probably more than on an undictated first draft. Taping is only a means of shortening the first step of the writing process; the same distance has to be covered whatever your method. As you gain experience at it, handling the mechanics of writing as you formulate your thoughts should become easier and easier, making a tape recorder unnecessary. This electronic aid can serve a purpose, but it is no substitute for the regular method of writing. You should learn to organize your thoughts quickly and write without too much hesitation, for much of your written work in college will be done in class as short compositions and essay exams. Using the key thought words and other devices of organization explained in this book should help you to write a first draft that needs little or no revision.

PROOFREADING

However you compose your work, with a tape recorder or without, proofread it carefully! Many of the mistakes that appear in writing can be traced to careless proofreading. (When a written work is a transcription, gross omissions or substitutions are particularly likely.) One of the best ways to proofread involves using a blank piece of paper or some other straight-edged object to cover up the line or lines below the one you are reading. This "cover up" method helps you to focus on each word and thus to see mistakes (such as spelling errors) that you might not see otherwise. It is also a good idea to proofread aloud, thereby making it easier to check style as well as accuracy. When you come across a word or passage that does not sound right, you should assume that it will be a stumbling block for other readers. Such impediments, of course, should be removed.

In the chapters that follow, we shall devote much attention to the key thought words. Once you acquire the knack of using them in a question related to your topic, you should find your writing not only easier but much improved. Again, we suggest that you commit these words to memory. Perhaps the easiest way to remember them is alphabetically:

HOW   IF   WHAT   WHEN   WHERE   WHO   WHY

SUGGESTED TOPICS FOR PARAGRAPHS
AND COMPOSITIONS

Many composition students faced with an assignment complain, "My teacher said that we could pick our own topic, but I can't think of anything to write about." To help you with this dilemma, we are listing below a number of topics that you might consider if your teacher does not assign a specific topic. They are presented in no particular order. Most of them, by the way, relate to personal experience and do not require any special knowledge.

Being the Oldest (Middle, Youngest) Child
Being a Twin
An Unforgettable Experience
Television and Maturity
A Visit to a Large City
An Outstanding Speaker
My Favorite Writer
My Best High-School Teacher
A Group Activity in Which I Participated
The Difference Between High School and College
Giving and Receiving Advice
Learning Away From School
My Favorite Sport
Succeeding in College
Young People and Their Music
Attending a Local College
Attending an Out-of-Town College
People and Conformity
An Important Decision in My Life
My Goal in Life
Changes I Would Like to See Made in Government
Motorcycle Riding
My Favorite Season of the Year
Choosing a Car
Admirable Personality Traits
My Best Friend
Experience Is the Best Teacher

How I Spend My Leisure Time
An Unusual Incident
A Foreign Country I Would Like to Visit
My Home Town
A Family Custom
My Interest in Nature
Changing Fashions
What I May Live to See
What the Future Holds
My First Job
My Present Job
An Unforgettable Experience
A Humorous Incident
An Outstanding Movie
A Poor Movie
My Favorite Music
A Time When I Was Really Scared
An Obstacle I Overcame
An Experience on Water
Overcoming Prejudices
Gaining a Sense of Identity
An Embarrassing Moment
The Need for Self-Confidence
Spring in the Air
A Day in Autumn
Never Again
Raising a Family
Honesty Is the Best Policy
Qualities of a Good Teacher
A Business Venture
My Greatest Ambition
Having Good Friends
If I Were a Millionaire
A Sporting Event I Will Never Forget
Safe Driving
Giving a Party
A Day at the Zoo
Jury Duty
Camping
My Favorite Television Show
Umpiring Softball

EXERCISE 1

Using the seven key thought words, formulate questions on seven different topics. The topics may be taken from the list given at the end of this chapter, or you may pick your own or use those assigned by your instructor. Answer each of the questions with an appropriate generalization. This exercise is designed to give you practice in formulating main idea (or thesis) statements and topic sentences. Make sure that you avoid the pitfalls that have been explained under the heading *What Not to Do*.

Topic_____

Question_____

Statement_____

_____

Topic_____

Question_____

Statement_____

_____

Topic_____

Question_____

Statement_____

_____

Topic_____

Question_____

Statement_____

_____

Topic_____

Question_____

Statement _____

_____

Topic _____
Question _____
Statement _____

_____

Topic _____
Question _____
Statement _____

_____

 © 1981 HBJ

2: The Paragraph

BASIC ELEMENTS

If you can write good paragraphs, you should have little or no trouble in writing a successful composition. The standard paragraph consists of one or more sentences. It is always begun on a new line and is usually indented about half an inch if you are writing in longhand or five spaces if you are typing. Most standard paragraphs develop a single topic, which is usually mentioned at the beginning of the paragraph. However, a topic sentence may relate to more than one paragraph in a series. The writer may decide to divide an excessively long paragraph into shorter units to make the writing easier to read. In such a case, the shorter paragraphs may or may not have subtopic sentences. Listed below are the five basic elements of a standard paragraph:

Topic Sentence   A lone paragraph or the first paragraph in a series of paragraphs should have a topic sentence. A good way to compose a topic sentence is to formulate a question related to your topic using one of the key thought words. Answer the question with a general statement; this generalization is your topic sentence. It is all right to use questions as the first sentences in your paragraphs—as long as you do not overuse them.

An outline can be of great help in writing topic sentences; for if it is a clear blueprint of what you intend to communicate, the main and subordinate ideas should inspire an appropriate generalization. In some instances the topic is implied rather than stated directly, but use of this technique is not recommended until you have gained proficiency in writing the standard paragraph where the topic sentence appears at the beginning or the end.

Sufficient Details   A paragraph should contain enough details to develop the topic or subtopic sentence. Unless general ideas are backed up with specific details, the writer runs the risk of creating overlapping generalizations, which represent a serious flaw in writing. The best way to avoid this problem is to plan your paragraphs carefully by means of a topic outline. This technique will be discussed at length in the next chapter.

Unity   Make sure that every idea and fact in your paragraph is related to the topic sentence. One of the most common problems in writing is digression (straying from the topic)—the tendency to include ideas and facts that are not directly related to the topic sentence. This problem will not occur if you test the relevance of the details in your outline before you write your paragraphs.

Logical Order   The sentences of a paragraph should be arranged in a logical order. The first sentence should come first for some logical reason; the second should come next for some logical reason, and so on. Sometimes the order of the middle sentences makes little or no difference from the standpoint of logic, but it may matter stylistically. You should always test the order of your sentences to make sure that the most understandable and most pleasing arrangement has been achieved.

Coherence   The logical relationships within a sentence or between sentences should be clearly implied or stated. The best way to achieve this important quality in your writing is to strive for unity and logical order. Another good way is to use transitional words and phrases. Transitionals should not be overused, however; and, of course, only the appropriate word or phrase should be chosen. Listed below are some of the transitional words and phrases you will find most helpful.

TRANSITIONAL WORDS AND PHRASES

1. To indicate an *order* of arrangement (importance, time, etc.)

after	from now on	prior
afterward	in the days ahead	recent
at other times	in the future	simultaneously
at the same time	later	someday
before	meanwhile	soon
constantly	next	still
eventually	now	subsequently
finally	over the years	then
first, second, third	presently	thereafter
for the time being	previously	ultimately
frequently		until

2. To indicate an *addition*

additionally	as well as	just as
again	besides	likewise
along with	further	moreover
also	furthermore	similarly
and	in addition	too
another	in like manner	what is more
	in the same way	

3. To indicate an *alternative, contrast,* or *exception*

although	instead	rather
at any rate	lest	still
but	neither	though
despite	nevertheless	unless
either	nor	unlike
except	not	when
however	on the other hand	where
if	or	whereas
in contrast	otherwise	while
in spite of		yet

4. To indicate a *conclusion, effect,* or *summary*

accordingly	in consequence
all in all	in short
as a result	so
consequently	the point is
hence	therefore
in brief	thus
in conclusion	to sum up

5. To indicate *how* or *why*

as	for
because	in order
by	since

6. To introduce an *example* or *illustration*

for example	namely
for instance	that is

7. To *emphasize* or *clarify*

actually	in other words
as a matter of fact	indeed
in fact	of course

8. To indicate an *afterthought* or *something of minor importance*

by the way
incidentally

9. To indicate a *generalization*

as a general rule	in general
generally	on the whole

10. To indicate a *possibility* or *probability*

apparently	possibly
if	presumably
maybe	probably
perhaps	usually

11. To indicate a *certainty* or *likelihood*

certainly	obviously
evidently	surely
naturally	unquestionably
no doubt	without a doubt

12. To refer to *something previously mentioned*

it	they
such	this
that	where
the former	which
the latter	who
there	whom
these	

The rules for punctuating transitional phrases will be explained fully in the chapters on sentence structure and punctuation. The following lists and guidelines should help you to understand the basic differences among those words and phrases that function within a sentence as conjunctions.

1 *Coordinate* *Conjunctions*	2 *Correlative* *Conjunctions*	3 *Subordinate* *Conjunctions*
and	not only . . . but also	if
but	neither . . . nor	when
for	either . . . or	after
nor	both . . . and	while
or		until
		since
		before
		unless
		because
		whether
		although

4
Conjunctions that are preceded by a semicolon
when used to join two independent clauses
(*So* and *yet* are sometimes considered coordinate conjunctions.)

so	however
yet	moreover
thus	therefore
then	furthermore
hence	consequently
	nevertheless

Guidelines

1. A semicolon generally comes before words from List 4 when they join two independent clauses.
2. A comma is usually placed after the longer words (two or more syllables) from List 4 when they join two independent clauses.
3. A comma is *not* usually placed before or after words from List 3.
4. A comma is usually placed before words from List 1 when they join two independent clauses.
5. A comma is *not* usually placed before or after words from List 2 (conjunctions used in pairs).

LENGTH

The typical paragraph in your composition—thus excluded are introductory, transitional, or concluding paragraphs—should be more than one or two sentences long. If your composition consists mainly of paragraphs of less than three sentences, your major points will probably be underdeveloped. You will not have presented sufficient details to back up your topic sentence. On the other hand, you should avoid making your paragraphs too long. A 500-word composition written in longhand with some paragraphs a page or more in length is likely to be a burden on the reader. Even when typed, excessively long paragraphs are often difficult to read. You should always consider dividing an overly long paragraph into two or more parts. Of course, if you regroup your sentences after they have been written, some of your paragraphs will not contain strong topic sentences. This shortcoming is acceptable, however; the newly created paragraphs in effect share the topic sentence of the paragraph from which they came.

PATTERNS OF ORGANIZATION

It is wise—whenever possible—to use a discernible pattern of organization in presenting points within a paragraph. The patterns most easily perceived by the majority of readers are those based on standard measuring systems: time, size, distance, geographical direction, importance, and worth. The following outlines and paragraphs are examples of some of these patterns. (In each paragraph, the underlined sentence is the topic sentence.)

TIME

What happened to me on my first day at boot camp?

I. My first day at boot camp
   A. Got up at 5:00 A.M.
   B. Dressed and marched to breakfast
   C. Took physical exam
   D. Went to lunch
   E. Received clothing and equipment
   F. Marched to permanent barracks

> *My first day at boot camp was a hectic experience.* Oh, how I hate to get up in the morning. Nevertheless, like the other recruits, I had to hit the deck at 5:00 A.M. The temporary quarters were crowded, and there was little time to dress. So there was a great deal of confusion. But soon we were on our way to the mess hall, where for the first time in my life I had beans for breakfast. Then we marched to the medical center for our final physical exams. After lunch we were issued clothing and other gear and marched to our permanent barracks. Our arrival there was the official beginning of six weeks of training on how to become "admiral of the fleet."

IMPORTANCE

How was European society organized during the Middle Ages?

I. European social structure during the Middle Ages
   A. Lord
   B. Vassal
   C. Knight
   D. Serf

> *During the Middle Ages, European society was organized along very rigid lines, the nobility wielding great power while the lowest class was all but enslaved.* There was no local government as we know it today. Instead, most lands were ruled under a system called feudalism. A large tract would be owned by one nobleman, who was considered lord of that piece of land. If he rented part of it to another nobleman, that nobleman was thereby the lord's vassal. A vassal did not pay a monetary rent for his parcel of land. Rather, he compensated the lord by supplying a certain number of knights to fight in the lord's battles. The common people were known as serfs, and most were farmers living in villages surrounding the estate of a lord. They came under the lord's rule at birth and were compelled to stay on his land and work for him. In return, the lord protected them from outside attack.

SIZE

How vast is the universe?

I. The vastness of the universe
   A. The universe (everything in space, including space itself)
   B. The Milky Way (the galaxy in which our solar system is located)
   C. The sun (a star that controls our solar system)
   D. The earth (the planet on which we live)

> *It is difficult—perhaps impossible—for most people to comprehend the vastness of the universe.* Just what is the universe? It has been defined as everything in space, including space itself; but how much "everything" is there? Scientists maintain that the Milky Way, one of many galaxies, is a huge collection of billions of stars. One of those stars is the sun that sustains life on this planet. Thus the earth, which is dwarfed even by this sun, is a mere speck in relation to the total universe, a system whose vastness is truly awesome.

GEOGRAPHICAL DIRECTION: EAST TO WEST

What large cities did we visit on our drive from Boston to San Diego?

I. The large cities we visited between Boston and San Diego
   A. New York
   B. Washington, D.C.
   C. St. Louis
   D. Oklahoma City
   E. Phoenix

> *On our trip from Boston to San Diego, we visited a number of large cities.* The first stop on our carefully planned itinerary was New York City, which is always an exciting place to us. In one day, we visited the Metropolitan Museum, shopped at three department stores, saw a new Broadway show, and ate dinner at a lovely restaurant with an old friend. The next day we drove to Washington, D.C., where we spent a few hours sightseeing. Leaving Washington about six that same evening, we drove straight through to St. Louis and spent the night at a charming little hotel. From St. Louis, we moved on to Oklahoma City, where we ate lunch and relaxed for several hours before departing for Phoenix; there we spent the weekend with my sister and her husband. On Monday morning we started the last leg of our journey to San Diego, reaching it by evening, as scheduled, after an easy day's drive. Overall, though somewhat hectic, the trip was a most enjoyable cross-country adventure.

THE ABSENCE OF AN ORGANIZATIONAL PATTERN

Although it is often useful to have an organizational pattern for your paragraph, it is not always necessary. As a matter of fact, most of the paragraphs you will need to write will not lend themselves to the sort of familiar patterns illustrated in the previous section. Such patterns guide the reader; the absence of them makes it all the more vital that the writer strive for unity, logical order, and coherence. The two sample paragraphs that follow do not have discernible patterns of organization. (Note that the topic sentence, though appearing only in the first paragraph, governs the succeeding paragraph as well. As explained previously, the material relating to one topic sentence is often divided into several paragraphs for the sake of readability.)

NO ORGANIZATIONAL PATTERN

If I had plenty of leisure time and money, *what* would I do?

I. Using my leisure time and money
  A. Traveling
    1. Spain
    2. Puerto Rico
  B. Exercise
    1. Golf
    2. Tennis
  C. Cultural interests
    1. Creative writing
    2. Music

If I had plenty of leisure time and money, I would do more of those things that give me a sense of accomplishment. First, I would travel more. Ever since I took my first high-school course in Spanish, I have had a yearning to visit a place where mainly Spanish is spoken. Spain would be my choice for a long trip, but I might get to Puerto Rico for a week or so since it is closer to home. I would like to spend several months in Spain to become more proficient in the Spanish language.

Another of my hopes for the future is to have more time to play golf and tennis. If I could play these sports every day or so, I think I would become good enough to play in some of the amateur tournaments.

Of no less importance to me is an increase in my cultural pursuits. I long for the day when I will have time to do extensive research in colonial history, enabling me to write a novel about the revolutionary war. Also I hope someday to have enough time to learn how to play a guitar. I have no interest in becoming a professional guitarist, but I think my understanding of all music would increase substantially if I could play a stringed instrument.

NO ORGANIZATIONAL PATTERN

What are the most common eye defects that cause people to wear glasses?

I. Common eye defects
  A. Nearsightedness (myopia)
    1. Eyeball elongated or cornea too curved
    2. Light rays focus in front of retina
  B. Farsightedness
    1. Eyeball too short or cornea not curved enough
    2. Light rays focus behind retina
  C. Astigmatism

1. Surface of the eye not smooth
2. Light rays not diffused
D. Combination of defects
   1. Nearsightedness and astigmatism
   2. Farsightedness and astigmatism

There are a number of eye defects that require people to wear glasses. One of them is nearsightedness (sometimes called myopia). The eyeball of some-one with this defect is longer than normal, causing the light rays to focus in front of the retina. Another common eye defect is farsightedness. The prob-lem here is just the opposite. The eyeball is shorter than normal, and the light focuses behind the retina.

The third common eye defect is astigmatism. An astigmatic eye has an uneven or wavy surface. As a result, the light rays are not evenly focused but diffused, causing vision to blur. Frequently people have astigmatism along with nearsightedness or farsightedness. At present, eyeglasses or con-tact lenses are the only means of correcting these common defects.

TOPIC QUESTION

As previously stated, the topic question is not generally used in the final draft of a paragraph; it is mainly a tool to help you get started and to limit your topic. Sometimes, however, you may want to use a topic ques-tion at the beginning of your paragraph, for direct questions tend to get the reader's attention. But they succeed only when kept to a minimum; the overuse of questions can become boring and annoying to the reader.

Since the ability to write a well-constructed paragraph is essential to writing a superior composition, research paper, or essay examination, you should make every effort to master this aspect of writing. Begin by remembering the principles that have been explained in this chapter:

1. A paragraph (or the first paragraph in a series) should have a clear topic sentence.
2. A paragraph should have sufficient details to develop the topic sen-tence.
3. A paragraph should have unity. Every sentence in the paragraph should be directly related to the topic sentence.
4. The sentences in a paragraph should have a logical order. The first sentence should come first for some logical reason. The second should come next for some logical reason, and so on. (However, sometimes the order of sentences other than the topic sentence makes little or no difference.)
5. The sentences in a paragraph should exhibit coherence, the rela-tionships between them being made clear by means of transitional words or phrases.

If you compose one good paragraph at a time, your final work is al-most bound to be impressive.

EXERCISE 2

Writing is often difficult, but knowing how to get started makes it much easier. This exercise is intended to give you practice in limiting your topic and in writing topic sentences for a paragraph or series of paragraphs. Choosing your own topics, write a topic question and a topic sentence for each of the seven key thought words. Use the examples given below each key thought word as your guide.

1. HOW
How do you change a flat tire?
To change a flat tire you must follow a few simple steps.

_____

_____

_____

2. IF (. . . WHAT)
If I had a choice, *what* would be my career?
If I had a choice, I would be an electronics engineer.

_____

_____

_____

3. WHAT
What do I remember most about my trip to New England?
Recalling my trip to New England, I remember most the historical places of interest that I visited.

_____

_____

_____

4. WHEN
When did I feel a sense of accomplishment?
I felt a sense of accomplishment when my fellow high-school students picked me to be president of the senior class.

_____

_____

_____

© 1981 HBJ

5. WHERE
Where would I like to go on my summer vacation?
I would like to spend my summer vacation visiting England and France.

_____

_____

_____

6. WHO
Who do you think will be the Democratic and Republican candidates for governor?
In my opinion, when the primary elections are over, the Democratic candidate for governor will be James Irwin and the Republican candidate will be Jean Harris.

_____

_____

_____

7. WHY
Why do I enjoy playing tennis?
I enjoy playing tennis for a number of reasons.

_____

_____

_____

          © 1981 HBJ

EXERCISE 3

Presenting sufficient details to develop generalizations is one of the basic concerns in paragraphing. The use of a three-level outline, even for short compositions, is usually helpful. The following skeleton of such an outline has only its first level completed. Complete the other levels by adding the names of favorite celebrities and by providing details about them. Feel free to give more than two details about each celebrity or to add to the outline in any other way.

Topic question: *Who* are some of my favorite celebrities?
Topic sentence: Like most people, I have favorite stars in the movies, on television, in the theater, and in sports.

   I. In the movies

      A. _____

         1. _____

         2. _____

      B. _____

         1. _____

         2. _____

  II. On television

      A. _____

         1. _____

         2. _____

      B. _____

         1. _____

         2. _____

 III. In the theater

      A. _____

         1. _____

         2. _____

      B. _____

         1. _____

         2. _____

IV. In sports

    A. _____

        1. _____

        2. _____

    B. _____

        1. _____

        2. _____

© 1981 HBJ

EXERCISE 4

Complete the following three-level outline with appropriate details on the topics. Do not hesitate to increase the number of subtopics if you want to include more facts than indicated.

Topic question: *What* might a stranger want to know about my home town?

Topic sentence: A stranger might be interested in learning certain facts about my home town.

I. Size and location

    A. _____

        1. _____

        2. _____

    B. _____

        1. _____

        2. _____

II. Business and commerce

    A. _____

        1. _____

        2. _____

    B. _____

        1. _____

        2. _____

III. Educational institutions

    A. _____

        1. _____

        2. _____

    B. _____

        1. _____

        2. _____

IV. Amusement and recreation

    A. _____

© 1981 HBJ

         1. _____

         2. _____

B. _____

         1. _____

         2. _____

                    © 1981 HBJ

EXERCISE 5

In a unified paragraph or series of paragraphs, every idea and fact is related to the main topic. The following outline includes items that are *not* logically related to the main topic suggested by the title and the main divisions. Place an *X* next to each of these inappropriate items.

GIVING AND TAKING TESTS IN COLLEGE

I. Advantages

_____A. Motivates student to study

_____B. Causes teacher much extra work

_____C. Helps student to learn from mistakes

_____D. Interferes with student's recreation

_____E. Develops the student's attention span

_____F. Helps student to gain self-knowledge

_____G. Takes time away from study of new material

_____H. Enables school to maintain higher standards

II. Disadvantages

_____A. Sometimes causes friction between student and teacher

_____B. Gives student something to talk about

_____C. May destroy student's intrinsic interest in the subject

_____D. Gives student excuse for not going home on the weekend

_____E. May cause bitter competition among students

_____F. May foster dishonest practices

_____G. May frustrate student's creative capacities

EXERCISE 6

In a unified paragraph or series of paragraphs, every idea and fact is related to the main topic. The following outline includes items that are *not* logically related to the main topic suggested by the title and the main divisions. Place an *X* next to each of these inappropriate items.

THE ADVANTAGES OF LIVING IN A METROPOLITAN AREA

I. Educational

_____A. Generally higher quality of elementary schools and high schools

_____ 1. Better equipment

_____ 2. Better teachers

_____B. Closer relationship between teacher and student in small towns

_____C. Opportunity to attend college or university while living at home

_____D. Variety of educational programs on noncommercial radio and TV

_____E. Higher quality of newspapers to inform the citizens

_____F. Fewer distractions in small towns, thus more opportunity to study

II. Cultural

_____A. Closer proximity to museums and other cultural centers

_____B. Presence of local symphony orchestra and theater groups

_____C. Greater opportunity in small town to associate with people of similar interests

_____D. Many cultural activities in connection with municipal college or university

_____E. More time in small town for those who want to belong to cultural group

_____F. Appearance of outstanding personages in arts and sciences in big cities

© 1981 HBJ

III. Occupational

_____ A. Better opportunity to choose the type of job you want

_____ B. Better opportunity to choose the particular company you want to work for

_____ C. Better opportunity in small town to own your own business

_____ D. Larger size of company offers greater chance for promotion

_____ E. Lower cost of living in small town permits salary to go further

_____ F. Better opportunity to change jobs if you are dissatisfied

IV. Recreational

_____ A. Activities of social clubs such as American Legion and Elks better developed in small town

_____ B. Opportunity to see variety of professional entertainers in all fields

_____ C. Not necessary to travel to larger cities for entertainment

_____ D. Better opportunity for outdoor sports such as hunting and fishing in small town

    © 1981 HBJ

EXERCISE 7

The sentences of a paragraph should be arranged in a logical order. One of the most frequently used is chronological order. Rearrange the following outline so that the items appear in order of occurrence, with the most recent last.

I. John F. Kennedy—the 35th president of the United States
   A. Founded the Peace Corps
   B. At age 29 elected to U.S. House of Representatives
   C. Succeeded by Vice President Lyndon Johnson
   D. Born in Brookline, Massachusetts
   E. At age 35 elected to the U.S. Senate
   F. Assassinated in Dallas, Texas, November 22, 1963
   G. Elected president of the U.S. in 1960
   H. Served in U.S. Navy during World War II

EXERCISE 8

The sentences of a paragraph should be arranged in some logical order. One of the most frequently used is chronological order—what happened first, then second, third, and so on. Put the items of the following sentence outline in such an order. It may be helpful first of all to divide them into two processes: (1) taking off the flat tire and (2) putting on the spare tire.

I. Changing a flat tire
    A. Loosen the lug nuts one turn before jacking up the car
    B. Remove the flat tire
    C. Remove the jacking equipment and spare tire from the trunk
    D. Tighten the lug nuts one turn before jacking down the car
    E. Remove the hub cap with the jack handle or some other instrument
    F. Remove the lug nuts from the hub
    G. Put the jacking equipment and flat tire into the trunk
    H. Jack up the car
    I. Tighten the lug nuts all the way after the tire is on the ground
    J. Jack down the car
    K. Replace the hub cap
    L. Put the spare tire on the hub

EXERCISE 9

One of the best ways to achieve *logical coherence* in writing sentences and paragraphs is to use transitional words and phrases. In each of the following sentences at least one conjunction has been omitted. Consider the logical relationship between the parts of the sentence. Then choose an appropriate conjunction from the lists on pages 12–13. In making your choice, pay close attention to how the blank spaces in the exercise are punctuated.

1. The president is convinced that the peace conference will be a success, _____ he believes that the Soviet Union will cooperate in promoting disarmament.

2. A protest was registered _____ by the students _____ by the teachers.

3. The parents of the schoolchildren became angry _____ the federal government curtailed the school milk fund.

4. A number of civic groups in the city urged Judge Finley to run for Congress; _____, he declined because of his judicial duties.

5. The court would not grant Mary Johnson custody of her children _____ she could prove herself able to provide for them.

6. The two boys were caught throwing lighted firecrackers at pedestrians from a roof; _____ they were arrested and later placed on probation.

7. The senator criticized the policies of the administration _____ of the steady rise in the cost of living.

8. Philadelphia was the first capital of the United States; _____, the capital was moved to Washington in 1799.

9. Chicago had been hit by the worst snowstorm in its history; _____, the president declared it a disaster area.

10. The company did not deliver the office equipment on time _____ its truck broke down.

11. It is generally agreed that smoking is a health hazard _____ millions of people continue to smoke.

12. My handwriting is hard to read; _____, I decided to take a course in typing.

13. I can swim across the pool; _____ I am afraid to jump off the diving board.

© 1981 HBJ

14. All flights were canceled _____ of the heavy snowstorm.

15. The drive to help the needy children was announced all week on radio and television; _____ on Sunday volunteers went from door to door soliciting donations.

 © 1981 HBJ

EXERCISE 10

One of the best ways to achieve *logical coherence* in writing sentences and paragraphs is to use transitional words and phrases. In each of the following sentences at least one conjunction has been omitted. Consider the logical relationship between the parts of the sentence. Then choose an appropriate conjunction from the lists on pages 12–13. In making your choice, pay close attention to how the blank spaces in the exercise are punctuated.

1. Professor Ellwanger knows her subject throughly, _____ she has a lively sense of humor.

2. The man was arrested _____ he was indicted by the grand jury.

3. The space vehicle will not be launched _____ the weather is ideal.

4. Robert Eiler was _____ a Republican _____ a Democrat; he was a socialist.

5. Gwendolyn achieved a very high score on the English placement test; _____ , she did not have to take freshman composition.

6. I am a very poor golfer _____ I am good in other sports.

7. James does not have superior intelligence; _____ he has a great deal of determination.

8. The movie was given an Academy Award _____ of its superb photography.

9. Ronald did not get an acceptable grade on his math placement test; _____ , he had to take a review course in algebra.

10. We were forced to take the train to New York, _____ all the flights were canceled because of the heavy snowstorm.

11. The business district of Anchorage was in shambles _____ the devastating earthquake.

12. The umpire's decision was disputed _____ by the base runner _____ by the manager of the team.

13. Senator Cammack was scheduled to speak at the banquet; _____ , due to illness, he could not appear.

© 1981 HBJ

14. It would be unwise to say what caused the plane crash _____ the wreckage is carefully examined.

15. The judge ruled that an impartial jury could not be secured among the townspeople; _____ the trial was moved to another county.

 © 1981 HBJ

3: Organizing the Composition

Several years ago on the main campus of Indiana University a newspaper reporter asked a number of straight-A students to enumerate the reasons for their success in schoolwork. Although many different reasons were given, all of the students placed one factor at or near the top of their lists: I am well organized.

Much of the work done in college is written, and superior writing must be well organized. The student of average intelligence can often surpass the "brilliant" student by becoming more proficient at organizing a composition. This skill usually comes through learning how to prepare an outline.

In the minds of some students the term *outline* is a dirty word. However, unless you can outline in your head (more or less unconsciously), you should get into the habit of outlining on paper as a step in prewriting. If you do not learn this technique, chances are you will have trouble when it comes to writing long papers, especially reference or research papers. Even though you can write short compositions based on personal experiences without the help of outlines, you would be wise to use such assignments to learn the fundamentals of outlining before you are called upon to write more complex compositions. Once you have learned to outline, you can use this skill not only in writing but in summarizing reading and in taking lecture notes. The following is the skeleton of an outline for a complete composition. The main topics and subtopics are indicated by the use of Roman numerals, capital letters, Arabic numerals, and small letters.

Main idea question:
Main idea statement:

Introduction
  I.
    A.
      1.
      2.
        a.
        b.
          (1)
          (2)
            (a)
            (b)
    B.
  II. A.
      B.
  III.
      A.
      B.
      C.
Conclusion

Some implications of this outline form—which differs slightly from comparable forms found in other textbooks on writing—should be noted:

(1) We have included a main idea question. Using a question related to one of the key thought words (as explained in Chapter 1) will help you in getting started and in limiting your topic. Some teachers may prefer that you *not* include the question. Although it is a great help in organizing your composition, the question does not have to appear with your outline.

(2) The main idea statement does generally appear with your outline. However, your instructor may want you to label it differently—for example, Thesis Statement, Main Idea Sentence, or Central Idea.

(3) Some textbooks on writing place a Roman numeral before the labels *Introduction* and *Conclusion*. This practice can sometimes be confusing, for often (as we shall explain in the next chapter) the main divisions of an outline are mentioned as part of the introduction and conclusion. You should, though, write the words *Introduction* and *Conclusion* on your outline to remind yourself that every composition—short or long—should have three distinct parts:

Introduction
Main Body
Conclusion

However, do not write out the introductory and concluding parts of your composition on your outline.

(4) The numbering in your outline does not appear in your composition. Do not begin regular paragraphs and sentences with designating numbers or letters.

(5) Except for the main idea question, do not use questions in your outline.

(6) Except for the main idea statement, do not use complete sentences in your outline. The main idea statement should also appear in the introduction (first paragraph) of your composition.

(7) The main idea statement should be only one sentence.

(8) The title should be as brief as possible but should clearly indicate the theme of your composition. It should not be underlined or enclosed in quotation marks. All the words in your title should be capitalized except articles (*a, an, the*) and short prepositions (*of, at, in*, etc.); even an article or preposition is capitalized if it is the first word in the title.

(9) Capitalize *only* the first word (and proper nouns) of each main topic and subtopic.

(10) The main topics and subtopics of your outline, like the title, should be brief but as clear as possible.

(11) In the first main division of the skeletal outline, there are six levels:

1st
I.
   2nd
   A.
      3rd
      1.
         4th
         a.
            5th
            (1)
               6th
               (a)

In your short compositions (say 300 to 500 words) you will probably not have to go beyond the third level of subordination. Even in your long papers you will probably not have to go beyond the fourth level.

(12) Different topics lend themselves to different types of outlines. That is, a one-level outline may be sufficient for certain topics:

   I.
   II.
  III.
  IV.
   V.

Other topics may require a two-level outline:

I.
   A.
   B.

II.

    A.

    B.

    C.

III.

    A.

    B.

    C.

Other topics may lend themselves to a three-level outline:

I.

    A.

        1.

        2.

    B.

        1.

        2.

II.

    A.

        1.

        2.

    B.

        1.

        2.

(Note that the fewer main divisions, the more likely you are to move to the second and third levels.)

(13) An outline for a composition (even a short one) should have at least two main divisions.

(14) Subtopics should also come in groups of two or more. Do not use an *A* unless you use a *B*. Do not use a 1 unless you use a 2. Do not use an *a* unless you use a *b*.

LOGICAL COORDINATION

Since the most important quality of an effective outline is logical coordination, the most serious problem in outlining is faulty or overlapping coordination; this problem can also occur in writing sentences. In fact, this principle might be easier to understand if first we relate it to sentences and then show how it carries over to outlining.

In a sentence, *overlapping coordination* occurs when the elements joined by a coordinate conjunction (*and, but, for, or, nor*) or the elements that follow correlative conjunctions (*not only . . . but also; either . . . or; neither . . . nor*) do not have the same logical value: one of the elements is more important or more abstract than another:

    Overlapping
    Coordination   I like camping and outdoor recreation.

    Analysis   The overlapping coordination in this sentence is easy to detect. Obviously, *camping* and *outdoor recreation* are not of the same value or scope. Camping is generally considered one of the many types of outdoor recreation. Using the coordinate conjunction *and* to join the two noun constructions makes the sentence illogical.

Overlapping
Coordination I admire Ruth Jones because of her sense of humor, her friendliness, and her personality.

Analysis The first two elements, *sense of humor* and *friendliness*, are coordinate. However, the third element is more abstract than the first two. Sense of humor and friendliness could be considered aspects of personality.

Overlapping
Coordination The essay "A Modest Proposal" is not only excellent satire but also first-rate literature.

Analysis This example is somewhat different from the preceding examples; instead of a coordinate conjunction, there are correlative conjunctions: not only . . . but also. Grammatically and logically, it is necessary to have parallel elements after these conjunctions. *Excellent satire* and *first-rate literature* overlap, but the sample sentence gives the impression that they are two distinct qualities.

LOGICAL COORDINATION AND OUTLINING

The main divisions of an outline (I., II., III., etc.) should be logically coordinate with one another. Indeed, the items at any level should be coordinate. The problem of overlapping coordination in an outline is the same at any level. Thus, for the sake of simplicity, the following examples deal only with main divisions:

THE ART EXHIBIT

I. Paintings
II. Portraits
III. Sculpture
IV. Watercolors

Analysis Some of these main divisions overlap. Paintings and sculpture are coordinate, but watercolors could be a subtopic under paintings. Also, portraits are not logically coordinate with the other three main divisions since a portrait can be both a painting and a watercolor. In addition, portraits could conceivably be a subtopic under sculpture.

MY FAVORITE SPORTS

I. Golf
II. Driving and putting
III. Tennis

Analysis Golf and tennis are logically coordinate. But driving and putting are not of the same scope as golf and tennis. They are aspects of the former and should have been made a subtopic under the first main division.

WOMEN COMPETING FOR JOBS

 I. Managerial
 II. Business
III. Professional

Analysis The three main divisions are not logically coordinate. A person with a managerial position could be a professional. Also, someone in a managerial (and professional) position could be in business.

LIVING IN THE COUNTRY

 I. Less traffic
 II. Less pollution
III. Lower crime rate

Analysis The three main divisions are logically coordinate because they are separate and distinct concepts related to the topic in the same way.

GETTING RID OF MY OLD CAR

 I. Because the oil pan was leaking
 II. Because the carburetor was defective
III. Because the door latch was broken

Analysis The three main divisions in this outline appear to be logically coordinate, even though the third is not as serious a problem as the first and second.

SISTERS AND BROTHERS

 I. As children—fighting
 II. As teenagers—being envious
III. As adults—being mature and understanding

Analysis These three main divisions are logically coordinate, indicating that the writer can think clearly and—no doubt—write effectively.

GRAMMATICAL PARALLELISM

The second necessary quality of a well-constructed outline is *parallelism*. The main divisions of a topic outline should be logically coordinate and grammatically parallel. Of the two qualities, coordination is the more important, for an outline is mainly a conceptual tool, not a stylistic one. It can be useful even though it is not grammatically correct. Nevertheless, it is important to try to make your outline parallel; indeed, parallelism increases the chance that your outline will also be logically coordinate. Let us consider some brief outlines:

MY FAVORITE OUTDOOR SPORTS

I. To hunt
II. Swimming
III. To fish

> *Analysis* These three main divisions are logically coordinate—involving three separate and distinct outdoor sports of approximately the same scope—but they are not grammatically parallel. *To hunt* and *to fish* are infinitives while *swimming* is a gerund.

MY FAVORITE HIGH-SCHOOL TEACHER

I. Sponsor of the yearbook
II. Personality traits

> *Analysis* These two main divisions are grammatically parallel—the key word in each (*sponsor* and *traits*) is a noun—but they are not logically coordinate. The first is a specific fact, one that will probably generate no more than one or two sentences; the second is a broad category that might take several paragraphs to develop.

In studying the parts of speech in elementary school and high school, you may have asked yourself why you had to learn them. There are several reasons to be thankful if you did. Certainly knowing the parts of speech will make an important difference in your ability to construct a good outline and write a smooth sentence. To devise an outline that is logically coordinate and grammatically parallel, you must be able to identify a complete sentence, a clause, and a phrase, as well as the parts of speech.

Let us illustrate the principles of grammatical parallelism using the following three-level outline, an outline that is not parallel:

POLLUTION—THE DEATH OF US YET

Main idea question: What is one of the most serious health problems in the United States today?
Main idea statement: Pollution (air, water, and noise) is one of the most serious health problems in the United States today.

Introduction
I. Air pollution is a serious problem in the United States.
   A. Causes
      1. Factories
      2. Vehicles
   B. Effects
      1. Air pollution gives rise to health problems.
      2. Destroys plant life

C. What are the remedies?
    1. We need better education.
    2. Better government regulation
II. Water pollution
  A. What are the causes?
    1. Contaminated industrial waste
    2. Garbage from swimmers and boats
  B. Effects
    1. Destroying marine life
    2. Water pollution is contaminating the water we drink.
    3. To reduce opportunities for outdoor recreation
  C. Remedies
    1. Stiffer penalties for violations
    2. More media efforts to educate people
III. Can noise pollution be considered a problem?
  A. Causes
    1. Loud music
    2. Motorcycles
    3. Trucks and buses
    4. Jet planes
  B. What are the effects of noise pollution?
    1. Nervous disorders may be caused by noise pollution.
    2. Impairment of hearing
  C. Remedies
    1. Strict laws to control noise
    2. We need an all-out effort to warn people of the danger.
Conclusion

Complete sentences (which includes questions) should not be used in a topic outline—except in the main idea question and the main idea statement. Therefore, the main divisions of the sample outline should be changed as follows:

    I. Air pollution
   II. Water pollution
  III. Noise pollution

The same principle applies to the second-level items, which should read as follows:

  A. Causes
  B. Effects
  C. Remedies

The subtopics under "Causes" in the first main division are grammatically parallel, for both *factories* and *vehicles* are nouns. The first item under "Effects" is a complete sentence; it should be changed to parallel the second item:

    1. Gives rise to health problems
    2. Destroys plant life

The key words (*gives* and *destroys*) are both verbs in the present tense. The first item under "Remedies" needs to be changed from a complete sentence to a compatible phrase:

1. Better education
2. Better government regulation

When such changes are made throughout the outline, a grammatically parallel version results:

POLLUTION—THE DEATH OF US YET

Main idea question: (Same as before)
Main idea statement: (Same as before)

Introduction
  I. Air pollution
    A. Causes
      1. Factories
      2. Vehicles
    B. Effects
      1. Gives rise to health problems
      2. Destroys plant life
    C. Remedies
      1. Better education
      2. Better government regulation
 II. Water pollution
    A. Causes
      1. Contaminated industrial waste
      2. Garbage from swimmers and boats
    B. Effects
      1. Destroying marine life
      2. Contaminating the water we drink
      3. Reducing opportunities for outdoor recreation
    C. Remedies
      1. Stiffer penalties for violations
      2. More media efforts to educate people
III. Noise pollution
    A. Causes
      1. Loud music
      2. Motorcycles
      3. Trucks and buses
      4. Jet planes
    B. Effects
      1. Nervous disorders
      2. Impairment of hearing
    C. Remedies
      1. Strict laws to control noise
      2. All-out effort to warn people of the danger
Conclusion

The outline below is logically coordinate but not grammatically parallel. Let us see what we have to do to solve the problem.

OWNING YOUR OWN HOME

Main idea question: *What* are the advantages and disadvantages of owning your own home?

Main idea statement: There are a number of advantages and disadvantages in owning your own home.

Introduction
 I. There are a number of disadvantages in owning your own home.
   A. Financial
     1. Property tax
     2. Have to pay cost of maintenance and upkeep
   B. What are some of the other disadvantages?
     1. Cutting grass, etc.
     2. Cannot move at will
       a. Undesirable neighbors
       b. Commercial buildup
 II. Advantages
   A. What are some of the financial advantages?
     1. Increases in value of property
     2. Tax write-off
     3. Your house payments are fixed for time span of mortgage
   B. Other
     1. Remodel and decorate at will
     2. Have more privacy than in apartment
     3. Have yard for children to play in
     4. Can raise garden
     5. It is easier to have pets if you have your own home.
Conclusion

Except for the main idea question and statement, all the complete sentences should be eliminated from this topic outline. Therefore, main divisions I and II should be made parallel as follows:

 I. Disadvantages
 II. Advantages

The same principle applies to B under I, where the question should be replaced:

 A. Financial
 B. Other

In the third level, the items under IA are not parallel: the key word in 1 (*tax*) is a noun; the key word in 2 (*have*) is a verb. They can be made parallel in the following manner:

 1. Have to pay property tax
 2. Have to pay cost of maintenance and upkeep

The same principle applies to 1 and 2 under IB. Item 1 would be parallel with 2 if both started with a verb:

    1. Have to cut grass, etc.
    2. Cannot move at will

On the fourth level, a and b are parallel. The key words (*neighbors* and *buildup*) are both nouns.

When similar changes are made in the second main division, a grammatically parallel outline is produced:

OWNING YOUR OWN HOME

Main idea question: (Same as before)
Main idea statement: (Same as before)

Introduction
  I. Disadvantages
    A. Financial
      1. Have to pay property tax
      2. Have to pay cost of maintenance and upkeep
    B. Other
      1. Have to cut grass, etc.
      2. Cannot move at will
        a. Undesirable neighbors
        b. Commercial buildup
 II. Advantages
    A. Financial
      1. Increase in value of property
      2. Tax write-off
      3. Fixed house payments for time span of mortgage
    B. Other
      1. Remodel and decorate at will
      2. Have more privacy than in apartment
      3. Have yard for children to play in
      4. Can raise a garden
      5. Is easier to have pets
Conclusion

There is a good reason for using a topic outline even for a relatively short composition. For example, with the outline above, a composition of 500 words or so called "Owning Your Own Home" becomes much easier to write; the writer now knows what he or she wants to say. You have probably heard this old complaint (or spoken it yourself): "I know what I want to say—but I can't say it." There is usually some truth in this cry of agony, but there may also be some self-deception. In most cases, writing is difficult because you do not know what you want to say. If you solve this problem in the pre-writing stage, you can give greater attention to the mechanics of writing correct sentences and logical paragraphs when you write your first draft. For most people, outlining not only eliminates the necessity for time-consuming revisions but improves the writing style as well.

USING 3" X 5" CARDS

Some students find the use of 3" x 5" cards a great help in constructing a topic outline, especially if they have only a vague idea of what they want to write. Before using this technique, it is a good idea to limit your topic by formulating a main idea (or thesis) statement. Relate your topic to one of the key thought words: *how, if, what, when, where, who, why.* Ask a pertinent question. Answer the question with a broad generalization, as explained in Chapter 1; this sentence is your main idea statement.

Then start writing on 3" x 5" cards whatever comes to mind about your topic. Make sure that you do not put more than one idea on a card. However, if you are noting facts, you can put several related facts on one card. You should not worry about spelling, punctuation, or grammar. Just relax! Let your thoughts flow freely. In a short time you should have fifteen or twenty cards on which you have written relevant ideas and facts.

After writing everything that comes to mind, separate the cards into two or more groups, each group representing a possible main division in your outline. For a short composition, one under 500 words, you should have no more than three or four groups.

As you arrange the cards, you may discover that a few do not fit into any of the large groups. Put such cards aside. Considering only the cards that can be grouped, ask yourself *why* you put them together, that is, *what* common factor makes them fit into a particular group. Answering this question about each group should provide you with statements that can be reduced to main divisions for your outline. After you have the main divisions, arrange them in logical order. Sometimes the order makes no difference, but you should always give it some thought.

The next step is to study the cards with the idea of expanding your outline. Keep in mind the fact that sufficient details are a hallmark of a good paragraph. You are more likely to develop your topic sentence adequately if you make every effort to have a second and third level under each main division, even for a short composition.

EXERCISE 11

Arrange the following items in a two-level topic outline. The following suggestions may be helpful:

1. A two-level outline may have more than two main divisions.
2. An outline is usually easier to construct if the main divisions are first listed in logical order.

THE TRAFFIC PROBLEM IN METROPOLITAN AREAS

Main idea statement: Although the traffic conditions in most large cities are deplorable, a number of steps can be taken to improve them.

Introduction
Inadequate public transportation
More expressways
Increase in auto accidents
Remedies
Increase in population
Waste of valuable time going to and coming from work
Wider use of car pools
Effects
Prohibition of trucks on main streets during rush periods
Improvement of public transportation
Causes
Increase in car ownership
Prolonged traffic jams
Conclusion

_____

_____

_____

_____

_____

_____

_____

_____

_____

_____

_____

_____

© 1981 HBJ

© 1981 HBJ

EXERCISE 12

Rework the following outline to make it parallel. (The present chronological arrangement should not be changed.) The following suggestions may be helpful:

1. Complete sentences or questions should not be used in a topic outline (except as the main idea statement or the main idea question).
2. Main divisions should be parallel with each other—but not necessarily parallel with their subtopics.

OUR SENIOR TRIP

Main idea statement: We debated the question for several months before we finally agreed to go to New York City on our senior trip—an experience that I am not likely soon to forget.

Introduction
  I. We boarded the train at one o'clock on Sunday afternoon.
      A. Spent several hours observing the countryside
      B. Playing cards and chatting
      C. We took catnaps after the lights on the train were turned down.
 II. Activities in New York
      A. We arrived on Monday morning.
          1. Boat trip around Manhattan
          2. We spent the evening at Radio City Music Hall.
      B. Tuesday
          1. Made a tour of United Nations building
          2. Stroll through Central Park
          3. Visiting Museum of Modern Art
          4. We had our farewell dinner at Sardi's.
Conclusion

_____

_____

_____

_____

_____

_____

_____

_____

_____

© 1981 HBJ

EXERCISE 13

Arrange the following items in a three-level topic outline form. The following suggestions may be helpful:

1. The number of main divisions and the levels of subordination in an outline may be the same in number or they may be different.
2. An outline is usually easier to construct if the main divisions are first listed in logical order.

TEEN-AGE CRIME

Main idea statement: People who have studied the problem have suggested a number of reasons for the alarming increase in teen-age crime in today's society.

Introduction
Burglaries
Employment of both parents
Competitive sports for teen-agers
Causes
Municipal agency to help teen-agers find full-time and part-time jobs
Lack of trade and vocational schools
Traffic violations
Separation of parents
Effects
Vandalism
Sex crimes
School life
Misdemeanors
Lack of counseling and aptitude testing
Home life
Felonies
Remedies
Conclusion

_____

_____

_____

_____

_____

_____

_____

© 1981 HBJ

EXERCISE 14

Rewrite the following outline to make it parallel. (The order of the items should not be changed.) The following suggestions may be helpful:

1. Complete sentences or questions should not be used in a topic outline (except as the main idea statement or the main idea question).
2. Main divisions should be parallel with each other—but not necessarily parallel with the subtopics.

A BUSINESS VENTURE

Main idea statement: There are a number of basic steps that should be followed in organizing a new business if it is to be successful.

Introduction
  I. Where can the operating capital be secured?
    A. Sold stock to friends and relatives
    B. The organizer of the company borrowed $10,000 from the First National Bank.
 II. Suitable store
    A. Good location in retail area
    B. There should be an adequate facility for loading and unloading merchandise.
    C. Elevator to move merchandise to second floor
    D. There should be ample customer parking.
III. Much effort should be expended in recruiting and hiring competent personnel.
    A. The store manager should have broad experience and good references.
    B. College students as part-time employees
IV. Advertising and promotion of merchandise
    A. Attractive neon sign in front of store
    B. It would be a good idea to put a full-page ad in the Sunday edition of the local newspaper.
    C. Soft-sell commercials on radio and television
Conclusion

_____

_____

_____

_____

_____

_____

© 1981 HBJ

© 1981 HBJ

EXERCISE 15

Arrange the following items in a two-level topic outline form. The following suggestions may be helpful:

1. The number of main divisions and the levels of subordination in an outline may be the same in number or they may be different.
2. An outline is usually easier to construct if the main divisions are first listed in logical order.

SHORTAGES OF BASIC COMMODITIES

Main idea statement: In some parts of the world there are acute shortages of basic commodities.

Introduction
Construction materials
Grain
Energy
Petroleum
Dairy products
Paper
Food
Natural gas
Wood
Electricity
Beef
Conclusion

_____

_____

_____

_____

_____

_____

_____

_____

_____

_____

© 1981 HBJ

EXERCISE 16

Rewrite the following outline to make it parallel. (The order of the items should not be changed.) The following suggestions may be helpful:

1. Complete sentences or questions should not be used in a topic outline (except as the main idea statement or the main idea question).
2. Main divisions should be parallel with each other—but not necessarily parallel with their subtopics.

THE VARIOUS WAYS TO TRAVEL

Main idea statement: Each of the popular ways to travel has distinct advantages and disadvantages.

Introduction
  I. Car
    A. The traveler will have transportation on arrival at destination.
    B. The driver and passengers will have more flexibility in sightseeing.
    C. Gets boring and fatiguing if distance great
    D. Greater risk of accidental death
 II. Traveling by bus has its advantages and disadvantages.
    A. Cheapest if traveling alone
    B. Going by bus is usually a good way to see the countryside.
    C. Uncomfortable if traveling long distance
    D. Going by bus is usually a slow way to travel.
III. What are the advantages and disadvantages of going by train?
    A. Can sit back and relax
    B. Can get up and move around
    C. Does not provide convenient schedules
    D. The incessant noise and vibration make it difficult to sleep.
 IV. Plane
    A. Usually the fastest way to reach one's destination
    B. Many people find it a glamorous way to travel.
    C. Air sickness
Conclusion

_____
_____
_____
_____
_____
_____

© 1981 HBJ

EXERCISE 17

Arrange the following items in a three-level topic outline form. The following suggestions may be helpful:

1. The number of main divisions and the levels of subordination in an outline may be the same in number or they may be different.
2. An outline is usually easier to construct if the main divisions are first listed in logical order.

TELEVISION AND MATURITY

Main idea statement: Many programs that appear on television have a high level of maturity, while others are an insult to the intelligence of a moron.

Introduction
Buy merchandise not needed
Classical music
News reports by expert analysts
Oversimplify complex social and psychological problems
Speeches by President and other high government officials
Fosters maturity
Simple-minded soap operas
Informative programs
Gives false picture of reality
Hinders maturity
Cultural programs
Are duped by contests and other gimmicks
First-rate dramas
Panel discussions such as "Meet the Press"
Vulgar advertising
Conclusion

_____

_____

_____

_____

_____

_____

_____

_____

© 1981 HBJ

EXERCISE 18

Rework the following outline to make it parallel. (The present order of the main divisions and subtopics should not be changed.) The following suggestions may be helpful:

1. Complete sentences or questions should not be used in a topic outline (except as the main idea statement or the main idea question).
2. Main divisions should be parallel with each other—but not necessarily parallel with their subtopics.

LEARNING AWAY FROM SCHOOL

Main idea statement: For a person who has an inquiring mind, it is possible to learn a great deal from sources other than the usual classroom experience.

Introduction
  I. Belonging to social clubs
     A. Develop the ability to get along with people
     B. A person can learn the techniques of conducting a meeting.
 II. One can learn a great deal by working at a part-time job.
     A. What is expected of an employee
     B. How to spend and save money earned
     C. What plans to make for future career
III. What can one learn from television and radio?
     A. Important issues of the day
        1. "Meet the Press"
        2. Local and national news reports
     B. If one is selective one can learn much about the fine arts.
        1. Serious music programs
        2. Drama programs (such as *Hamlet* and *Hedda Gabler*)
 IV. Reading nonclassroom material
     A. Newspapers
        1. Local
        2. *The New York Times*
     B. Can magazines be tools for learning?
        1. Monthly—*Atlantic*
        2. Each week I read *Newsweek* magazine.
Conclusion

_____

_____

_____

_____

© 1981 HBJ

4: Introduction and Conclusion

THE INTRODUCTION

The introduction is a very important part of your composition. Since readers often pass judgment on a piece of writing after reading only the first paragraph, you should make your introduction as attractive as possible. It should stimulate interest while telling in a general way what your composition is about.

APPROPRIATE TITLE

Choose the title of your composition with care, striving for one that is clear, pointed, and brief. A well-chosen title can ease the burden on your introduction. You may even want to make it the focus of your first sentences. However, do not assume that the title is grammatically part of the introduction. Such an assumption leads to ambiguous opening sentences:

Title	A Passion for the Ugly
Poor	This seems to have been a problem of our American forebears if the architecture of our cities and towns can be used as an indication.
Better	A close look at the architecture to be seen in American cities and towns suggests that our forebears had (to adapt a phrase from H. L. Mencken) a passion for the ugly.
Comment	In the poor example the writer apparently tries to save time by

letting "This" refer to the title instead of stating the theme in the first paragraph.

Title   Our Hectic Senior Trip

Poor   This was one of the most enjoyable trips I ever took in my life although I was exhausted by the time I got back home.

Better   When the bus, crowded with sixty screaming teen-agers, pulled out of the Evansville station for New York City, the driver probably wished he had taken a nice quiet job in a boiler factory.

Comment   As in the other poor example, the writer makes the mistake of assuming that the title is grammatically part of the introduction.

POOR INTRODUCTIONS

Do not call the reader's attention to the fact that you are writing a composition.

Title   Cheating in College

Poor   The purpose of my composition is to convince the reader that cheating in college has a bad effect on people who do this type of thing.

Better   Students who cheat in college are actually cheating themselves. True happiness in life depends largely on being honest with others as well as with oneself.

Title   Attending College Away From Home

Poor   In this theme I am going to discuss the financial disadvantages of attending an out-of-town college or university.

Better   The soaring cost of living (better known as "inflation") makes it increasingly difficult to attend an out-of-town college or university.

Do not apologize for not being an expert. Your teacher is not likely to expect you to be an authority on your topic.

Title   The Firearms Issue

Poor   Although I haven't had a chance to read very much about the topic, I feel that guns and ammunition should not be sold to anyone who does not have a permit.

Better   The assassination of President John Kennedy brought into sharp focus in the minds of many Americans a question that for too many years had been brushed aside: Should firearms be sold on the open market to anyone who wants to buy them?

Do not complain about your lack of interest in the topic.

Title   "No Man Is an Island"

Poor   Since I don't have much interest in British literature, my interpretation of John Donne's prose poem might not be exactly what you want.

Better   You do not have to be an expert in British literature to understand the message of John Donne's beautiful prose poem "No Man Is an Island." The poem tells us that all human beings belong to the same family because we all have the same Heavenly Father.

EFFECTIVE INTRODUCTIONS

Now that we have discussed what *not* to do, let us concentrate on the positive considerations in writing an effective introduction. How long should it be? The length of your introduction depends on the length of your paper. A short composition may need just two or three sentences; sometimes just one sentence will do. A longer composition, on the other hand, may require half a page or even a whole page.

How should your introduction be indicated on your outline? In constructing an outline, it is best *not* to put a Roman numeral before the words *Introduction* and *Conclusion*. Although some composition teachers may instruct otherwise, using the Roman numerals may cause a problem. One of the basic principles in devising an outline for a composition requires that there be at least two main divisions; that is, if there is a I, there must be a II. If you put a Roman numeral before the words *Introduction* and *Conclusion*, you are more likely to violate this basic principle in this way:

     I. Introduction
    II. Attending college away from home
   III. Conclusion

Although it uses three Roman numerals, the outline above has only one main division. To help avoid this problem, omit Roman numerals before the labels for introductory or concluding material; write only the words *Introduction* and *Conclusion* to remind yourself that every composition (short or long) must have these three components: introduction, main body (with at least two main divisions), and conclusion.

Your main idea (or thesis) statement, which should appear on your outline below the title, may become part of your introduction. For a short composition, it may be the whole introduction. A reference to the main divisions of your outline may also be included in your introduction to give the reader an understanding of what ground will be covered in the main body of your composition. In most cases, the main idea (or thesis) question is not included in the introduction although it may be used to attract the reader's attention—as we shall explain later in this chapter.

Each of the following sample introductions includes both a main idea statement and the main divisions of the outline:

POLLUTION—THE DEATH OF US YET

Main idea (or thesis) statement: Pollution is undermining the quality of
    life in the United States and throughout the world.

Introduction
  I. Air pollution
 II. Water pollution
III. Noise pollution
Conclusion

Pollution is undermining the quality of life in the United States and throughout the world. On certain days in some urban areas it is dangerous for people with respiratory problems to go outdoors. In rural areas as well as urban ones, polluted water is destroying many forms of marine life. And in all large cities, noise, perhaps the most noticeable pollution of all, is impairing the ability to hear and listen, especially among young people.

The next sample introduction includes not only a main idea statement and the main divisions of the outline but also subtopics A and B under the main divisions. However, as a general rule you will need to use only main divisions.

OWNING YOUR OWN HOME

Main idea question: What are the advantages and disadvantages of owning your own home?

Main idea (or thesis) statement: There are both advantages and disadvantages in owning your own home.

Introduction
 I. Disadvantages
    A. Financial
    B. Other
 II. Advantages
    A. Financial
    B. Other
Conclusion

There are both advantages and disadvantages in owning your own home. The most obvious are financial. However, there are also other important factors to be considered.

The type of introduction shown above—one that uses the main idea statement along with the main divisions and/or subtopics of the outline— is adequate for most compositions. But experienced writers sometimes use "gimmicks" in their introductions to get the reader's attention. These devices include the arresting question, the apt quotation, and the narrative hook.

ASKING A QUESTION AT THE BEGINNING OR END OF THE INTRODUCTION

The introductory "gimmick" most often used by writers is probably the question.

POLLUTION—THE DEATH OF US YET

What is one of the most serious problems facing humankind today? Pollution!—the often unseen force that is undermining the quality of life not only in the United States but throughout the world. On certain days in some urban areas it is dangerous for people with respiratory problems to go outdoors. In rural areas as well as urban ones, polluted water is destroying many forms of marine life. And in all large cities, noise, perhaps the most noticeable pollution of all, is impairing the ability to hear and listen, especially among young people.

AN APT QUOTATION

An apt quotation that appears before or after the main idea statement may also be a useful device in getting the attention of the reader.

A CURE FOR INFLATION

"People are rich in proportion to the number of things they can afford to leave alone." These profound words written by Henry David Thoreau in the first half of the nineteenth century suggest that he was a prophet far ahead of his time. Today, government economists have finally been more or less forced to agree that easy credit, which entices people to buy things they don't actually need or can't afford, is one of the principal reasons for double-digit inflation. Accordingly, interest rates have been raised to discourage people from living beyond their means.

THE NARRATIVE HOOK

Another "gimmick" used to get the reader's attention is called the *narrative hook*, a word picture (such as a brief scene from a play) that is related to the main idea the writer wants to convey. In writing a short composition, you would probably be well advised *not* to use this device; the introduction would probably be too long for the composition.

AN UNUSUAL EXPERIENCE

About a dozen people scampered off the bus as its doors swished open. When I reached the sidewalk, I stopped for several seconds before deciding to go into the corner restaurant and have a cup of coffee. As I entered the crowded restaurant and moved toward the lunch counter, a well-dressed elderly man (who seemed to have appeared out of nowhere) put his hand on my shoulder and said, "Young man, how would you like to make a lot of money?" This was the beginning of one of the most unusual experiences I ever had.

THE CONCLUSION

Having written your introduction and presented enough ideas and facts to develop your main idea statement, you are ready to write a conclusion. The length of your paper is an important factor in deciding what type of conclusion to use. If you have written a long paper, you will probably need a summary conclusion restating the main points of your paper. But if you have written a short composition, that is, one of less than five hundred words, a summary conclusion may be awkward. Let us consider some ways to avoid poor conclusions.

POOR CONCLUSIONS

Do not mechanically sum up the main ideas of your paper.

MY FAVORITE SPORTS

Introduction
 I. Swimming
 II. Tennis
III. Golf
IV. Bowling
Conclusion

> *Poor*   My favorite sports, therefore, are swimming, tennis, golf, and bowling.
>
> *Better*   Although I will never match the professionals in swimming, tennis, golf, or bowling, I enjoy participating in these sports as a dedicated amateur. They provide not only enjoyment but the exercise I need to help me stay in good physical condition.

Do not belabor the fact that you are writing a conclusion.

FASHION TRENDS

Introduction
 I. Among men
 II. Among women
Conclusion

> *Poor*   In conclusion I would like to say that if the present fashion trends continue, in future years it will be difficult to distinguish men from women simply by the clothes they wear.
>
> *Better*   If the present fashion trends continue, in future years it will be difficult to distinguish men from women simply by the clothes they wear.

Do not apologize for your lack of knowledge regarding the subject on which you are writing.

STEREOTYPED THINKING

Introduction
 I. Because of a biased home environment
 II. Because of a lack of liberal education
Conclusion

> *Poor*   As I said at the beginning of this theme, I am not certain that I understand what Walter Lippmann means by stereotyped thinking.
>
> *Better*   Realizing that many of our strong convictions result from environmental influences—many people are Republicans or Democrats because their parents were—we should as students in college make a special effort to study both sides of controversial issues. It is only through such effort that we can develop the objectivity that is the hallmark of a well-educated person.

EFFECTIVE CONCLUSIONS

Now let us concentrate on the positive goals in writing a good conclusion. Remember that the conclusion is important because it represents your last chance to impress the reader and win him or her to your way of thinking.

Your final statement should be emphatic and clearly related to the main idea stated in the introduction. The superior conclusion usually goes beyond what has already been said in the main body of the composition by expressing a judgment or an opinion that logically follows from the ideas and facts developed previously. In other words, a good composition reaches a definite conclusion instead of ending as if the writer ran out of time or paper.

The summary conclusion is highly recommended for a lengthy composition, such as a reference or research paper. Referring to your outline, you should sum up each main division in one or more sentences. Then you should reach a conclusion that goes beyond what has been said in the introduction and main body of your paper. In this regard, the rhetorical devices or "gimmicks" mentioned in connection with the introduction are often effective; a rhetorical question, an apt quotation, or a narrative hook can be used to end a composition as well as to begin one. In the conclusion that follows, three rhetorical questions are used to relate the problem to the reader.

POLLUTION—THE DEATH OF US YET

Main idea statement: Pollution is undermining the quality of life in the United States and throughout the world.

Introduction
  I. Air pollution
 II. Water pollution
III. Noise pollution
Conclusion

> Every year the air over the United States becomes more and more polluted, and new forms of contamination find their way into the nation's lakes, rivers, and streams. Birds and marine life suffer and die, and Americans are forced to place new restrictions on their food supply and aquatic recreations. The nation's noise pollution is having a devastating effect on the average student's ability to hear and concentrate, and the quality of education in our schools is declining accordingly. And yet most of us sit back and do nothing to help solve these problems. Is our nation dying a slow death? In a few years will life on this planet be impossible? What price must we pay to remedy these deplorable conditions?

SHORT CONCLUSIONS

Many papers of the type you write in English Composition and other college courses will be relatively short, say three to five hundred words.

These usually will not require a summary conclusion similar to the one presented above. However, you will still need a conclusion that clearly gives the impression that you are bringing your paper to an end. Do not just stop after your last subtopic.

OWNING YOUR OWN HOME

Main idea statement: There are both advantages and disadvantages in owning your own home.

Introduction
 I. Disadvantages
    A. Financial
    B. Other
 II. Advantages
    A. Financial
    B. Other
Conclusion

> After considering the advantages and disadvantages of buying our own home, my wife and I decided that we should wait no longer. Now all we have to do is worry about getting a loan, which should not be too difficult, for we have an excellent credit rating. We are looking forward with great joy to this "once in a lifetime" experience.

GETTING RID OF MY OLD CAR

Main idea statement: I decided to get rid of my old car for a number of reasons.

Introduction
  I. Because the oil pan was leaking
 II. Because the carburetor was defective
III. Because the door latch was broken
Conclusion

> Now that I have definitely made up my mind to get rid of my old car, I can start looking around for a new or used one that I can afford. I care about style, but my most important consideration is fuel economy. The last thing in the world I want is a gas guzzler.

Remember, then, that a composition—no matter how long or short—should have an introduction, at least two main divisions, and a conclusion. The introduction should give the reader a general idea of what you are going to discuss or try to prove in the body of your paper. The main divisions should develop your main idea statement by presenting sufficient details to back up your general assertions. The conclusion should remind the reader once more of your main idea and go a step beyond what you have said in the introduction and main body of the composition. The extra time you spend writing the best possible introduction and conclusion may mean the difference between a poor and superior composition.

EXERCISE 19

For each outline below, write a brief introduction and a brief conclusion based on the title and main divisions. To get the main idea (or thesis) statement for your introduction, relate one of the key thought words— *how, if, what, when, where, who, why*—to the title. Then ask a question. Answer the question with a generalization. In the conclusion, try to go a step beyond what you would have said in the main body of the composition.

THE NEED FOR A CAMPUS BEEF (OR RAP) SESSION

Introduction
 I. For students
II. For teachers
Conclusion

Introduction

_____

_____

_____

_____

_____

Conclusion

_____

_____

_____

_____

_____

CHANGING FASHIONS IN CLOTHES

Introduction
 I. Men's
II. Women's
Conclusion

Introduction

_____

_____

_____

_____

_____

Conclusion

_____

_____

_____

_____

_____

 © 1981 HBJ

EXERCISE 20

For each outline below, write a brief introduction and a brief conclusion based on the title and main divisions. To get the main idea (or thesis) statement for your introduction, relate one of the key thought words— *how, if, what, when, where, who, why*—to the title. Then ask a question. Answer the question with a generalization. In the conclusion, try to go a step beyond what you would have said in the main body of the composition.

AN OUTSTANDING MOVIE

Introduction
  I. Excellent acting
 II. Superb photography
III. Effective music
Conclusion

Introduction

_____

_____

_____

_____

_____

Conclusion

_____

_____

_____

_____

CONSUMER EXPLOITATION

Introduction
 I. Products
II. Services
Conclusion

Introduction

_____

_____

_____

_____

_____

Conclusion

_____

_____

_____

_____

_____

© 1981 HBJ

EXERCISE 21

For each outline below, write a brief introduction and a brief conclusion based on the title and main divisions. To get the main idea (or thesis) statement for your introduction, relate one of the key thought words— *how, if, what, when, where, who, why*—to the title. Then ask a question. Answer the question with a generalization. In the conclusion, try to go a step beyond what you would have said in the main body of your composition.

PROBLEMS OF THE ELDERLY

Introduction
  I. Nutrition
 II. Housing
III. Medical care
Conclusion

Introduction

_____

_____

_____

_____

_____

Conclusion

_____

_____

_____

_____

WORLD SHORTAGES

Introduction
  I. Food
 II. Wood
III. Energy
Conclusion

Introduction

_____

_____

_____

_____

_____

Conclusion

_____

_____

_____

_____

_____

© 1981 HBJ

EXERCISE 22

For each outline below, write a brief introduction and a brief conclusion based on the title and main divisions. To get the main idea (or thesis) statement for your introduction, relate one of the key thought words—*how, if, what, when, where, who, why*—to the title. Then ask a question. Answer the question with a generalization. In the conclusion, try to go a step beyond what you would have said in the main body of the composition.

HOPES FOR THE FUTURE

Introduction
  I. Elimination of war
 II. Elimination of poverty
III. Improvement in health care
Conclusion

Introduction

_____

_____

_____

_____

_____

Conclusion

_____

_____

_____

_____

_____

A PERSON I ADMIRE

Introduction
 I. Personality
II. Character
Conclusion

Introduction

_____

_____

_____

_____

_____

Conclusion

_____

_____

_____

_____

_____

  © 1981 HBJ

5: Logic for Composition

What is logic? Putting this question to different people would probably yield very different answers:

A college professor who teaches an academic course in logic: Logic is the science concerned with the principles of valid reasoning and correct inference, either deductive or inductive.

A copywriter in an advertising agency: Logic is a part of the mental anguish I go through for several hours a day while writing radio commercials on why people should own their own homes. Personally, I would rather live in an apartment. It's a lot more convenient.

An automobile mechanic: Logic is something I use all the time in figuring out what is wrong with a car or truck and how to fix it. If a car won't start, I check the most obvious cause. If that is all right, I know something else is wrong. So I keep checking. By the process of trial and error, I eventually find what is causing the trouble.

A judge giving instructions to a jury at the end of a trial: Logic should be the basis on which you reach a verdict of guilty or not guilty. One of the most important principles of logic is evidence. To return a verdict of guilty, you must be convinced beyond a reasonable doubt that the evidence logically proves that the defendant committed the crime of which he is accused. Otherwise, you must return a verdict of not guilty.

Logic is used in various ways in many of our daily activities. It is an integral part of reading, listening, speaking, and writing. A basic understanding of the principles of logic can thus be of great help in improving your skills in these areas. In writing, it will help you to anticipate the type of criticism that is likely to be made of your compositions. Thus you will have a chance to qualify your language so that the potential reader will not be able to discount your statements on logical grounds. Indeed, a basic understanding of logic will help you to look at and present many aspects of life more realistically. This understanding is one of the hall-marks of an educated person, and it should be one of the main goals of higher education.

Francis Bacon, the famous English statesman and philosopher, in-sisted that people in all walks of life should study facts carefully before reaching conclusions. He deplored the habit of "unscientific" thought, the gathering of facts to support preconceived ideas rather than the drawing of conclusions after careful study of the facts. Bacon held that ingrained prejudice on the part of individuals is a great obstacle to cor-rect reasoning.

Many problems in logic can be traced to unexamined assumptions, conclusions, or judgments. As Bacon rightly observed, people search for examples to support their opinions; they disregard examples that contra-dict those opinions even "though there be a greater number and weight of instances to be found on the other side." This illogical thinking is quite common in dealing with controversial subjects such as race, religion, pol-itics, economics, arts, music, and so on. Naturally, the lack of logic often causes bitter conflicts.

What are some of the specific causes of illogical thinking? In the essay "Idols of the Mind," Bacon says that wishful thinking is one of the main causes of unreasoned opinion: "For what a man had rather were true he more readily believes."

Another stumbling block to logic, according to Bacon, is the unrelia-bility of each of our five senses: "For the sense by itself is a thing infirm and erring." Bacon contended that our senses, especially sight and hear-ing, often play tricks on us.

There is still another reason for caution in drawing conclusions and making judgments based on sensory experience. Even though accurate, what we think we see and hear at any instant may be an exception rather than the rule. To be judged properly, the experience of the moment must usually be compared to similar perceptions or experiences. Choosing the right experiences to compare and making the right conclusions about them is the essence of logic. Errors in either of these processes are consid-ered logical fallacies.

What can you do to avoid logical fallacies in your own writing? Don't be overly positive in your assertions; strive for a tone of moderation. Don't hesitate to admit that an issue is complex. And don't be afraid to admit that you are not absolutely certain about your conclusions.

You should make a conscious effort to avoid logical fallacies because they tend to suggest that the writer is dishonest, ignorant, or stupid—or a combination of the three. The critical reader, who is usually disagree-able, may pounce on just one logical fallacy as the reason for rejecting an otherwise flawless piece of writing. The logical fallacies most frequently found in student writing are faulty generalization, *post hoc*, begging the question, *non sequitur, argumentum ad hominem*, false or imperfect analogy, and improper appeal to authority.

FAULTY GENERALIZATION

The most common logical fallacy in speech and writing is probably the faulty generalization, sometimes called the hasty or unqualified generalization. It is very difficult to make a generalization that is airtight, especially regarding a controversial topic. Experienced writers are aware of this fact and try to make their generalizations as limited as possible. The broader the generalization, the more likely it is to be in error.

Writing in a cocksure, dogmatic tone, one that suggests shouting or pounding on a table, often leads to faulty generalizations. This type of diction usually coincides with sloppy and uncritical thinking. A moderate tone gives the impression that the writer is a responsible authority who has taken both sides of the question into consideration.

Perhaps the best way to understand the reasons for faulty generalizations is to study some examples:

Faulty Generalization	All people with red hair have hot tempers.
Comment	Faulty generalization can frequently be traced to the unqualified use of such absolute words as *all, always, anyone, best, every, everyone, everything, greatest, least, most, never, no, none, nothing,* and *worst.* In many cases, eliminating the unqualified word solves the problem.
Improved	Some people with red hair have hot tempers.
Faulty Generalization	Shakespeare's *Hamlet* is the best play ever written in the English language.
Comment	Many scholars and critics would take issue with the assertion that *Hamlet* is the best play, arguing, for instance, that Shakespeare's *King Lear* is a better play than *Hamlet.* Some scholars would even argue that *Hamlet* is inferior to plays by other English-speaking writers.
Improved	Most scholars agree that Shakespeare's *Hamlet* is one of the best plays ever written in the English language.
Faulty Generalization	Everyone in the world wants peace.
Comment	Obviously not everyone in the world wants peace—or we would have it. Some people make large fortunes by stirring up armed conflict, and some others—such as power-crazed dictators—get perverted pleasure from conquering other nations.
Improved	Most people throughout the world seem to want peace.

Faulty	
Generalization	The thirst for knowledge is something that every college student will never lose.
Comment	Unfortunately, this statement is not quite true. Some college students will never lose their thirst for knowledge; some others never really had one.
Improved	College students with a true thirst for knowledge look upon learning as a lifelong commitment.

POST HOC
After the Fact;
Therefore, Because of the Fact

The writer who commits the *post hoc* fallacy illogically assumes that one fact is the cause of another simply because it preceded the other in time, as in the following examples:

> George had a heart attack shortly after he walked through the park. Thus, walking through the park must have caused his heart attack.

> Rome fell after the introduction of Christianity. Thus, Christianity no doubt caused the fall of Rome.

> The winter weather in the United States in the year following extensive hydrogen bomb tests in the South Pacific was very severe. Obviously, these tests were responsible for this unusual weather.

As with other logical problems, the best way to avoid the *post hoc* fallacy is to back up your general assertions with facts and examples. If the writer of the sentences linking severe weather and bomb testing had presented data from, say, the United States Weather Bureau indicating that the unusual winter was in fact caused by the extensive exploding of hydrogen bombs, the reader would be more inclined to accept the statement as logically sound.

Much scholastic and professional writing is concerned with cause-and-effect relationships. If you are not careful, you can easily make an illogical statement by positing a cause for an effect merely because the assumed cause precedes the effect in time. Usually a combination of factors causes any one result. Although it is sometimes easy to identify the immediate cause of an effect, it is often difficult to explain the underlying causes.

Also you should be careful not to confuse a cause with an effect, as the writer of the following sentence has done:

> Since most financially secure people are productive, the way to make all citizens productive is to redistribute the wealth so that every adult will have approximately the same amount of money.

The writer of this illogical assertion overlooked or ignored the fact that many people are financially secure because they are productive.

ARGUMENTUM AD HOMINEM
Discrediting a Person
Associated with the Issue
Rather Than the Issue Itself

The *argumentum ad hominem* attempts to disprove or cast doubt on an issue by discrediting the person or persons associated with the issue. This logical fallacy is sometimes difficult to identify, for the criticism of the individual may be relevant to the issue being considered, as in the following example:

> I am opposed to the appointment of John Brown as chief of police, for it is well known that until recently he ran the biggest bookmaking operation in town. Also it is suspected that a couple of years ago he was involved in the selling of illegal drugs.

In this case the criticism of the individual is relevant to the issue under consideration. As chief of police, Brown would have to enforce the laws on gambling and drugs and would be expected to set an example for the rest of the community.

The criticisms in the following sentences are not relevant. Each sentence is an example of the *argumentum ad hominem*, which is often used as a way of evading the issue.

Argumentum ad Hominem	The theories of Karl Marx are obviously immoral and detrimental to the welfare of humankind because he failed miserably to provide a decent living for his own family.
Comment	Attacking Karl Marx as an individual weakens rather than strengthens the writer's argument. Presenting published historical facts that directly refute the theories of Marx would have been more convincing.
Argumentum ad Hominem	Inasmuch as Freud was an atheist, his therapeutic methods have little value in treating nervous disorders.
Comment	The logical fallacy in this statement is not quite as clear-cut as the previous one, for it contains certain implied premises. But as it stands, the intelligent reader would probably reject it because of the hostile attitude toward Freud based on a difference of opinion about religion.
Argumentum ad Hominem	The legislation that Senator Smith proposes to reduce unemployment is obviously a farce. For it is well known that he is a man of expensive tastes with a private fortune of several million dollars. Just how did he amass such a huge fortune?
Comment	This statement does not argue to the point, for it does not present relevant facts that discredit the legislation. Rather it makes an illogical attack on the character and finances of Senator Smith.

BEGGING THE QUESTION
Saying More or Less the Same Thing
in the Beginning
That You Say in the End

Begging the question is another logical fallacy in speech and writing. It can be traced to one of the most basic problems in communication: the failure of the speaker or writer to present enough facts and examples to support the original assertion. You beg the question when you say more or less the same thing in your premise as in your conclusion. Begging the question is arguing in a circle. The writer tries to prove the premise by the conclusion and the conclusion by the premise—and ends up proving nothing at all. The examples of begging the question that follow are typical of the fallacious thinking that is often found in speech and writing:

Begging the Question Being on time for work is important because no one should be late for work.

Comment If you read the first part of this statement carefully, you will see that the writer did not answer the important question, "Why is it important?"

Begging the Question The belief in justice is universal, for everyone believes in justice.

Comment If you examine the statement with a critical eye, you will see that the writer only seems to present evidence for an assertion. The would-be evidence is actually a rewording of the opening generalization.

Begging the Question Roast beef is my favorite meat because I like roast beef better than any other meat.

Comment The second clause in the sentence serves no logical purpose. To improve the sentence, the writer needs to suggest why roast beef is the favorite.

FALSE OR IMPERFECT ANALOGY
Comparing Unlike Things
That Have Implied Similarities

An analogy is a figurative or metaphorical contrast between things or concepts based not on an actual likeness but upon implied similarities that may be common to the things or ideas being compared—for instance, comparing the buttons on a coat to the coordinate elements of a sentence or comparing a single atom to the solar system.

The vivid use of analogy is an effective technique in writing. As the proverb states, "One picture is worth a thousand words." A good analogy is sometimes useful in clarifying factual evidence, but arguments based solely on analogy are not desirable. Although a properly drawn analogy may enhance an argument, there is general agreement among logicians that analogy is not valid as evidence or proof in an argument. The comparison of dissimilar things—such as learning to be a lawyer and learning to play tennis—generally breaks down under careful examination; the differences are usually more important than the similarities. In ignoring the differences, the person using the analogy as evidence in an argument usually oversimplifies the issue.

False Analogy   Writing is a skill like bowling or playing tennis. A person becomes skillful in sports only through actual practice. Therefore, studying textbooks on writing is a waste of time.

False Analogy   If a man has a new car, he should drive it. If a woman has a new dress, she should wear it. If a nation has a new ballistic missile, it should use it.

IMPROPER APPEAL TO AUTHORITY

After you complete your basic courses in composition, most of your out-of-class writing for other courses will be in the form of reference papers, usually on topics related to the course. Although the success of these papers will depend to a large degree on your skill in organizing and marshaling facts to support generalizations, every reference paper you write should closely follow the rules of logic. Usually you will be digesting, summarizing, and quoting the published works of writers, who, to varying degrees, are considered authorities on the topic of your paper. Thus, before attempting the writing necessary in your advanced courses, you would be wise to learn what constitutes an improper appeal to authority—the logical fallacy that occurs often in academic reference papers and other reports.

When a writer is not an expert on a subject, he or she must depend on reliable authorities. But who should be considered an authority? This is not an easy question to answer. Some of the heated debates in law courts have concerned whether or not a certain individual was qualified as an authority. But usually an authority is determined more informally, through recognition in the given field. In the field of chemistry, for instance, James B. Conant might be considered an authority: he has written a number of books on chemistry and was one of the key figures in the development of atomic energy at the beginning of the Second World War. Similarly, Erich Fromm might be considered an authority on psychology: he practiced psychiatry and was the author of a number of highly regarded books on the subject. An authority, then, is a person who is proficient in a special field and articulate in communicating knowledge of it to others.

We commit the improper appeal to authority fallacy in a number of different ways: (1) by citing persons or groups who are not qualified to be called authorities:

It is absolutely necessary that a federal tax refund be given to stimulate the economy. Dr. Harris, my dentist, said that such a refund is crucial to the future of this country.

(2) by appealing to an authority that may have been competent at one time but is no longer accepted because of a change in time or circumstances:

The founders of the Republic were vigorously opposed to a strong federal government; therefore, the bill now before the Senate to regulate interstate commerce should be rejected.

and (3) by appealing to an authority that may be legitimate in one field but not qualified in another:

The space program should be discarded. Guy Strong, a former All-American football player and now a top television sportscaster, has said that it is a waste of the taxpayer's money.

NON SEQUITUR
It Does Not Follow

The last logical fallacy that we shall discuss, *non sequitur* (it does not follow), tends to occur when the writer is not quite certain as to what he or she is trying to say. You have committed the *non sequitur* fallacy when your conclusion does not logically follow from your premise or premises: "John is a very handsome man. He is also poor. Therefore, he has obviously wasted his talents."

Everyone who has ever seen John may agree that he is handsome; the fact that he recently declared bankruptcy may confirm that he is poor; and those people who know John best may agree that he has wasted his talents. But the statement is illogical (a *non sequitur*) because the premises provide no basis for the conclusion. The same is true of the following sentences:

Non Sequitur   The other day Jack bought a motor scooter. Obviously he hates automobiles.

Non Sequitur   The man sitting across the aisle from me on the train has a long beard; hence he must be poor.

Non Sequitur   Larry does not have a girl friend; so he must be going to college after he graduates from high school.

Non Sequitur   Leona is not only kind but also intelligent; her parents must be college graduates.

Non Sequitur   Jim is a terrific football player; undoubtedly his IQ must be below average.

In a broad sense, almost any logical fallacy can be called a *non sequitur*, because for one reason or another its conclusion "does not logically follow." There is, for example, often only a fine line of difference between a faulty generalization and a *non sequitur*. In some cases, the logical fallacy is as much one as the other.

Faulty logic of any type is a more serious problem in writing than most composition students realize. For most purposes, content (the logical ordering of parts and the truth of all assertions) is perhaps more important than mechanics (punctuation, spelling, grammar, and so on). By underestimating the *what* and overestimating the *how*, writers can fail to give proper consideration to the opposite side of a debatable question; they can jump to conclusion without giving sufficient evidence or reach a conclusion that is not justified by the premises; they can use imprecise or inappropriate figures of speech and be grossly prejudiced, considering only their own feelings or beliefs. All these errors in logic can be avoided in your writing if you place proper emphasis on improving the content, as well as the style, of your compositions. Objectivity and reason are expected of the college student in all written assignments.

EXERCISE 23

Each of the following sentences contains a fallacy. Identify the fallacy by its letter on the following list, and place that letter in the left-hand column opposite the sentence.

U. Unqualified or Hasty Generalization
P. *Post Hoc* (after the fact; therefore, because of the fact)
A. *Argumentum ad Hominem* (discrediting the individual rather than the issue)
B. Begging the Question
F. False Analogy
I. Improper Appeal to Authority
N. *Non Sequitur* (it does not follow)

_____ 1. Susan lives alone, proving that she dislikes people.

_____ 2. This tax on gasoline will reduce the consumption of petroleum, for less gasoline will be used if such a tax is imposed.

_____ 3. The human eye is like a camera; therefore, defective parts of the eye can be readily replaced.

_____ 4. Everyone should learn to drive an automobile.

_____ 5. Since Senator Smith is being sued for divorce by his second wife on the grounds of mental cruelty, I am opposed to his plan for national health insurance.

_____ 6. Well-groomed people make friends easily.

_____ 7. The ambassador to the United Nations Organization is opposed to high interest rates. Therefore, the present rate of interest should be held steady or reduced.

_____ 8. Everyone enjoys being with relatives on holidays.

_____ 9. The prices charged for oil by the OPEC countries are outrageous. Consequently, the United States should immediately stop buying oil from this cartel.

_____10. The other day Lucy bought a Volkswagen, proving that she hates big automobiles.

_____11. After Joe learned to play the guitar he stopped drinking. It is remarkable that a hobby can have such a great influence on your life.

© 1981 HBJ

_____12. People who live in apartments do not like to do yard work.

_____13. The desire for happiness is universal since most people want to be happy.

_____14. The improvement of the transit system will attract many more shoppers to the downtown business district.

_____15. Aristotle invented the science of physics. Einstein's theory of relativity contradicts some of Aristotle's basic principles. Hence Einstein's theory must be fallacious.

_____16. United States senators do not give a hoot for the average taxpayer.

_____17. After being in an auto accident, Mary had a nervous breakdown. It is sad that an auto accident has a severe emotional effect on a person's life.

_____18. The only reason people work is to make money.

_____19. The bill offered by Senator Knight to reduce waste in the federal government is unsound, for before he became a senator he was the president of a company that went bankrupt.

_____20. Everyone enjoys watching television.

 © 1981 HBJ

EXERCISE 24

Each of the following sentences contains a fallacy. Identify the fallacy by its letter on the following list, and place that letter in the left-hand column opposite the sentence.

   U. Unqualified or Hasty Generalization
   P. *Post Hoc* (after the fact; therefore, because of the fact)
   A. *Argumentum ad Hominem* (discrediting the individual rather than the issue)
   B. Begging the Question
   F. False Analogy
   I. Improper Appeal to Authority
   N. *Non Sequitur* (it does not follow)

_____ 1. People cannot see themselves as others see them.

_____ 2. Henrik Ibsen fathered a child out of wedlock. Consequently, the social criticism in his plays should not be taken seriously.

_____ 3. Yolanda is very pretty. She is also very quiet. So she must be conceited.

_____ 4. The postal service in the United States needs to be improved, for it should be better than it is.

_____ 5. Jane, who is single, dropped out of college. Thus she will probably never get married.

_____ 6. Tony likes to fish. So he must be lazy and without ambition.

_____ 7. Before writing my reference paper on drug abuse, I talked with my uncle, who is a building contractor, to get some ideas I might use.

_____ 8. Frank Harris drives a 1975 Ford. So he must not have a very good job.

_____ 9. Becoming a competent writer is like becoming a good tennis player. It takes a lot of practice. So rather than waste my time studying textbooks, I will just write.

_____10. There are advantages and disadvantages to everything in life.

_____11. Larry is not handsome. So he will not make a very good lawyer.

_____12. Howard Jones is not competent to serve on the school board. Ten years ago he was fined for double-parking his car in front of the elementary school.

_____13. Before I began writing my research paper on police brutality, I talked with my grandfather, a retired bank president, to get some information that I might use.

_____14. Everyone should drink a cup of black coffee every morning.

_____15. A semester after the new president took office, the enrollment at our college increased by ten percent. It is amazing what one person can do to improve an institution.

_____16. Jim is a very friendly young man. He should make an outstanding teacher.

_____17. College professors are detached from reality.

_____18. As Shakespeare wrote, "All the world's a stage, and all the men and women merely players." Thus, people who have not been to acting school will have a hard time in life.

_____19. Home cooking is better than the food you can get in restaurants.

_____20. Poor achievement in school is often caused by poor housing conditions, for an uncomfortable domicile often causes poor academic achievement.

  © 1981 HBJ

EXERCISE 25

Each of the following sentences contains a fallacy. Identify the fallacy by its letter on the following list, and place that letter in the left-hand column opposite the sentence.

U. Unqualified or Hasty Generalization
P. *Post Hoc* (after the fact; therefore, because of the fact)
A. *Argumentum ad Hominem* (discrediting the individual rather than the issue)
B. Begging the Question
F. False Analogy
I. Improper Appeal to Authority
N. *Non Sequitur* (it does not follow)

_____ 1. Paul bought a shortwave radio. Obviously he hates to watch television.

_____ 2. Before he entered politics, Harry Truman failed in business. It is no wonder that the economy suffered a mild depression after he became president of the United States.

_____ 3. Everyone hates to get up in the morning.

_____ 4. Yesterday I got up feeling depressed. On my way to work I had a flat tire. It is strange how your moods can effect almost everything that happens to you.

_____ 5. Mr. Douglas is talkative. He also has a ruddy complexion. Consequently, he must have a violent temper.

_____ 6. A dictionary is like a miniature encyclopedia. Therefore, you can get all the factual information you need by consulting a good dictionary.

_____ 7. With a bike there is never a parking problem as there is with a car.

_____ 8. A proper diet is necessary for sound teeth, for dental health requires the right kind of food and drink.

_____ 9. Harold is deeply religious. He would make an excellent lawyer.

_____ 10. Tomorrow afternoon our debating team is going to debate Western State on the petroleum issue. I am on my way to talk with the pastor of my church to get some information I can use.

_____11. Everyone knows the difference between right and wrong.

_____12. Let's not have lasagna, for everytime we do it rains.

_____13. I am strictly opposed to the snow removal plan that Alderman Rainbolt supports. When he was a young man he was dismissed from West Point for cheating on an exam.

_____14. You have to pay income tax on the interest you receive on money in a bank. Therefore, a savings account is not a good form of investment.

_____15. Making a garment is a creative act like painting a picture. If a person does not have artistic talent, he or she should not attempt to make a suit.

_____16. The Parthenon, an ancient Greek temple, was the most splendid building ever constructed.

_____17. Bowling is an enjoyable pastime, for it is fun to bowl.

_____18. Mary is an only child. She must be very selfish.

_____19. I have to write a reference paper on child abuse as a social problem. I will talk with my uncle, who is a dentist, to get some ideas.

_____20. Serial dramas, which were formerly heard on the radio and are now seen on television, have no literary value.

 © 1981 HBJ

6: Using Precise Words

How can you improve your ability to speak and write with clarity and precision? One of the best ways is to form the dictionary habit in your reading. Of course, it is sometimes impractical to look up the meaning of every word that is unclear to you. Moreover, you will often be able to guess the meaning of an unfamiliar word from its context. But in most instances, the time it takes to confirm the meaning of a word is well worthwhile.

If periodically—say once a week—you were to read a well-written essay and underline and analyze all the words that are not in your active vocabulary, in a matter of time your language skills would improve. Looking up the words in your dictionary or in a thesaurus will yield a brief definition or synonym that can be substituted for the underlined word. You will also get valuable writing experience by composing sentences in which you use the "new" words. If you keep a record of such words and review them from time to time, they will soon become part of your active vocabulary, improving all your communication skills—reading, writing, speaking, and listening.

Besides forming the dictionary habit, anyone who is anxious to speak and write with greater precision should avoid the major pitfalls in word selection: wrong words, weak words, and overemphatic words.

WRONG WORDS

A large vocabulary can be an asset to any speaker or writer. However, some people attempt to appear intellectual by using uncommon words (and/or words they do not fully understand) when more familiar words would suffice. This tendency can be seen among college students who are consciously trying to improve their writing. Struggling to impress the reader, many students choose a word for its complexity or rarity and give too little thought to its meaning.

Poor	An *extenuating* vocabulary is an asset in all forms of verbal communication.
Better	An extensive vocabulary is an asset in all forms of verbal communication.
Poor	Schizophrenia destroys reason, a precious human *commodity.*
Better	Schizophrenia destroys reason, a precious human faculty.
Poor	A decline in *immortality* is one of the reasons for the population explosion.
Better	A decline in the death rate is one of the reasons for the population explosion.
Poor	John Wallace, while running for governor, said that he would call out the national guard if the laws of the state were *vexed.*
Better	John Wallace, while running for governor, said that he would call out the national guard if the laws of the state were violated.
Poor	The effects of air pollution have been *awesome.*
Better	The effects of air pollution have been alarming.
Poor	Divorce is usually a tragic *experiment* for the people involved.
Better	Divorce is usually a tragic experience for the people involved.
Poor	I hope to gain a *desirable* education in college.
Better	I hope to gain a useful education in college.

The use of the terms *wrong words*, *weak words*, and *overemphatic words* in this chapter is a good example of the problems involved in using words precisely. In one sense, weak words and overemphatic words may be considered wrong. However, in another sense they may be considered only imprecise, not wrong. There is also a problem of overlapping coordination. In some cases it is possible for a word to be equally weak and/or overemphatic.

WEAK WORDS

Weak words are often difficult to distinguish from specific and precise words, for context largely determines (or should determine) the appropriate language to use. For instance, in a letter to a friend you may deliberately use imprecise and exaggerated words to achieve a humorous or ironic effect, and this informal style may make your letter readable and entertaining.

But most of the writing you do in college and the letters and reports you will write after you leave college will require a more exact vocabulary than does a breezy letter to a friend. As you advance in college your written assignments will be increasingly based on books and periodicals; the diction you use in this type of writing should be more specific than the vocabulary you use in an informal letter.

The same high standards will be expected of the professional writing you will do after you leave college. As a social worker you will probably be expected to use mature language in writing your case reports and other correspondence. As a business executive writing letters for your company, you will be expected to write like a well-educated adult—not a high-school freshman. As a certified public accountant you may retain or lose a client because of the exactness or vagueness of your audit report. As a laboratory scientist your lengthy report based on months of research may be accepted or rejected because of the precision of the language.

In most practical writing situations clarity and exactness in diction are important; for before readers can judge the merit of your conclusions, they must have a clear understanding of what you are saying. Thus in advising you to eliminate weak words from your writing and to substitute more concrete and precise words, we are referring to a particular type of writing—the more formal essays and reports you will have to do in school and the letters and reports that you will have to compose in your professional work.

The clarity of your writing depends to a large extent on whether you use specific words or general ones that have lost their vigor because of overuse. Some of the words usually considered weak are *awful, bad, beautiful, big, fine, funny, good, great, interesting, lovely, nice, pretty, swell, thing, wonderful.* The following sample sentences show ways to avoid such words.

Poor   Susan said that she had an *awful* time at the homecoming dance.
Better   Susan said that she had a boring time at the homecoming dance.

Poor   The starting pay isn't *bad*, but they hold back your first paycheck for one month.
Better   The starting pay is adequate, but the company holds back your first paycheck for one month.

Poor   Stella Hardin achieved a *big* success when she ran for president of the student council.
Better   Stella Hardin was elected president of the student council by an overwhelming majority.

Poor   The college provided the students with some very *fine* programs.
Better   The college provided the students with some very stimulating programs.

Poor   It is *funny* how some people achieve financial success and others do not.
Better   It is hard to understand how some people achieve financial success and others do not.

Poor   We had a *good* time on our fishing trip to Dale Hollow.
Better   We had an enjoyable time on our fishing trip to Dale Hollow.

Poor	The movie had an *interesting* plot.
Better	The movie had a suspenseful plot.
Poor	Mr. Green, the manager of the supermarket, has a *nice* personality.
Better	Mr. Green, the manager of the supermarket, has a friendly personality.
Poor	During our vacation in Maine, we had a very *pretty* view of the Atlantic Ocean from our hotel room.
Better	During our vacation in Maine, we had a splendid view of the Atlantic Ocean from our hotel room.
Poor	There are certain *things* I look for in judging a person's character.
Better	There are certain traits I look for in judging a person's character.

OVEREMPHATIC WORDS

The distinction between weak words and overemphatic words is sometimes a matter of opinion. Whereas weak words generally dull the sharpness and incisiveness of writing by not saying enough, overemphatic words say more than is appropriate. Enthusiasm is an admirable quality; but unrestrained enthusiasm or a lack of moderation in speech and writing may lead to illogical assertions. In addition, the immoderate use of extreme words and phrases can be a handicap in developing a mature style of writing. The italicized words in the following sentences are frequently misused in speech and writing. Each word is overemphatic in the context in which it appears.

Poor	The county agent gave a *magnificent* talk on the need for crop rotation.
Better	The county agent gave an informative talk on the need for crop rotation.
Poor	I was *amazed* at the differences between high school and college.
Better	I was surprised at the differences between high school and college.
Poor	The author's description of the five characters killed when the bridge collapsed is *terrific*.
Better	The author's description of the five characters killed when the bridge collapsed is impressive.
Poor	During our visit to New Orleans, we had a *fabulous* dinner at a famous French restaurant.
Better	During our visit to New Orleans, we had a delicious dinner at a famous French restaurant.
Poor	The governor gave a *tremendous* speech at the graduation exercises.
Better	The governor gave an inspiring speech at the graduation exercises.
Poor	I was *astonished* by the ability of my math teacher to solve difficult problems quickly.
Better	I was impressed by the ability of my math teacher to solve difficult problems quickly.

The difference between poor and superior writing is often a matter of using words precisely. Experienced writers may use the words we have labeled weak and overemphatic, but they tend to use them with discretion. Inexperienced writers have a tendency to overuse such words. The clarity and style of your writing should improve if you begin to judge each word for precision and suitability and keep your use of marginal words to a minimum.

EXERCISE 26

Substitute more precise words and phrases for those italicized.

1. Alcoholism is more *popular* among the upper classes.

   _____

2. When I visited Paris for the first time, I was *astonished* by the amount of boat traffic on the Seine.

   _____

3. One of the *things* that impressed me most about New Orleans was the statue of Andrew Jackson in the middle of the square that bears his name.

   _____

4. The governor seemed *pretty tired* after his long speech.

   _____

5. A college is what its *inhabitants* make it.

   _____

6. My high-school English teacher wrote a *nice* letter wishing me success in college.

   _____

7. Dr. White gave an *interesting* talk on the need for a balanced diet.

   _____

8. The increase in crime in our city during the past ten years has been *amazing*.

   _____

9. I feel that many television programs are *unhealthy* for children.

   _____

10. It seems *funny* that the ambulance didn't arrive on the scene until an hour after the accident.

   _____

© 1981 HBJ

11. The actors in the movie were miscast, but it had a *fabulous* plot.

_____

12. The loss of electricity due to the *bad* tornado made it necessary to impose a curfew.

_____

13. John Kennedy had *extreme* intelligence.

_____

14. I am confident that if Coleman is elected he will do a *magnificent* job as mayor.

_____

15. The Gilberts said they had an *awful* time at the party.

_____

 © 1981 HBJ

EXERCISE 27

Substitute more precise words and phrases for those italicized.

1. I am going to vote for Harriet Luckett because I think she will make a *fine* governor.

   _____

2. People are usually not happy unless they receive some sort of *retribution* for their efforts.

   _____

3. Automation has affected the economy of the country *tremendously*.

   _____

4. I was surprised at the *bad* housing conditions that exist throughout the valley.

   _____

5. The committee appointed by the mayor played a *magnificent* role in curbing false advertising.

   _____

6. Senator Patterson gave a *wonderful* speech on the need for economy in government.

   _____

7. The search for a leading lady was one of the most extensive ever *inaugurated* by a film company.

   _____

8. In my opinion, Johnny Carson is the most *interesting* talk-show host on television.

   _____

9. Irene has a *terrific* idea for a short story about teen-age marriages.

   _____

© 1981 HBJ

10. We can learn a *very good* lesson from the story.

_____

11. My pastor has *enhanced* me into thinking about my real purpose in life.

_____

12. Our view of the Grand Canyon at sunset was *beautiful*.

_____

13. The president talked about many *things* in his recent speech before Congress.

_____

14. Sue told me that she had an *awful* time during her first year as vice-president of the company.

_____

15. The Empire State Building affords a *nice* view of New York City.

_____

   © 1981 HBJ

EXERCISE 28

Substitute more precise words and phrases for those italicized.

1. The social worker devised a *wonderful* plan to rehabilitate convicts.

   _____

2. My friend, Jean, has a *nice* personality.

   _____

3. The *dialogue* of Jimmy Stewart clearly sets him apart from other actors.

   _____

4. I was *astonished* that only a small number of people attended the game.

   _____

5. The scenery of the Swiss Alps is *beautiful.*

   _____

6. The talent of the choreographer was a *prevailing* factor in the success of the musical.

   _____

7. I have always been *tremendously* interested in history.

   _____

8. I have not found enough material on the subject in the branch library to write a *good* research paper.

   _____

9. The movie had a plot that *demonstrated* a great deal of suspense.

   _____

10. The food served in the restaurant at the state park was *terrific.*

    _____

© 1981 HBJ

11. Clint Eastwood had a *big* role in the movie.

_____

12. If I am to return to school in the fall, I must find a summer job that pays a *feasible* salary.

_____

13. It is *amazing* that so many qualified college graduates are unable to find employment.

_____

14. Gary's high-school principal wrote a *fine* recommendation for him.

_____

15. One of the most important *things* a job can teach a young person is the value of money.

_____

   © 1981 HBJ

EXERCISE 29

Substitute more precise words and phrases for those italicized.

1. We had a *very pretty* view from the window of our seaside hotel.

    _____

2. Karl Jaspers says that people find the future so *disastrous* that it fills them with dread.

    _____

3. Driving to Chicago isn't too *bad* since it is only fifty miles away.

    _____

4. The City Council submitted a *fabulous* plan for the construction of a garbage disposal facility.

    _____

5. Senator Harris developed an *awful* headache and was unable to keep his speaking engagement.

    _____

6. The electronics company in our city has announced some *terrific* plans for expansion.

    _____

7. The judge had to use a great deal of care in making her decision, for the custody of a child is a *funny thing*.

    _____

8. The candidate for governor avoided giving direct answers to *prominent* questions of the day.

    _____

9. I like the book because of its suspenseful plot and its *good* setting.

    _____

10. Jennifer wrote an *interesting* article on the need for federal aid to private schools.

    _____

© 1981 HBJ

11. I was *astonished* by the amount of business we were able to transact at our last meeting.

———————————————————————————————————

12. When administered properly, urban renewal has a *gratifying* effect on a community.

———————————————————————————————————

13. Tom told me many *things* about farming that have been a great help to me.

———————————————————————————————————

14. In my estimation Judge McGuire handed down a *perfect* decision in the antitrust suit.

———————————————————————————————————

15. An aspiring actor can gain *wonderful* experience by participating in amateur theatricals.

———————————————————————————————————

 © 1981 HBJ

EXERCISE 30

Substitute more precise words and phrases for those italicized.

1. The mayor did his best to remedy the *bad* conditions in the slum areas.

   _____

2. The networks did a *stupendous* job covering the political convention.

   _____

3. Macomb has some *good* farmland on the outskirts of town.

   _____

4. I was *astonished* that Dr. Vetter did not require regular classroom attendance.

   _____

5. My visit to the museum proved to be very *interesting*.

   _____

6. Few historians depict Adolph Hitler as a *commendable* person.

   _____

7. On our way to Denver, we had a *nice* visit with relatives who live in St. Louis.

   _____

8. Ewing made a *tremendous* effort to clear his garden of weeds.

   _____

9. The energy crisis is one of the *things* that the candidates talked about in their debate.

   _____

10. Jones was a *terrific* leader of the subcommittee on ethics.

   _____

© 1981 HBJ

11. The small car had some *discouraging* features.

_____

12. The governor gave a *wonderful* speech on the need to control strip mining.

_____

13. The Red Cross was *tremendous* in bringing relief to the flood victims.

_____

14. Elmhurst is a *beautiful* town overlooking the Illinois River.

_____

15. The traveling nurses made an *enormous* effort to help the sick people they visited.

_____

© 1981 HBJ

EXERCISE 31

Substitute more precise words and phrases for those italicized.

1. I was *amazed* to discover that Thomas Edison's New Jersey laboratory can now be seen at the Greenfield Village in Dearborn, Michigan.

_____

2. The *bad* storm did much damage to the tobacco crop.

_____

3. Carl Price wrote a *magnificent* essay on the Civil War.

_____

4. Dr. Bradley's teaching methods were *very good.*

_____

5. Our pastor gave a *terrific* sermon on helping your neighbor.

_____

6. The movie had an *interesting* plot.

_____

7. After I paid all my bills, all worries were *neglected* from my mind.

_____

8. The economist gave an *interesting* speech on the dangers of inflation.

_____

9. A person is handicapped without a *reliable* background in writing.

_____

10. My father received a *nice* bonus at the end of the year because his company made windfall profits.

_____

11. Where the facts end and the fiction begins is not *decipherable.*

_____

12. One of the *things* that the party out of power exploits during an election is the economic unrest of the people.

_____

13. Clear writing is a *symbol* of a well-educated person.

_____

14. Television may prove to be a *good* medium for adult education.

_____

15. John Keats wrote a *stupendous* poem, "Ode to a Nightingale," about a man who is deeply depressed.

_____

 © 1981 HBJ

7: Deadwood

serious problem in writing is *deadwood:* needless words, phrases, and sentences that impede the smooth flow of language. As a writer, you should always strive to express your ideas clearly. This means getting rid of any dead branches and useless limbs that may clutter your writing.

Deadwood in writing can be divided into broad categories: branches and twigs—unnecessary words and phrases that clog sentences; and limbs—unnecessary sentences or paragraphs. The latter type of deadwood (also called digression) can usually be traced to poor organization; the writer in all probability has not organized the ideas in logical sequence before composing the first draft.

In this section, however, we are mainly concerned with unnecessary twigs and useless branches that clutter sentences and paragraphs. Perhaps the easiest way to solve this problem is to understand *why* deadwood is so common in writing.

Deadwood may result if the writer fails to use pronouns in references to previous noun constructions.

Poor The athletes who make up the swimming and track and tennis teams are usually very fond of their sport. For the athletes who participate in these sports as a general rule receive neither financial help nor recognition.

Better The athletes who make up the swimming, track, and tennis teams are usually very fond of their sport. In most cases they receive neither financial help nor recognition.

Poor   The Red Cross volunteers deserve a great deal of credit for the help they gave during the recent tornado. The Red Cross volunteers staffed the rescue centers that provided housing, food, and clothing for the victims of the disaster.

Better   The Red Cross volunteers deserve a great deal of credit for the help given during the recent tornado. They staffed the rescue centers that provided housing, food, and clothing for the victims of the disaster.

Deadwood may result when modifiers are used that do not add to the meaning of the sentence.

Poor   I had a *very* difficult time getting my car started.
Better   I had a difficult time getting my car started.

Poor   We *really* had a wonderful time at the dance.
Better   We had a wonderful time at the dance.

Poor   I am *surely* glad I learned to swim when I was a kid.
Better   I am glad I learned to swim when I was a kid.

Poor   I was not *actually* surprised when I heard Joan got the lead in the play.
Better   I was not surprised when I heard Joan got the lead in the play.

Poor   I was *merely* sitting in class, letting my mind wander, when the professor asked me to explain the principle.
Better   I was sitting in class, letting my mind wander, when the professor asked me to explain the principle.

Poor   I was *simply* too tired to go to the dance after studying for the midterm exams.
Better   I was too tired to go to the dance after studying for the midterm exams.

Deadwood may result from needless repetition before examples or illustrations.

Poor   We had to sacrifice a great deal in order to win the district contest. Some of the sacrifices made were omitting a few lunches, study periods, and history classes.
Better   We had to sacrifice a great deal to win the district contest, for example, study periods, history classes, and (most important) a few lunches.

Poor   The novel was outstanding for several reasons. One reason it was outstanding is that everything had a meaning and a place.
Better   I thought the novel was outstanding because every element was logically related to the theme.

Deadwood may result when words and phrases are awkwardly inserted rather than implied.

Poor   Huntsville is a very interesting city to live in because of the many interesting and varied people living there.
Better   Huntsville is an interesting city to live in because of its diversified population.

Poor   One of the most difficult decisions I have ever made in my life is whether or not I should go to college after high school or not go to college after high school.

Better   I had a difficult time deciding whether or not to go to college right after high school.

Deadwood may result when related ideas are expressed in more than one sentence.

Poor   The car my mother owns is in perfect running order. One of the reasons it is in perfect running order is the fact that she has it serviced every thousand miles.

Better   The car my mother owns is in perfect running order because she has it serviced every thousand miles.

Poor   The students gave up their leisure time to sell magazines. Most of the people bought the magazines. Some who did not need magazines bought them just to help the class.

Better   The students gave up their leisure time to sell magazines, and many people in the neighborhood bought them mainly to help a worthy cause.

You can see in comparing the poor examples with the better ones that the elimination of deadwood not only shortens a sentence but makes it more readable. If you try to avoid useless words and roundabout sentence structure, your writing should become more precise. Unfortunately, deadwood is not always easy to spot. It is easy enough for a sharp reader to see the deadwood in another's writing; but it is difficult—unless you make a special effort—to see it in your own. Perhaps the easiest way to detect wordiness is to proofread your writing out loud, looking for words and phrases and even complete sentences that are nonessential. The best time to do this is just before you write the final draft of your composition.

EXERCISE 32

Rewrite the following sentences, eliminating the deadwood (1) by using a pronoun to take the place of a wordy noun construction, (2) by deleting nonessential modifiers, (3) by striking words or phrases that can be easily inferred, (4) by combining the closely related thoughts of two or more sentences into one, or (5) by using any other method that seems practical. Before you begin the exercise, study the following example.

> *Poor*   There are also many people who can't afford to go to a college out of town.
>
> *Better*   Many people cannot afford to attend an out-of-town college.

1. Bears that have just come out of hibernation are usually very hungry for food. The bears are usually very dangerous at this time of year.

   _____

   _____

2. We were actually astonished when we discovered that the teacher was really strict in requiring very regular attendance.

   _____

   _____

3. We took several different tests. These tests included math, English, and science.

   _____

4. Birth control is a topic that creates a great number of controversial arguments.

   _____

5. After the hunter tramped all day in the woods, the hunter came home.

   _____

6. We all were surely surprised when the small Indiana college very nearly upset Michigan State.

   _____

   _____

7. I believe every person on earth should have his or her chance to decide what kind of job or work to do.

_____

_____

8. You must first choose a theme or caption for your float. This is usually a clever saying that will impress the judges.

_____

_____

9. The student body was simply overjoyed when the dean announced that there would be a holiday because of our very excellent play in the tournament.

_____

_____

10. Some of the members of the cast made the audience actually like and respect them in many ways due to the superb acting they did or the characters they portrayed.

_____

_____

11. We were really amazed at the very large crowd on hand for the ceremony.

_____

12. The men in the volunteer fire department deserve a lot of credit. The volunteer firemen answer the alarm any time day or night and in all kinds of weather.

_____

_____

13. An insurance company is a very interesting place to work because of the many varied interesting business transactions that are made there.

_____

_____

 © 1981 HBJ

14. I believe television does foster maturity for the following reasons: television is informative, it is educational, and it is entertaining.

_____

_____

15. Children who live together daily learn to share and to respect the rights of others. Sharing and respecting the rights of other people are important qualities in any society.

_____

_____

© 1981 HBJ

EXERCISE 33

Rewrite the following sentences, eliminating the deadwood (1) by using a pronoun to take the place of a wordy noun construction, (2) by deleting nonessential modifiers, (3) by striking out words or phrases that can be easily inferred, (4) by combining the closely related thoughts of two or more sentences into one, or (5) by using any other method that seems practical. Before you begin the exercise, study the following example.

> *Poor*   One of the finest aspects that football helps to create in a person is the ability for a person to learn to get along with other types of people.
>
> *Better* Playing football helps a person learn to get along with others.

1. Our baseball team was very good for several reasons. One of the reasons it was outstanding was because of the almost flawless fielding of the infield.

   _____

   _____

2. One of the most important things to do in writing a theme is to develop the topic so that unity exists throughout the theme.

   _____

   _____

3. The thing we had to decide on next was in what place we would be able to give our high-school play and in what fashion we would sell the tickets.

   _____

   _____

4. As an individual Dr. Seymore is a very congenial woman.

   _____

5. I am very much interested in the fund-raising drive. One of the reasons I am interested is that I enjoy helping other people.

   _____

   _____

6. Lincoln High School has a faculty of teachers who do their job well,

and the academic standards are high. I think the school is a good one to attend.

_____

_____

7. There are several advantages of living in a small town. One of the advantages is that you know practically everyone who lives in the town.

_____

_____

8. Our team fought hard to win the basketball game. To win the game they had to press the guards of the other team as soon as they put the ball into play.

_____

_____

9. There are many different reasons for buying a house and many against buying one, which I will discuss, pointing out the advantages and disadvantages.

_____

_____

10. The beggar came up to me as I was walking along, and he asked me if I would give him some money to buy something to eat because he was hungry.

_____

_____

11. The ages between three and six are when a child needs to be with other children. If he is not around other children, he is not likely to adjust properly.

_____

_____

12. Giving to the United Fund should be something that everyone does. Then a person won't have to give to every so-called worthy cause that comes along.

_____

_____

 © 1981 HBJ

13. After most of the things were taken care of, the final thing we had to do was spray the float with an electric paint sprayer.

_____

_____

14. If I were a physical fitness teacher, I would help young people accomplish the goal of exercising to help them keep fit.

_____

_____

15. We couldn't decide if we should go shopping in the suburban shopping center or drive downtown to the business district and shop.

_____

_____

EXERCISE 34

Rewrite the following sentences, eliminating the deadwood (1) by using a pronoun to take the place of a wordy noun construction, (2) by deleting nonessential modifiers, (3) by striking out words or phrases that can be easily inferred, (4) by combining the closely related thoughts of two or more sentences into one, or (5) by using any other method that seems practical. Before you begin the exercise, study the following example.

> *Poor*   Many charts about the human anatomy were placed on the walls. These charts contained detailed information on our bodies.
>
> *Better*   Many detailed charts on the human anatomy were placed on the walls.

1. People who both work and go to school have many problems. These people don't have much time for recreation. Often they don't get enough sleep.

   _____

   _____

2. Tornadoes and hurricanes are exceedingly dangerous storms, and one should take every safety precaution when warned of their approach.

   _____

   _____

3. After the theme of the parade was chosen, several students went to work designing the float. Designing the float was not an easy job.

   _____

   _____

4. The object of this lesson on the sentence is to teach us what things are important in writing a good sentence.

   _____

   _____

5. We went on a picnic Sunday. The weather was ideal. We had a good time.

   _____

6. Jack decided to sell his car. He said the reason for selling the car was that he had lost his job and was not able to make the payments.

7. Our English class stressed vocabulary development. One way we added words to our vocabulary was by finding synonyms for uncommon words in our reading manual.

8. I had to sacrifice many things in order to go to college. Some of the sacrifices were new clothes, a summer vacation, and weekend trips to the city.

9. In constructing an outline writers should make sure that their main divisions are coordinate. They should also make sure that these divisions are grammatically parallel.

10. Wildwood is a lively town with an attractive beach. We spend our summer vacation there almost every summer.

11. Recently Louise joined a social club. The club that she joined raises money for the care of needy children. They get together every Tuesday evening.

12. The important thing to remember is that a person should always try to do the proper thing at the proper time.

    © 1981 HBJ

13. We had to do many things before we left. Some of the things we had to do were pack, make reservations, and ask our neighbors to watch our house.

_____

_____

14. Saturday night we went to the holiday dance. While we were there we saw several of our friends from high school.

_____

_____

15. There were many things to consider before we could prepare to go. Some of the considerations were stopping the milk delivery and asking our neighbor to forward our mail.

_____

_____

© 1981 HBJ

EXERCISE 35

Rewrite the following sentences, eliminating the deadwood (1) by using a pronoun to take the place of a wordy noun construction, (2) by deleting nonessential modifiers, (3) by striking out words or phrases that can be easily inferred, (4) by combining the closely related thoughts of two or more sentences into one, or (5) by using any other method that seems practical. Before you begin the exercise, study the following example.

> *Poor*   These improvements are things that all citizens will benefit from.
> *Better*   All citizens will benefit from these improvements.

1. In Houston, Lyndon Johnson acquired the support of the Mexican-Americans. This support would later prove useful to him in his political career.

   _____

   _____

2. If people have the characteristics of being sincere and honest, one can depend on them to do what they say.

   _____

   _____

3. The subject I will present to you for reading will be a short explanation of how I really feel about being an elder brother.

   _____

   _____

4. In recent years and up to the present time smoking has been considered by many people dangerous to the health.

   _____

   _____

5. The character of Abraham Lincoln was described in the book before he was elected president and after he was elected president.

   _____

   _____

© 1981 HBJ

6. The person or persons who chose the actors for the movie knew what they were doing when they picked such convincing characters for the parts.

_____

_____

7. To me, the essay was very entertaining. I guess I thought it was entertaining because it was so descriptive.

_____

_____

8. I want to be able to look into the future and see that I will be able to offer security to myself or anyone else I might have to support in the future.

_____

_____

9. The essay was written in chronological order, and because of this order it was very understandable.

_____

_____

10. One of the requirements was a term paper. It was to consist of fifteen hundred words on a subject of our choice.

_____

_____

11. The reason I chose this subject to write about is because I know more about gymnastics than I know about practically anything else.

_____

_____

12. The words and actions of the politicians brought to mind things that I have observed to be prominent in politicians' words and actions.

_____

_____

 © 1981 HBJ

13. College students must plan their time wisely. Also, students in college must often make certain changes in their habits.

_____

_____

14. The main reason that the movie was so interesting to me was the suspense that I was in from the beginning to the end.

_____

_____

15. The swarm of bees was about a foot wide, and it was about as long as a yardstick.

_____

_____

© 1981 HBJ

EXERCISE 36

Rewrite the following sentences, eliminating the deadwood (1) by using a pronoun to take the place of a wordy noun construction, (2) by deleting nonessential modifiers, (3) by striking out implied words or phrases that can be easily inferred, (4) by combining the closely related thoughts of two or more sentences into one, or (5) by using any other method that seems practical. Before you begin the exercise, study the following example.

> *Poor*   But rich people are unhappy at times just as the average person finds himself not too happy at times.
>
> *Better*   But rich people—just like ordinary people—are not always happy.

1. Some people have made the claim that the violence one can see on television is the main cause for the rise of juvenile delinquency that exists in the world today.

   _____

   _____

2. I cannot live in the town that I would like to live in because I cannot find a good job there.

   _____

   _____

3. It was my turn to have the potluck dinner. I was undecided as to what meat to serve for the main course. I wanted to serve roast beef, turkey, or pork.

   _____

   _____

4. Her first job which lasted a duration of six months was nothing but a total bore to Hedda.

   _____

   _____

5. The interior decorator decided on a basic color scheme of blue and white for the room. The room was meant to give the impression of happiness.

_____

_____

6. Some of the characters won the hearts of the audience by the sincerity of the characters they portrayed.

_____

_____

7. I took part in two types of recreation. One was water-skiing. Another was horseback riding.

_____

_____

8. A quality most important in teaching to me is a knowledge of the subject being taught.

_____

_____

9. We had a wonderful Thanksgiving dinner. We had turkey and dressing and all the trimmings that go with a typical Thanksgiving dinner.

_____

_____

10. Joe and Kathy went to the dance with us. We drove our new car. On the way we had a slight accident.

_____

_____

11. In order to buy the new car we had to cut down on expenses. Some ways we did this were by staying home nights and cutting down on smoking.

_____

_____

© 1981 HBJ

12. I noticed the color of almost all the lawns. They looked so yellow that they reminded me of the hay you would find in a barnyard.

_____

_____

13. It has long been a fact that travel is perhaps one of the best means of broadening a person intellectually.

_____

_____

14. One of the classes he taught was typing which was the first class I had under him.

_____

_____

15. Yesterday we went fishing in the pond. While we were fishing we caught several bass. We also caught a catfish.

_____

_____

EXERCISE 37

Rewrite the following sentences, eliminating the deadwood (1) by using a pronoun to take the place of a wordy noun construction, (2) by deleting nonessential modifiers, (3) by striking out implied words or phrases that can be easily inferred, (4) by combining the closely related thoughts of two or more sentences into one, or (5) by using any other method that seems practical. Before you begin the exercise, study the following example.

> *Poor*　Several qualities of *West Side Story* show why it was an outstanding movie. Three of these qualities are acting, photography, and choreography.
>
> *Better*　Superb acting, excellent photography, and unique choreography made *West Side Story* an outstanding movie.

1. She wanted to make things better for herself, because she saw that making things better for herself would also make things better for others.

   _____

   _____

2. A career in the navy has both advantages and disadvantages. The return to civilian life from the military also has advantages and disadvantages.

   _____

   _____

3. Sharing an apartment near work with my friend promised many important advantages. These advantages included help in driving and less distance to drive.

   _____

   _____

4. The major decision in my life which I contributed the most thought to, perhaps, is the decision of what I wanted to do with my life after graduating from high school.

   _____

   _____

5. There is no sport that I know of today that doesn't have some aspect of teamwork involved either directly or indirectly.

_____

_____

6. We had a good basketball team last year. They were good because they had the right attitude and much determination.

_____

_____

7. One of the greatest-known group efforts is in sports. Two of the most important phases of group effort in sports are teamwork and sportsmanship.

_____

_____

8. College is a difficult thing to adjust to. One reason it is difficult is that you are left on your own to solve many problems.

_____

_____

9. My particular case, which I will deal with in this essay, presented a very important question for me to deal with.

_____

_____

10. I understand people better after I have had a chance to talk with them than I understand them before I have talked with them.

_____

_____

11. The trouble with censorship is that it cannot work in practice. Censorship cannot work because it would be strictly against the American way of life.

_____

_____

  © 1981 HBJ

12. In order to get what he wanted accomplished, the governor placed his men in every strategic state government job.

_____

_____

13. Helen was afraid to climb stairs because of the cast she had on her leg. She had to wear the cast on her leg because she broke it playing hockey.

_____

_____

14. Getting the door opened was the hardest part of getting into the room. To get it open you had to hit the top part of it with your fist. Apparently it was warped.

_____

_____

15. I realized many more and better reasons why I should further my education. The reasons were that by going to college I would acquire much valuable knowledge and not have inferior feelings when I met college students.

_____

_____

© 1981 HBJ

8: Inflated Diction

The term *inflated diction* as used in this discussion means awkward, unnatural, flowery, pretentious, or overly formal writing, as exemplified by the following sentences:

Inflated Diction   Unimpeachable integrity in our business dealings with others will produce results of a more substantial nature.

Inflated Diction   Insofar as hesitation may incapacitate my progression, it creates my biggest problem.

Inflated Diction   The undesirables abide in neighborhoods befitting their position of social retardation.

Why do people write such abominable sentences? Primarily, we assume, because they are trying to impress the reader, failing to realize that most people do not enjoy the backtracking and hair-pulling that are needed to understand this type of jargon. Therefore, your writing is likely to be more effective if you make a conscious effort to avoid contrived writing and develop a style that is more in keeping with your speech patterns. If you detect inflated diction in your composition and want to revise it, ask yourself this question: "How would I express this idea in speech?" Take another look at the examples above. Don't you agree that the revisions below represent a definite improvement in clarity as well as in style?

Better   Honesty in our business dealings is more productive than deception.
Better   Hesitation is my biggest problem because it impedes my progress.
Better   Social misfits often live in the slums of big cities.

In stressing the close relationship between conversation and writing, we do not mean to imply that they are the same. If you were sitting at a table in the student lounge with several of your friends, having a cup of coffee and a little friendly chat, and if one of the group got the conversation down on tape and later transcribed it on paper, you might note certain features of the dialog that should be avoided in writing: (1) The speakers will probably jump from one topic to another. (We expect writing to be better organized than speech.) (2) The speakers will probably use many short, simple sentences. (We expect the sentence patterns in writing to be longer, with more complex and compound sentences.) (3) The speakers' sentences will often contain deadwood. (We expect writers to prune the deadwood from their sentences.) (4) The language of the speakers—unless they are exceptional—will be studded with clichés. (This problem will be discussed in the next chapter.)

Informal speech, quite naturally, will differ from careful writing for at least two reasons. In conversation, a person often says the first thing that comes to mind in order to avoid long pauses or awkward stammering. A writer, on the other hand, can usually stop time and search for a precise word or phrase. Of even greater importance, the impromptu speaker must mentally outline a pattern of thoughts on the spur of the moment; whereas the writer can (and should) spend considerable time arranging ideas and facts before composing the first draft of a piece of writing. So we expect writing to be a more effective form of communication than unplanned conversation.

But such a pat conclusion is sometimes misleading, for many people (perhaps most people) speak better than they write. To avoid inflated diction in your writing, make a conscious effort to have your writing conform more to your speech patterns. Knowing the following causes of inflated diction should help you to overcome this problem:

Deadwood

In getting rid of deadwood you may at the same time eliminate inflated diction.

Poor The subject of teen-age marriage is a topic that has created a magnitude of controversial arguments.

Better The pros and cons of teen-age marriage have been widely debated.

Poor When I have attained the goal of my desire, there will be even greater understanding between us.

Better After I have reached my goal, we should understand each other better.

Poor I found that establishing myself a budget was the only way to manage profitably on a small income.

Better Sticking to a budget was the only way I could manage on a small income.

Cloudy thinking

Clarity is one of the most important qualities of effective writing. Inflated diction often acts as a smoke screen, obscuring your precise meaning.

Poor   Bob Kelly could present his subject with a persuasive attitude.
Better   Bob Kelly was a very persuasive salesman.

Poor   Professor Jones dealt with her students on an equal basis of intelligence.
Better   Professor Jones did not belittle her students.

Poor   In the play the hero is described as a character of perfection.
Better   In the play the hero is portrayed as a perfectionist.

Awkward use of passive voice

When the subject of a sentence does the acting, the verb is said to be in the active voice: "John drove the automobile." When the subject receives the action, the verb is said to be in the passive voice: "The automobile was driven by John." We form the passive voice by combining some form of the helping verb *to be* (*be, am, is, are, was, were, being, been*) with the past participle of the main verb.

Both speaking and writing are more natural when we use the active rather than the passive voice. People sometimes use the passive voice to achieve a literary effect. But instead of impressing their readers, they often confuse them. As a rule of thumb, never use the passive voice when the active voice would sound more natural.

Poor   This tournament had long been awaited by me.
Better   For weeks I had looked forward to the tournament.

Poor   First, my associate's degree in physical therapy must be obtained.
Better   First, I must obtain my associate's degree in physical therapy.

Poor   The early train was taken, and Nashville was reached around five in the afternoon.
Better   We took an early train and reached Nashville around five in the afternoon.

Putting the cart before the horse

Our sense of logic or sense of proportion will help us to put first things first.

Poor   Realism is the main reason that the story is my favorite.
Better   The story is my favorite because of its unique realism.

Poor   The pronounced characteristics of this outstanding movie were excellent photography, fine acting, and realism.
Better   The movie was outstanding because of its excellent photography, convincing acting, and stark realism.

Poor   Organization is one of the better ways to have a successful program.
Better   A successful program usually depends on advanced planning.

Awkward use of the negative

Using too many negative words often results in awkward as well as vague writing. Thus it is a good idea to heed the advice of a song that was popular some years ago, "Accentuate the positive—eliminate the negative."

Poor   It is not seldom that we find hate as a characteristic of belligerent people.
Better   Belligerent people are often filled with hate.

Poor   The unconscious mind plays an unnegligible role in human life.
Better   The unconscious mind plays a vital role in human life.

Poor   Ed Moore's teaching methods were not subordinate to his attitude and personality.
Better   Besides being a first-rate teacher Ed Moore had a friendly personality and an optimistic view of life.

Euphemism

The term *euphemism* may be unfamiliar to you. It is defined by one dictionary—Funk & Wagnalls *Standard College Dictionary*—as a "substitution of a mild or roundabout word or expression for another felt to be too blunt or otherwise distasteful or painful." In most writing situations, it is assumed that writers will use discretion in their choice of words. However, there is a danger of being too polite and ending up with a lifeless euphemism, as in the three poor sentences below.

Poor   Since my financial status was small, I decided to attend a state university.
Better   Since I didn't have much money, I decided to attend a state university.

Poor   Two people expired in the car accident.
Better   Two people died in the car accident.

Poor   By then he will be of an age that will keep him from enjoying his money.
Better   By then he will be too old to enjoy his money.

Inflated diction, then, as you can see from the examples that we have given, detracts from the clarity and force of most writing. Ironically, you should view with suspicion any sentences of which you are exceedingly proud, for usually these are the ones that will seem inflated and pretentious to the reader.

Having decided that a sentence is inflated and wishing to revise it, ask yourself two important questions: (1) How would I express this idea in speech? (2) Can I express this idea in more concrete language that will be clearer to the reader?

EXERCISE 38

Rewrite the following sentences, using language more in keeping with ordinary speech patterns. Two pertinent questions may help you to improve these sentences: (1) How would I express this idea in speech? (2) Can I express this idea in more concrete language that will be clearer to the reader? Consider the following poor and better examples before doing the exercise.

Poor   The equation provoked the student into a dubious state of mind.
Better The student had a difficult time understanding the equation.

1. Illusions are the main problem for many Americans.

   _____

2. Several months ago industry moved to my town under the name of General Electric.

   _____

3. It is not frequent that we have an opportunity to witness a good play.

   _____

4. When I was of an early age my parents would not let me have any responsibilities.

   _____

5. The mountain climber was fearless of the journey.

   _____

6. They often try to discuss subjects above their category and usually make a fool of themselves.

   _____

   _____

7. Public opinion of Senator Keyes wasn't too high.

   _____

8. I found that the students from big cities are more adept at learning than I.

   _____

9. A life without purpose would not be demanding of human concern for the future.

_____

10. Being dishonest will dwell on your conscience.

_____

11. It is not unlikely that Jim will take advantage of his friends.

_____

12. The financial end is better for the person who has a college education.

_____

13. The situation of wearing hand-me-downs was my chief disappointment.

_____

14. For me the result of going too fast was a traffic fine.

_____

15. The thought of disciplining myself came into existence.

_____

 © 1981 HBJ

EXERCISE 39

Rewrite the following sentences, using language more in keeping with ordinary speech patterns. Two pertinent questions may help you to improve these sentences: (1) How would I express this idea in speech? (2) Can I express this idea in more concrete language that will be clearer to the reader? Consider the following poor and better examples before doing the exercise.

> *Poor*   The events that occurred surrounding my purchase of a used car a few months ago are events that I will never forget.
>
> *Better*   I will never forget what happened when I went to purchase a used car a few months ago.

1. After failing in scholastic training, Poe got a job in Richmond, Virginia, as an editor.

   _____

   _____

2. The newspaper editorials handled the controversial political issues on the basis of equal representation.

   _____

   _____

3. Elizabeth was possessed with many responsibilities.

   _____

4. When Gordon returned he found that his financial status was in a very bad condition.

   _____

   _____

5. It is not impractical that one should wear a hat when it rains.

   _____

6. An outstanding personality was another trait of my teacher.

   _____

7. Efficiency is the reason that I think Helen will make a good executive.

   _____

© 1981 HBJ

8. This job, though unsatisfactory to Mark's desires, allowed him time to work on his mathematical theories.

_____

_____

9. The essay was fully descriptive as to what the countryside looked like.

_____

10. The situation rendered it necessary to be less extravagant with money.

_____

11. The relatively unqualified hairdresser dealt with all customers using the same age-old methods.

_____

_____

12. It is not infrequent that we must make decisions by ourselves.

_____

13. The idea was formulated early in his mind to become wealthy.

_____

14. I believe the chief reason for the engrossment of the novel is that it is so true of everyday life.

_____

_____

15. I gained certain concepts of information that I believe are vital to every freshman.

_____

 © 1981 HBJ

EXERCISE 40

Rewrite the following sentences, using language more in keeping with ordinary speech patterns. Two pertinent questions may help you to improve these sentences: (1) How would I express this idea in speech? (2) Can I express this idea in more concrete language that will be clearer to the reader? Consider the following poor and better examples before doing the exercise.

Poor   For quite a lengthy period the joys of friendship escaped me.
Better For several years I was very unhappy because I had no close friends.

1. The television tower is not unnoticeable even from a long distance.

2. The bridge is the one sight along the highway that remains in memory.

3. The basketball game had been anticipated for a long time.

4. Mark's style of clothing fits the modern trend.

5. Brown's manner was one of utmost neatness.

6. Hiking, fishing, and boating were engaged in as soon as we arrived at camp.

7. Being a student, Max is faced with many problems related to the interference of his line of concentration.

8. To extricate myself from debt, I obtained employment with a construction company.

_____

_____

9. A revolver was needed to fulfill the undesirable goal of the robber.

_____

10. The typical rowdiness of boys at this age did not seem to show in Bob.

_____

11. Much of the admiration held by people for Major London was the result of bravery.

_____

12. The main purpose of the novel was to express an idea about a widower and his only child.

_____

_____

13. While watering the lawn or doing other such chores, faded blue jeans, a ragged shirt, and sloppy, worn-out shoes make up Tom's apparel.

_____

_____

14. The warm personality and marvelous sense of humor exhibited by Dr. Allen filled her classroom with a pleasant environment.

_____

_____

15. An increase in people traveling during the Christmas holidays causes an increase in traffic and accidents.

_____

_____

 © 1981 HBJ

EXERCISE 41

Rewrite the following sentences, using language more in keeping with ordinary speech patterns. Two pertinent questions may help you to improve these sentences: (1) How would I express this idea in speech? (2) Can I express this idea in more concrete language that will be clearer to the reader? Consider the following poor and better examples before doing the exercise.

> *Poor* A controversial figure would be an excellent description of Lawrence of Arabia.
>
> *Better* Lawrence of Arabia was indeed a controversial figure.

1. Dr. Green could present a speech with an intriguing effect on the audience.

2. Undemocratic practices, I observed, were found existing on the campus.

3. It is not infrequent that a teacher encounters students who have a natural talent for writing.

4. All the things that passed through my mind during the flight would be hard to recapitulate.

5. The wedding had long been awaited by me.

6. The force with which the rain was coming down was very rapid.

7. Now that you have reached the college era a sense of individualism should be prevalent.

_____

_____

8. The first time Frank met Dolores he was subjected to fondness for her.

_____

9. It is not seldom that the college seniors fail to attend their classes.

_____

10. As an individual, Alan had characteristic behavior that was well organized.

_____

11. As I began to advance in years I found myself to be inclined toward solving difficult problems.

_____

_____

12. Seat belts were fastened as we descended at the airport.

_____

13. Formal education in the life of Abraham Lincoln was little.

_____

14. My parents voiced a decision to spend a vacation in Florida.

_____

15. It is not unusual that we find alcoholic beverages the cause of broken homes.

_____

_____

 © 1981 HBJ

EXERCISE 42

Rewrite the following sentences, using language more in keeping with ordinary speech patterns. Two pertinent questions may help you to improve these sentences: (1) How would I express this idea in speech? (2) Can I express this idea in more concrete language that will be clearer to the reader? Consider the following poor and better examples before doing the exercise.

> *Poor* Mr. Jordan would talk to the students on an equal quality of thinking.
> *Better* Mr. Jordan lectured to the students on an adult level.

1. Drama programs give us a conception of what psychological problems exist in our environment.

   _____

   _____

2. The boy used many flirtatious techniques to find a girlfriend.

   _____

3. Skill was not possessed by those on whom the cameras were directed.

   _____

4. Sympathy and admiration sum up my feelings about the story.

   _____

5. We decided to further our plans concerning the birthday for Alex.

   _____

6. To covet happiness for oneself is a universal desire.

   _____

7. A resentment against Lincoln High School was prevalent at Eastern High School.

   _____

8. Beneath the surface both men harbored the same philosophy and ideas.

   _____

© 1981 HBJ

9. Recreation is sought on the golf courses and tennis courts.

_____

10. Harry's careless childhood training had resulted in a personality devoid of initiative.

_____

11. Next week my two-week vacation will be begun by me.

_____

12. Physically Phillip is described as an adult; however, we become aware that he still retains the immaturity of an adolescent.

_____

_____

13. The not unsubstantial number who were against the measure caused it to be rejected.

_____

14. A tree was crashed into by the car going ninety miles an hour.

_____

15. I felt the opportunity for more money was to be had as a college graduate.

_____

_____

 © 1981 HBJ

EXERCISE 43

Rewrite the following sentences, using language more in keeping with ordinary speech patterns. Two pertinent questions may help you to improve these sentences: (1) How would I express this idea in speech?
(2) Can I express this idea in more concrete language that will be clearer
to the reader? Consider the following poor and better examples before doing the exercise.

> *Poor*   Why isn't there individuality when facing the question of smoking
> and drinking?
>
> *Better*   Why do most teen-agers "follow the crowd" when it comes to drink-
> ing and smoking?

1. My feeling toward the foreign movies is one of approval.

   _____

2. Intercollegiate athletics should play a part which is second to the
   aspect of academic education.

   _____

   _____

3. I have had several occasions on which a decision on attending college had to be reached.

   _____

4. The wrong kind of television shows may disrupt our moral attitude.

   _____

5. One family, to create a prosperous impression, paid a large amount
   of money for their son to attend a private school.

   _____

   _____

   _____

6. Many troublesome thoughts arise in me as to the effect another
   major war could bring.

   _____

© 1981 HBJ

7. These lakes ideally provide us with the sports of water-skiing, swimming, and skin-diving.

_____

_____

8. Humorous would be a descriptive word for the play.

_____

9. Price displays a sarcastic attitude toward people educated at Eton and Oxford.

_____

_____

10. Most people experience self-doubt and lack of confidence on occasions of individually variable frequency.

_____

_____

11. The location of the plant in reference to my living quarters is only five miles.

_____

12. The talents and personality of my high-school teacher were of such a dynamic proportion that he vividly stands out in my mind.

_____

_____

13. Through his guidance and instruction he gave me an ample background for college.

_____

14. Centerville's growth pertaining to industry started soon after the Civil War.

_____

15. Because of my restricted financial status new clothing and such will be extremely scarce.

_____

_____

 © 1981 HBJ

9: Clichés and Expressive Phrases

AVOIDING CLICHÉS

Precise writers make an effort to avoid worn-out phrases—that is, clichés. The word *cliché* comes from the French verb *clicher*, meaning to stereotype. In simple language, a cliché is an expression that has become threadbare through excessive use. The following phrases are some current examples:

acid test
agree to disagree
all work and no play
as luck would have it
at a loss for words

better late than never
beyond a shadow of a doubt
bull in a china shop
burn the midnight oil
busy as a bee
by leaps and bounds
by the sweat of his brow

center of attention
chip off the old block
commune with nature
cool as a cucumber

crack of dawn
cream of the crop

darkness overtook us
depths of despair
doomed to disappointment

each and every week
easier said than done

fast and furious
feather in her cap
feeling under the weather
few and far between
financially embarrassed

goes without saying
golden opportunity
great deal to be desired

green with envy
growing by leaps and bounds

history tells us
home sweet home

in the final analysis
in this day and age

keeps abreast of the times

last but not least

making ends meet
method in his madness

never a dull moment
nipped in the bud
no news is good news
no sooner said than done

on the right track
out of this world

poet at heart
point with pride
pretty as a picture

ready and willing
rotten to the core

sadder but wiser
scratch the surface
selling like hot cakes
showed his true colors
sigh of relief
slowly but surely
sly as a fox
sober as a judge

the finer things in life
through thick and thin
too funny for words
to the bitter end
trials and tribulations

variety is the spice of life

words cannot express

We hope that you will add other clichés to this list as you come across them. To prove to yourself that these are commonplace expressions, try this experiment on one or more individuals. Read the first part of the phrase to someone, and see if he or she can supply the last part. It should make little or no difference whether the person is young or old. These verbal clinkers seem to smolder forever because they obviously serve a useful purpose.

In studying the chapters on inflated diction and weak words, you may have discovered what appears to be a contradiction. In the former, we advised you to write more as you speak; whereas, in the latter, we admonished you to avoid in writing both the weak words and the overemphatic words that you may frequently use in speech. Now we tell you to make a conscious effort to avoid clichés in your writing, expressions that you would also use in speech.

This apparent contradiction can be explained. In writing, your primary goal is (or should be) to communicate clearly your ideas and facts. Inflated diction, as we have shown, can be a serious barrier in achieving this end. Writing more as you speak can often solve the problem quickly and effectively.

On the other hand, writing should be more original and more precise than unprepared speech; in your writing, you can pause and spend several seconds or minutes searching for the best word or phrase. In speech you more or less have to say the first thing that comes to your mind or else risk awkward pauses or stammering. Frequent hesitations can be very irritating to the listener and embarrassing, especially if you are speaking before a group. To avoid the "uh, uh, I mean, you know" habit, the speaker may reluctantly use a cliché, fully realizing that it is a trite expression.

A similar but somewhat different problem may occur in writing. Say, for instance, a professional journalist is writing an editorial for a high-quality newspaper. There is a deadline to meet; time is an important factor. The writer composes a sentence and stops abruptly, realizing that he has used a cliché. He racks his brain to think of a more original expression and puts it down on paper. But it strikes him as awkward, flowery, pretentious—inflated. Glancing at the clock on the wall, he decides to use the cliché as *the lesser of two evils*. [Note that we have used a cliché ("the lesser of two evils") in a similar situation.]

However, a careless writer is likely to use one cliché after the other with no conscious effort to avoid them. In such cases, the sophisticated reader will probably conclude that the writer lacks originality or has not given the topic serious thought. So if you are trying to make a favorable impression on the reader, try to get rid of your clichés or at least use them with discretion. Often you can solve the problem by striking out one or more words in the expression.

Poor   My mother was *busy as a bee* preparing the Thanksgiving dinner.
Better   My mother was very busy preparing the Thanksgiving dinner.

Poor   Louis had a blowout on the highway, but *as luck would have it* a state trooper came along and helped him change the tire.
Better   Louis had a blowout on the highway, but luckily a state trooper came along and helped him change the tire.

Poor   *Last but not least* I stopped by the bank to get some traveler's checks before I left on my vacation.
Better   Finally, I stopped by the bank to get some traveler's checks before I left on my vacation.

Poor   *History tells us* that most wars are fought for economic reasons.
Better   History indicates that most wars are fought for economic reasons.

Poor   Our basketball team has improved since losing its first game, but there is still *a great deal to be desired*.
Better   Our basketball team has improved since losing its first game, but we still have a number of problems to solve.

Poor   We rose at the *crack of dawn* to get started on our trip to Virginia Beach.
Better   We rose at dawn to get started on our trip to Virginia Beach.

Poor   *Each and every week* Dr. Jordan has a personal conference with his students.
Better   Every week Dr. Jordan has a personal conference with his students.

Poor   After many *trials and tribulations* Mary developed a stoical attitude toward life.
Better   After many painful trials Mary developed a stoical attitude toward life.

Poor	In order to finish my term paper, I had to *burn the midnight oil.*
Better	In order to finish my term paper, I had to work through the night.
Poor	The detective was *sly as a fox* in getting the information he needed.
Better	The detective was very sly in getting the information he needed.
Poor	During the past twelve years Western State University has *grown by leaps and bounds.*
Better	During the past twelve years Western State University has grown rapidly.
Poor	The show I saw on television last night was *too funny for words.*
Better	The show I saw on television last night was hilarious.
Poor	I have read a couple of articles for my term paper, but I have just *scratched the surface.*
Better	I have read a couple of articles for my term paper, but I have just begun my research.

The sensitive reader will probably prefer the *better* example in every instance, for the diction is more original. Thus, if a composition is littered with clichés, the critical reader may judge the writer to be untrained or incompetent. The use of clichés by professional writers as a technique to delineate character, having the person think and speak in clichés, is further proof of this point. The author of a short story, for example, might have a character speak these lines:

> The main reason I watch the news programs on television is to keep abreast of the times. But I also enjoy watching the sport programs, for all work and no play makes Jack a dull boy. The other night, as luck would have it, I saw a terrific murder mystery on the late show in which the private eye was cool as a cucumber. Of course, I don't spend all my time watching television. On Sunday afternoon, if the weather is nice, I take a walk through the park and commune with nature.

The fiction writer is saying in effect that the character in the story is a person who has little originality or imagination. The stale ideas expressed in stereotyped language prove this fact. A writer whose composition is littered with clichés invites a similar judgment. So you should make a special effort to rid your writing of clichés by using more original language.

ACQUIRING NEW WORDS AND PHRASES

Most textbooks on writing advise you to avoid clichés as a way to improve your writing style. However, in a more positive vein, it is wise to imitate experienced writers as another way of improving your diction. Frequently, in listening or reading, we encounter a phrase that is especially pleasing, and we may think, "I wish I had said that."

Although plagiarism, the uncredited use of substantial portions of someone else's material, is a serious matter, there is nothing wrong in borrowing an expressive phrase from another writer. Perhaps he or she has acquired the phrase in the same way. But without a doubt you can improve your style by imitating other writers. To help you get started in this direction, at the end of this section we will list fifty expressive phrases and ask you to use them in sentences.

Another way to improve your writing is to add new words to your active vocabulary. One of the best ways to do this is to look for unfamiliar words in your reading. Set a goal; try to add a certain number of words to your active vocabulary each week. For this purpose, it is a good idea to read several articles or essays in a high-quality magazine or some other publication. Look up the unfamiliar words in your dictionary or thesaurus, and find a brief definition or synonym for each. The use of 3" x 5" cards in this procedure is recommended.

Write the unfamiliar word in the upper left-hand corner of the card. Paying close attention to how the word is used in the essay, use the word in a similar way in a sentence of your own and write it in the middle of the card. At the bottom of the card, if possible, write a memory aid such as the name of a person, object, or idea that you have associated with the word. On the back of the card write your synonym or brief definition. Review your cards whenever you add others to your collection. In a short time you should have several hundred cards, having developed a habit that will greatly improve your writing, speaking, reading, and listening.

USING EXPRESSIVE PHRASES

A similar technique can be used for acquiring expressive phrases. In one of the exercises at the end of this chapter, you will be asked to compose sentences using certain expressive phrases in order to make them part of your language. We have included them in this chapter because some of them come close to being clichés. But as we have already suggested, don't let the fear of using a cliché now and then cause a psychological block in your writing, especially in writing your first drafts.

There is an old saying that learning to write is like playing a trumpet. Before something comes out, you have to put something in. If you are really trying to improve your writing, you will not only try to eliminate clichés but you will make a conscious effort to add new words and expressive phrases to your active vocabulary. The following list of expressive phrases may be helpful to you:

1. in sharp contrast
2. the dominating factor
3. did exceptionally well
4. have changed markedly
5. with calm detachment
6. success turned into ashes
7. placed great stress on
8. must guard against
9. a crushing blow
10. was indeed touching
11. were jumbled together
12. was the big question mark
13. stood his (or her) ground
14. worked tirelessly
15. had nerves of steel
16. didn't have the foggiest notion
17. are closely linked
18. a picturesque description

19. is of first importance
20. lodged a complaint against
21. mixed feelings
22. with a burst of enthusiasm
23. lived in abject poverty
24. used various modes of flattery
25. reaped huge profits
26. was utterly corrupt
27. mustered up enough energy
28. searched industriously
29. of a short duration
30. squander our time
31. burning with anxiety
32. came to grips with the fact
33. buzzing with excitement
34. shrank from no effort

35. progress was painfully slow
36. a fog of confusion
37. a widespread belief
38. a wide departure from
39. cherished the hope
40. a compelling need
41. had an electrifying effect
42. made a clumsy mistake
43. the indispensable element
44. talked incessantly
45. a visible decline
46. a confused muddle
47. would tolerate no foolishness
48. hard-won victory
49. superficial comparison
50. calculated risk

EXERCISE 44

Refer to the preceding list of expressive phrases and compose sentences in which you use some of these phrases. Devise as many sentences as your instructor suggests.

_____

_____

_____

_____

_____

_____

_____

_____

_____

_____

_____

_____

_____

_____

_____

_____

_____

_____

_____

_____

_____

_____

_____

_____

_____

© 1981 HBJ

© 1981 HBJ

EXERCISE 45

Read two or more articles or essays in a high-quality publication and underline 25 or 30 unfamiliar words that you would like to make part of your active vocabulary. Look up each word in a dictionary and/or thesaurus and find a brief definition or synonym that you can substitute for the word in the sentence; then write an original sentence for each unfamiliar word in which it has the meaning it has in the published sentence.

1. _____

2. _____

3. _____

4. _____

5. _____

6. _____

7. _____

8. _____

9. _____

10. _____

11. _____

12. _____

13. _____

14. _____

15. _____

16. _____

17. _____

18. _____

19. _____

20. _____

21. _____

22. _____

23. _____

© 1981 HBJ

24. _____

25. _____

26. _____

27. _____

28. _____

29. _____

30. _____

© 1981 HBJ

EXERCISE 46

The italicized phrases in each of the following sentences are clichés. Try to improve each sentence by replacing the cliché with more original language. In most cases it will not be necessary to rewrite the entire sentence.

1. The real *acid test* in the game Saturday is how well our passing attack will work.

   _____

2. The student council and the president of the college *agreed to disagree* on the dorm regulations.

   _____

3. We try to have a party at least once a week, for we believe that *all work and no play* is not good for a person.

   _____

4. *As luck would have it*, a state trooper helped me to get my car started.

   _____

5. George Foster, *beyond a shadow of a doubt,* is a great hitter.

   _____

6. On the dance floor, Ted looks like a *bull in a china shop.*

   _____

7. To pass my chemistry course I had *to burn the midnight oil.*

   _____

8. The chef was *busy as a bee* getting everything ready for the banquet.

   _____

9. Over the past ten years, inflation has soared *by leaps and bounds.*

   _____

© 1981 HBJ

10. Kim earned enough money *by the sweat of his brow* to return to college for the fall semester.

   _____

11. The president was the *center of attention* on his recent trip to Egypt.

   _____

12. Our quarterback, whose father was an All-American at Notre Dame, is a *chip off the old block.*

   _____

13. Whenever possible, I like to walk in the woods and *commune with nature.*

   _____

14. The surgeon was as *cool as a cucumber* in performing the delicate heart operation.

   _____

15. We got up at the *crack of dawn* to get ready for our trip to the Smoky Mountains.

   _____

 © 1981 HBJ

EXERCISE 47

The italicized phrases in each of the following sentences are clichés. Try to improve each sentence by replacing the cliché with more original language. In most cases it will not be necessary to rewrite the entire sentence.

1. The Masters Tournament at Augusta, Georgia, draws the *cream of the crop* among professional golfers.

   _____

2. The man reached the *depths of despair* after his wife and two children were killed in the fire.

   _____

3. I thought I would be promoted to office manager, but I was *doomed to disappointment.*

   _____

4. *Each and every week* our committee meets to discuss matters related to safety at our plant.

   _____

5. Writing a superior composition is *easier said than done.*

   _____

6. The pace of the hockey game was *fast and furious.*

   _____

7. Lucy was *feeling under the weather* because of a bout with the flu.

   _____

8. Bowlers who can average two hundred are *few and far between.*

   _____

9. *In the final analysis,* it is the golfer who does well on and around the green who will probably win the tournament.

   _____

10. I think it *goes without saying* that Senator Hayes will be reelected.

_____

11. When I lived in England, I had a *golden opportunity* to visit a number of European cities.

_____

12. In recent years Atlanta has *grown by leaps and bounds.*

_____

13. *History tells us* that the conflict between the rich and the poor has been the cause of much unrest in the world.

_____

14. I enjoyed my vacation, but I was glad to see my *home sweet home* after living in a hotel for two weeks.

_____

15. *In this day and age* it is difficult to be optimistic about the future.

_____

  © 1981 HBJ

EXERCISE 48

The italicized phrases in each of the following sentences are clichés. Try to improve each sentence by replacing the cliché with more original language. In most cases it will not be necessary to rewrite the entire sentence.

1. *Last but not least,* we shall consider the short story as a modern literary form.

   _____

2. Today even many working people have a hard time *making ends meet.*

   _____

3. I think Dr. Perkins had a *method in his madness* when he gave low grades on the midterm exam.

   _____

4. When Susan is in the crowd, there is *never a dull moment.*

   _____

5. The plot to kill the dictator was *nipped in the bud.*

   _____

6. I asked the waitress to bring me another cup of coffee, and it was *no sooner said than done.*

   _____

7. That is not the correct answer, but you are *on the right track.*

   _____

8. The dinner we had last night at the Lobster Tail was *out of this world.*

   _____

9. The students can *point with pride* at their clean and orderly campus.

   _____

10. The president of the university is *ready and willing* to do all he can to help the students.

_____

11. The political group that controls Centerville is *rotten to the core.*

_____

12. My grandfather was *sadder but wiser* after being swindled by a confidence man.

_____

13. We had time only to *scratch the surface* of the complex problem.

_____

14. The tickets to the rock concert are *selling like hot cakes.*

_____

15. Tom *showed his true colors* when our team lost the final game in the district tournament.

_____

   © 1981 HBJ

EXERCISE 49

The italicized phrases in each of the following sentences are clichés. Try to improve each sentence by replacing the cliché with more original language. In most cases it will not be necessary to rewrite the entire sentence.

1. *Slowly but surely* I accumulated all the references I would read for my term paper.

   _____

2. The defense attorney was *sly as a fox* in getting his client acquitted.

   _____

3. After I graduate I hope to find a good job so I can afford *the finer things in life.*

   _____

4. The husband and wife stuck together *through thick and thin* until finally their financial situation improved.

   _____

5. The movie I saw on television last night was *too funny for words.*

   _____

6. After many *trials and tribulations,* we arrived in Florida for our spring vacation.

   _____

7. *Words cannot express* how sorry I was to hear about your accident.

   _____

8. *As luck would have it,* we found an attractive motel as soon as we arrived at Daytona Beach.

   _____

9. Interest in Frisbee has grown *by leaps and bounds.*

   _____

© 1981 HBJ

10. *Each and every week* during the warm months I wash my car.

_____

11. Getting a loan from a bank is *easier said than done.*

_____

12. It was a *feather in her cap* when Joan was elected president of the student council.

_____

13. It *goes without saying* that the economy of the United States is in dreadful shape.

_____

14. The ocean view from our hotel window was *pretty as a picture.*

_____

15. I was *sadder but wiser* after losing my week's pay at the race track.

_____

 © 1981 HBJ

10: Sentence Structure

The Sentence Fragment, the Run-Together Sentence, and the Comma Splice

The sentence fragment, the run-together sentence, and the comma splice are three of the most common errors in sentence structure. They are serious mistakes because they may detract from the clarity of a composition and suggest that the writer is untrained or careless. Be wise. Learn the fundamentals of sentence structure and avoid the mistakes that can be so damaging to an otherwise acceptable composition.

THE SENTENCE FRAGMENT

The sentence fragment or incomplete sentence or broken sentence (in our discussion and in the drills that follow we shall call them "fragments") is a word or group of words that lacks some feature of the conventional sentence pattern. The unintentional sentence fragment is a serious mistake, for such an error may cloud the meaning of what you are trying to say.

Perhaps the best way to avoid this error is to know the essential qualities of a complete sentence. It is difficult to give a brief definition of a sentence that will cover all forms of writing and speaking. Hence our definition is meant to be limited, relating to the types of compositions you will write in college.

A sentence is a unit of expression that is grammatically and logically complete. It should have at least one main clause that has a subject (the part about which something is said) and a predicate (the part that says something about the subject), and it should convey a complete thought. It is possible that subject and/or predicate may be implied, especially in writing answers to direct questions. But such condensed utterances should be avoided in college writing. It is best to stick to the sentence patterns that are usually considered proper.

USUAL PATTERNS

Declarative (makes a statement)	The opening-day game between the Reds and the Pirates was postponed because of rain.
Imperative (gives a command)	Please close the door.
Interrogative (asks a question)	Are you going to the dance next Saturday?

UNCOMMON PATTERNS

Subject implied	Walk. (I walk to school.)
Predicate implied	John Ford. (John Ford is president of the senior class.)
Subject and predicate implied	Chicago. (I am going to Chicago.)

It follows, then, from what we have said that a fragment is a word or group of words punctuated as a complete sentence that is only part of a sentence. Although fragments appear in a variety of forms, the most common are separated dependent clauses and detached phrases of various kinds. A writer can usually eliminate them by either joining them with a main clause or converting them into complete sentences.

SEPARATED DEPENDENT CLAUSE

One of the most common fragments is the dependent clause punctuated as though it were a complete sentence. It is an understandable mistake, because a dependent clause resembles a sentence: it has a subject and predicate. Still the separated dependent clause depends on a main clause for its meaning. Its first word is usually a subordinate conjunction or a relative pronoun (see the lists below). When you spot one of these words at the beginning of a would-be sentence, you should double-check to make sure the unit is properly joined to a main clause.

SUBORDINATE CONJUNCTIONS

after	before	until
although	except	when
as	if	where
as if	since	whereas
as though	though	whether
because	unless	while

that	whichever	whom
what	who	whomever
whatever	whoever	whose
which	whom	

SEPARATED PHRASES

Like separated dependent clauses, disjóined phrases are frequently punctuated as complete sentences. This error usually involves one of the following types of separated phrases: (1) the participial phrase, (2) the prepositional phrase, and (3) the explanatory phrase.

(1)

Contains a
Fragment (Wrong) Ellen returned the lost wallet to the man. Proving that she is an honest person.

Corrected Ellen returned the lost wallet to the man, proving that she is an honest person.

Corrected Ellen returned the lost wallet to the man. This act proves that she is an honest person.

Comment Recalling the definition of a sentence, you will note that the first part of the wrong example can stand alone as a complete unit. But the second part cannot stand alone because it is a dependent phrase. To remove the fragment the writer may either join the phrase to the main clause or convert the phrase into a sentence.

Contains a
Fragment (Wrong) We decided to drive to South Bend to see the Notre Dame–Ohio State game. Although the weather reports predicted snow and freezing temperatures.

Corrected We decided to drive to South Bend to see the Notre Dame–Ohio State game although the weather reports predicted snow and freezing temperatures.

Comment Recalling the definition of a sentence, you can see that the first statement is grammatically and logically complete. It has a subject and predicate, and it can stand alone as an expression of a complete thought. However, the last word group is not complete because it depends on the main clause for its full meaning. Thus the last group of words in the incorrect example is a fragment. You can avoid this error in sentence structure by joining the two clauses with a comma, as in the corrected example.

Contains a
Fragment (Wrong) I shall always remember the teacher in my business school. Who helped me to get a job with General Electric.

Corrected I shall always remember the teacher in my business school who helped me to get a job with General Electric.

Comment	If you analyze the first clause in the wrong example, you will see that it has the components of a complete sentence. But the same cannot be said of the second word group. It is dependent on the main clause for its meaning. The function of the clause is to describe *teacher;* therefore, it should be joined to the main clause, as in the corrected example.

(2)

Contains a	
Fragment (Wrong)	Bob signed a contract to play professional baseball. Without realizing that being considered a professional athlete would prevent him from playing basketball in college.
Corrected	Bob signed a contract to play professional baseball without realizing that being considered a professional athlete would prevent him from playing basketball in college.
Comment	If you know the basic requirements of a sentence, you will see that the first group of words in the wrong example is complete. However, the second group is not complete but depends on the preceding main clause for its full meaning. You can eliminate this fragment by joining it with the main clause.

(3)

Contains a	
Fragment (Wrong)	Some errors in writing are serious. For example, fragments and run-together sentences.
Corrected	Some errors in writing are serious, for example, fragments and run-together sentences.
Corrected	Some errors in writing are serious. Among these are fragments and run-together sentences.
Comment	In the wrong example the first group of words satisfies the requirements of a sentence, but the second group is not a complete thought. Therefore, it should not be punctuated as if it were a sentence. You can handle the phrase properly by either joining it to the main clause or converting it into a sentence.

Contains a	
Fragment (Wrong)	I told Ralph I was sorry that I could not attend the banquet. Because I had already made plans to visit some friends in St. Louis.
Corrected	I told Ralph I was sorry that I could not attend the banquet because I had already made plans to visit some friends in St. Louis.
Comment	In the wrong example the second clause is dependent on the first. Although it has a subject and a predicate, the second clause begins with a subordinate conjunction. By joining the dependent clause to the main clause, the writer removes the fragment.

Contains a *Fragment (Wrong)*	Although the extent of the damage will not be known until a more accurate survey is made. It is estimated that the property loss will be in the millions.
Corrected	Although the extent of the damage will not be known until a more accurate survey is made, it is estimated that the property loss will be in the millions.
Comment	The problem in this wrong example is the same as in the previous one. Dependent clauses should not be punctuated as complete sentences. They should be joined to a main clause or reworded to make a complete sentence.

Contains a *Fragment (Wrong)*	For many reasons we cannot expect a reduction in taxes this year. Although we do not expect an increase.
Corrected	For many reasons we cannot expect a reduction in taxes this year although we do not expect an increase.
Comment	If the word group does not have the components of a complete sentence, it should be joined to a main clause.

Contains a *Fragment (Wrong)*	A number of reasons for the protest have been suggested. The need for better housing, the need for equal educational opportunities, and the need for more jobs.
Improved	A number of reasons for the protest have been suggested: the need for better housing, the need for equal educational opportunities, and the need for more jobs.
Improved	A number of reasons for the protest have been suggested. They include the need for better housing, equal educational opportunities, and more jobs.
Comment	In the first improved example, the writer has placed a colon at the end of the main clause, indicating that a listing is to follow. If a colon is used in this way, it may be followed by part of a sentence. In the second improved example, the writer has made the listing of factors a complete sentence.

Contains a *Fragment (Wrong)*	Many of the graduate students disliked the dean for only one reason. The fact that he had given Clark preference over the other candidates who applied for the fellowship.
Improved	Many of the graduate students disliked the dean because he had given Clark preference over the other candidates who applied for the fellowship.
Improved	Many of the graduate students disliked the dean for only one reason. They knew that he had given Clark preferential treatment over the other candidates who applied for the fellowship.
Comment	Usually it is possible to combine the fragment with the main clause, but sometimes it is better to convert the fragment into a complete sentence.

Contains a *Fragment (Wrong)*	After the midterm exams our history teacher announced his new policy. Giving more objective tests as a means of motivating students to read assignments carefully.
Improved	After the midterm exams our history teacher announced his new policy, giving more objective tests as a means of motivating students to read assignments carefully.
Improved	After the midterm exams our history teacher told us that he was going to give more objective tests as a means of motivating students to read assignments carefully.
Comment	In the first improved example the fragment has been added to the second main clause. In the second improved example the fragment has been converted to an independent clause.

THE RUN-TOGETHER SENTENCE AND THE COMMA SPLICE

Another common and serious mistake in writing is the improper punctuation of independent clauses in compound sentences. This mispunctuation takes two forms: (1) the run-together (or fused) sentence and (2) the comma splice (or comma fault).

There are three basic types of sentences: simple, compound, and complex. A run-together sentence results when the writer fails to insert the necessary punctuation—a period or comma or semicolon—between clauses that could stand independently. A comma splice results when the writer uses a comma rather than a period or semicolon between independent clauses that are *not* joined by a coordinate conjunction (*and, but, for, nor, or*). If you are to avoid these errors you will need to know several rules that govern the punctuation of independent clauses. In explaining these rules, we shall try to avoid confusion by concentrating on the basic rules and not the exceptions.

When two or more independent clauses are combined in a compound sentence, they must be correctly punctuated. If they are joined by a coordinate conjunction (*and, but, for, nor, or*), a comma should be placed before the conjunction.

> We spent the night at the foot of the mountain, and the next morning we began our laborious ascent to the peak.

If two independent clauses are joined by a transitional word other than a coordinate conjunction (such words as *so, yet, thus, hence, however, moreover, consequently, furthermore, nevertheless, otherwise*), the independent clauses should be separated by a semicolon. If no coordinate conjunction or other transitional word joins the two independent clauses, they must be written as separate sentences or separated by a semicolon.

Example	I intend to spend my Christmas vacation working on my term paper; otherwise, I may end up with a failing grade in the course.
Comment	In the above example the writer correctly placed a semicolon after *paper* because *otherwise* is an adverbial conjunction. The

placement of a comma after *otherwise* also reflects a general practice among trained writers. However, a comma is not required after the shorter connectives, such as *so, yet, also, thus, hence,* and *then.*

Example   Perhaps it would be better to enroll at a university in my home state; the savings in tuition and transportation would be considerable.

Comment   If the second independent clause is not preceded by a coordinate conjunction (*and, but, for, nor, or*), a semicolon is required to punctuate the compound sentence correctly. In this example note the absence of any conjunction, in which case a semicolon is needed to separate the independent clauses.

Now that you are acquainted with the positive rules, let us see how these rules are violated. In correcting all the examples below we shall assume that the writer wants to combine the clauses in compound sentences rather than use separate complete sentences.

Run-Together   We spent the entire afternoon working on our pass defense for our coach felt that Lincoln High would exploit this weakness if their backs could not penetrate our line.

Improved   We spent the entire afternoon working on our pass defense, for our coach felt that Lincoln High would exploit this weakness if their backs could not penetrate our line.

Comment   The writer needs a comma before *for,* a coordinate conjunction joining the two independent clauses.

Run-Together   The boat was almost filled with water and we had to race full speed for the shore.

Improved   The boat was almost filled with water, and we had to race full speed for the shore.

Comment   We have two independent clauses joined by *and,* a coordinate conjunction. Thus a comma is needed before *and* to avoid a run-together sentence.

Run-Together   Dr. Collier attended the medical convention in London afterwards, he spent two weeks vacationing in France.

Improved   Dr. Collier attended the medical convention in London; afterwards, he spent two weeks vacationing in France.

Comment   In this example we have two independent clauses that are *not* joined by a coordinate conjunction (*and, but, for, nor, or*); therefore, they must be separated by a semicolon.

Run-Together   It is becoming increasingly difficult to obtain a good job without a college education therefore, more and more students are entering the colleges and universities of the United States.

Improved   It is becoming increasingly difficult to obtain a good job without a college education; therefore, more and more students are entering the colleges and universities of the United States.

Comment   In this example we have two independent clauses. The second is introduced by *therefore,* an adverbial conjunction, which must be preceded by a semicolon. The comma that follows is optional, but most experienced writers would use it.

Run-Together	Generally Dr. Brewer's lectures are not too stimulating however, now and then he gives one that is superb.
Improved	Generally Dr. Brewer's lectures are not too stimulating; however, now and then he gives one that is superb.
Comment	In the improved example the problem is solved by placing a semicolon before *however*.

When writers incorrectly punctuate a sentence by using a comma rather than a semicolon to separate independent clauses, they commit the comma splice error. Again, as in the case of the run-together sentence, we are concerned with punctuating independent clauses, groups of words that can stand alone as sentences. The positive rule has been previously stated: Independent clauses joined by coordinate conjunctions (*and, but, for, nor, or*) require a comma before the conjunction. Independent clauses joined by other conjunctions (such as *however, moreover, nevertheless, therefore*) or independent clauses that have no conjunctions must be separated by a semicolon.

Comma Splice	The number of commercial airliners that have crashed in recent months is shocking, nowadays, I am almost afraid to send a letter by air mail.
Improved	The number of commercial airliners that have crashed in recent months is shocking; nowadays, I am almost afraid to send a letter by air mail.
Comment	In the original example the writer has committed a comma splice; a semicolon rather than a comma is needed between the independent clauses.
Comma Splice	The number of holiday basketball tournaments is alarming, it is difficult to imagine when the players find time to catch up on their studies.
Improved	The number of holiday basketball tournaments is alarming; it is difficult to imagine when the players find time to catch up on their studies.
Comment	The two independent clauses are not joined by a coordinate conjunction. Therefore, they must be separated by a semicolon.
Comma Splice	The large number of high-school dropouts is indeed a problem that calls for serious study, a practical solution must be found to keep students in school.
Improved	The large number of high-school dropouts is indeed a problem that calls for serious study; a practical solution must be found to keep students in school.
Comment	There is a comma splice in the first version because of the writer's failure to join the independent clauses with a

comma and a coordinate conjunction or separate them with a semicolon.

Comma Splice   The pollution of our rivers and streams has been debated in the U.S. Congress and in the state legislatures, however, little has been done to solve this mammoth problem.

Improved   The pollution of our rivers and streams has been debated in the U.S. Congress and in the state legislatures; however, little has been done to solve this mammoth problem.

Comment   If the second independent clause is introduced by a conjunctive adverb (such as *however, moreover, consequently, nevertheless, therefore, furthermore*), a semicolon rather than a comma should be used to separate the clauses.

The *fragment*, the *run-together* sentence, and the *comma splice*—as we said at the outset—are serious sentence-structure errors that detract from the clarity of writing. They are considered gross errors in college composition; therefore, you would be wise to learn the correct structures so thoroughly that you can use them almost by reflex.

EXERCISE 50

Read each statement carefully; then decide whether it is correct or contains an error in sentence structure. No statement contains more than one error. Indicate your decision by placing the appropriate symbol in the left-hand column next to the sentence.

C   *Correct*
Frag.   *Sentence Fragment*
R.T.   *Run-Together Sentence*
C.S.   *Comma Splice*

_____ 1. Our basketball team missed fifteen foul shots, if we had made half of them, we would have won the game.

_____ 2. If it is going to be used for projects such as public works or roads.

_____ 3. At half time our team was behind by ten points however, we forged ahead with one minute to go on a hook shot by our center.

_____ 4. I like the way Mr. Clark taught his classes; he had no trouble holding the attention of his students.

_____ 5. Even though in the end the mayor was forced to compromise.

_____ 6. For a couple of weeks I spent much time looking at new cars, however, I finally decided to drive my old car for another year.

_____ 7. Remembering how the whole family had gone on a vacation to the Smoky Mountains.

_____ 8. Around noon the snow began to fall however, we went to the game anyway.

_____ 9. I went to a private boarding school from the seventh grade through high school.

_____10. For the past two days it has rained, therefore, I have not had a chance to play golf.

_____11. Not necessarily the student who makes the best grades in high school.

_____12. The repairman fixed the furnace on Tuesday but he had to return the following day to adjust the thermostat.

_____13. Their pleasure in recalling their honeymoon trip to Niagara Falls.

_____14. The patrol car rushed to the scene of the accident and arrived in time to give the necessary first aid to the victim.

_____15. Bill worked at a humdrum job for several years after he graduated from high school, finally, he decided to quit and go to college.

© 1981 HBJ

EXERCISE 51

Read each statement carefully; then decide whether it is correct or contains an error in sentence structure. No statement contains more than one error. Indicate your decision by placing the appropriate symbol in the left-hand column next to the sentence.

C   *Correct*
Frag.   *Sentence Fragment*
R.T.   *Run-Together Sentence*
C.S.   *Comma splice*

_____ 1. Because the examination was based on essays that most of the students did not understand.

_____ 2. Finally, the rain stopped although the river did not recede for several days.

_____ 3. The final exam covered all the stories we read during the semester, therefore, I had to spend the entire weekend studying my notes.

_____ 4. I cannot remember what actually happened for I was immediately knocked unconscious.

_____ 5. After all the votes were cast and the ballots were counted.

_____ 6. For three days in a row the rain came down in torrents.

_____ 7. Running back and forth like scared rabbits.

_____ 8. Terry decided not to swim across the river, much driftwood was floating downstream.

_____ 9. My uncle fell down the stairs, however, he didn't hurt himself seriously.

_____10. For example, those who have done very poorly in high school.

_____11. Calvin entered the store and bought some supplies for the picnic.

_____12. The captain became angry when he found some old newspapers consequently, our weekend liberty was canceled.

_____13. An individual groping toward understanding and learning.

_____14. We drove to Cincinnati last weekend and had a wonderful time.

_____15. Until recently the junior and senior high schools were in the same building now they are in different parts of town.

   © 1981 HBJ

EXERCISE 52

Read each statement carefully; then decide whether it is correct or contains an error in sentence structure. No statement contains more than one error. Indicate your decision by placing the appropriate symbol in the left-hand column next to the number.

C   *Correct*
Frag.   *Sentence Fragment*
R.T.   *Run-Together Sentence*
C.S.   *Comma Splice*

_____ 1. All the passengers on the plane except me were French and I did not have the slightest idea what any of them were saying.

_____ 2. Don excelled in most sports. Especially baseball, football, and basketball.

_____ 3. My favorite pastimes are boating and water-skiing on the Ohio River.

_____ 4. I believe there is a kind fate that guides my destiny, the trip to St. Louis had a happy outcome after all.

_____ 5. I prefer living in a large city however, life in a small town can be very pleasant.

_____ 6. Liz read rapidly. But with scant attention to what was between the lines.

_____ 7. We thought it would be impossible to buy tickets to the seventh game of the World Series, however, to our surprise we were able to walk right up to the box office and get them with no trouble.

_____ 8. The typical attic is drab, dusty, and poorly lighted.

_____ 9. Finally, I decided to accept the scholarship from Catholic University, I thought it would be exciting living in Washington, D.C.

_____10. In high school I read a great deal. Even books that were considered trash.

_____11. Carl failed the course not because he lacked intelligence, he failed because he did not do the required written work.

_____12. The role of the intellectual in our society has changed considerably in the past two decades.

_____13. I had planned a vacation in California but because of the airline strike I was not able to go.

_____14. The experience taught me a valuable lesson, never again will I disagree with a state trooper.

_____15. My adviser worked out my schedule. Which left all my afternoons free for study and recreation.

 © 1981 HBJ

EXERCISE 53

Read each statement carefully; then decide whether it is correct or contains an error in sentence structure. No statement contains more than one error. Indicate your decision by placing the appropriate symbol in the left-hand column next to the number.

C   *Correct*
Frag.   *Sentence Fragment*
R.T.   *Run-Together Sentence*
C.S.   *Comma Splice*

_____ 1. We had to spend the entire afternoon in our cabin for the rain was coming down in torrents.

_____ 2. All northbound traffic was blocked for over an hour. Until the police were able to remove the wreckage from the highway.

_____ 3. The tree outside my window was filled with sparrows with all the screeching I had a hard time sleeping.

_____ 4. Publicity is important in creating a movie star.

_____ 5. I plan to be a teacher, however, sometimes I wonder if I have sufficient patience.

_____ 6. When the driver lost control of his car and it hit a tree.

_____ 7. The realistic setting contrasted sharply with the movie's eerie plot.

_____ 8. The first-string quarterback broke his leg last Sunday therefore, his team does not have much chance to win the championship.

_____ 9. During my short stay in Las Vegas I visited several casinos, however, I did not try my luck except with the slot machines.

_____10. The lifeguard blew his whistle to call the man closer to shore. Because he was swimming alone in a restricted area.

_____11. We won the district championship, however, we lost in the state tournament.

_____12. Many citizens believe that such a plan would result in a sharp increase in taxes.

_____13. The sergeant told us we could fly on a commercial airline or we could travel by train.

_____14. Swimming is my favorite sport. Although this year I haven't had time to swim very often.

_____15. Dan was a superior science student, nevertheless, he had a difficult time writing a passable composition.

 © 1981 HBJ

EXERCISE 54

Read each statement carefully; then decide whether it is correct or contains an error in sentence structure. No statement contains more than one error. Indicate your decision by placing the appropriate symbol in the left-hand column next to the sentence.

C   *Correct*
Frag.   *Sentence Fragment*
R.T.   *Run-Together Sentence*
C.S.   *Comma Splice*

_____ 1. The house was destroyed by the tornado, miraculously, no one was injured.

_____ 2. Wishing that she would be able to go home for the weekend.

_____ 3. I went to the bank to cash my check then I drove to the supermarket to buy some groceries.

_____ 4. Usually, I wake up in the morning before the alarm goes off.

_____ 5. Jane was exhausted from jogging however, she felt a great sense of accomplishment.

_____ 6. To wait for the bus inside the drugstore to get out of the cold.

_____ 7. The Greyhound bus left Louisville at noon, it arrived in Chicago around six that evening.

_____ 8. Traffic moved slowly because of the snow and ice consequently, I was an hour late in getting to school.

_____ 9. After playing tennis for an hour, we sat on the ground under a shade tree to rest.

_____10. Straight from the library to the student union building.

_____11. Baseball is my favorite sport, I've played on baseball teams ever since I was seven years old.

_____12. Our debating team defeated all of our opponents therefore, we won the coveted trophy.

_____13. The salesman demonstrated the carpet sweeper to the young couple.

_____14. Ahead at the half but ten points behind when the basketball game ended.

_____15. Because of the snow and ice, Dr. Jones was delayed in getting to class however, the students waited for him patiently.

 © 1981 HBJ

EXERCISE 55

Read each statement carefully; then decide whether it is correct or contains an error in sentence structure. No statement contains more than one error. Indicate your decision by placing the appropriate symbol in the left-hand column next to the sentence.

C   *Correct*
Frag.   *Sentence Fragment*
R.T.   *Run-Together Sentence*
C.S.   *Comma Splice*

_____ 1. I did not take the direct route to Cincinnati rather I went by way of Lexington.

_____ 2. Final exam week beginning on December 15.

_____ 3. Doris had a pain in her stomach, consequently, she went to see her family doctor.

_____ 4. Many college students have a difficult time writing a composition.

_____ 5. Mrs. Thomas directed our senior play she also sponsored the yearbook.

_____ 6. Susan was endowed with a beautiful voice, she sang the national anthem before all our home football and basketball games.

_____ 7. Different from all the other teams in the conference.

_____ 8. Jane said she really enjoyed the opera however, the weather in New York City that weekend was dreadful.

_____ 9. I had to spend all of my money to get my car fixed; so I asked my dad to loan me a hundred dollars.

_____ 10. Helen was ready when I called for her at the sorority house, usually, I have to wait until she finishes dressing.

_____ 11. Of the ten sophomore girls who competed in the science contest.

_____ 12. I discussed my term paper with my English teacher she made a number of helpful suggestions.

_____ 13. I stopped in the service station and asked the attendant if I was going in the right direction to St. Louis.

© 1981 HBJ

_____14. To stop the water from leaking from the faucet.

_____15. Mary lives just a short distance from the campus, there-
fore, she doesn't have to worry about transportation.

© 1981 HBJ

II: Sentence Structure

Faulty Pronoun Reference

Faulty pronoun reference is another common error in sentence structure that detracts from the clarity and precision of writing. When such words as *it, he, she,* and *they* are used instead of noun constructions, the reader must be able to tell which of the preceding nouns is being represented by the pronoun—that is, which noun is the proper antecedent. Pronouns are of great help in avoiding awkward repetition, but they should be used with care. The pronoun reference that is perfectly clear to you may be misleading to your reader.

The essential cause of faulty pronoun reference can be traced to the manner in which we think. Much of our thinking is done in visual images that are captioned by pronouns rather than specific nouns. For example, a sailor walking through Times Square in New York may reflect, "I haven't heard from him for a long time." Simultaneously a picture of *him* (a former shipmate) comes to his mind. The same process undoubtedly takes place when we write. When we use a pronoun an image comes to our minds. However, we cannot be sure that a similar phenomenon will take place in the mind of the reader unless our pronoun clearly refers to a specific prior word, or antecedent.

In order to explain this principle more clearly we have divided faulty pronoun reference into three types: (1) *divided reference,* (2) *implied reference,* and (3) *broad reference.* The best way to understand these terms is to study examples, noting how the faulty reference is an obstacle to clear understanding and how the error may be corrected by rewriting the sentence or merely by supplying a specific word for the pronoun.

DIVIDED PRONOUN REFERENCE

Divided pronoun reference is also called *ambiguous reference*, for the vague pronoun can refer to more than one person, place, or thing, as in the following example:

Divided Reference   Mary told her sister that her car had been stolen.

The reader may wonder "Whose car was stolen? Did the car belong to Mary or did it belong to her sister?" Such a misuse of pronouns can make a statement in your theme baffling to the reader. Moreover, such a slip-up in business correspondence or in a legal document might cost an individual or a company considerable money or trouble. The examples and comments that follow demonstrate the need for careful pronoun reference. For if your reference is not clear, the reader has to guess what you are trying to say and may guess incorrectly.

Divided Reference	The members of the Senate tried in vain to convince the general public that they should assume the responsibility rather than the president of the United States.
Improved	The members of the Senate tried in vain to convince the general public that the people, rather than the president, should assume the responsibility.
Comment	In the divided example it is not clear who should assume the responsibility: the members of the Senate or the general public. To solve the problem no special rules need to be applied, except to ask yourself this practical question: How can I rewrite the vague statement so the meaning will be perfectly clear to the reader?
Divided Reference	Professor Desmond told David that his letter to the editor would be published in the school newspaper.
Improved	Professor Desmond told David that his (David's) letter to the editor would be published in the school newspaper.
Comment	The improved example may be a little awkward, but the meaning is clear, whereas the meaning in the divided example is ambiguous. Sometimes the preceding sentence will clarify the pronoun reference, but it is a risky business to leave too much to the imagination of the reader. Where clarity is involved, it is better to be too obvious than too subtle.
Divided Reference	Tom's brother told him that his income tax refund had come in the morning mail.
Improved	Tom's brother told him, "Tom, your income tax refund came in the morning mail."
Comment	Sometimes the use of dialogue is the best way to clarify divided pronoun reference, as seems to be true in this case.
Divided Reference	The sergeant told the corporal that his orders had finally been received, transferring him to Germany.
Improved	The sergeant broke the sad news to his assistant. "Cor-

	poral, I just received orders transferring you to Germany."
Comment	This example, of course, is comparable to the previous one. In the improved example, there is no doubt who is being transferred to Germany—just as there should be no possible doubt when you use a pronoun to refer to a preceding person, place, or thing.

IMPLIED PRONOUN REFERENCE

Implied pronoun reference is a problem in writing, for the imprecise use of pronouns is common in speech. This ingrained language pattern is bound to assert a strong influence on our writing style no matter what the occasion. But there are differences between ordinary speech and writing, one being the fact that writing should be more precise. Thus an implied pronoun reference that is acceptable in speech may be considered wrong in writing. Consider this statement:

Implied Reference	They make many poor movies in Hollywood.

The pronoun *they* is vague, for *they* implies a number of possibilities: the producers, the directors, the actors, and so on. As in divided reference, the reader has to guess what the writer means. The reader should not have to guess; the writer's thoughts should be expressed in precise language. Eliminating implied pronoun reference will help you to improve the clarity of your writing.

If you detect implied pronoun reference, all you have to do is remove the pronoun and substitute a specific word or phrase. In other words, you should clearly state what is implied.

Implied Reference	While traveling through Asia, we visited Japan and discovered that they are like Americans in many respects.
Improved	While traveling through Asia, we visited Japan and discovered that the Japanese are like Americans in many respects.
Comment	The meaning of the improved example is much clearer; the reader does not have to stop and try to figure out what the writer means by *they*.
Implied Reference	One of the most significant American space achievements took place on August 12, 1960, when they launched the Echo I balloon.
Improved	One of the most significant American space achievements took place on August 12, 1960, when the personnel of NASA launched the Echo I balloon.
Comment	We have solved the reference problem by getting rid of the pronoun and substituting "the personnel of NASA," which is more specific.
Implied Reference	A food shortage developed, and they had to import food to keep the people from starving.

Improved	A food shortage developed, and the government officials had to import food to keep the people from starving.
Comment	The problem was solved in the improved example by substituting a noun for the pronoun. If you make an effort to follow this principle, your writing is almost bound to improve in clarity and precision.

BROAD PRONOUN REFERENCE

The problem of *broad pronoun reference* is similar to that of *implied reference*, for the antecedent of the pronoun is implied rather than clearly stated. But an important distinction should be made. Whereas in implied reference no antecedent is stated, in broad reference the antecedent is a broad idea rather than a specific noun or phrase. In either case the reader is asked to do the writer's work, namely, to discover a relationship between a pronoun and an implied noun or between the pronoun and a broad idea.

You can easily solve the problem of broad pronoun reference if you will recall the definition of a pronoun: "A pronoun is a word that takes the place of a noun or another pronoun." Then when you use a pronoun, double-check to make certain that the reference is clear. If the pronoun does not refer to a specific word but to a general statement, you probably have broad pronoun reference, as in the following example:

Broad Reference	Working while going to college is difficult for most students, but *this* strengthens the will and often leads to success in life.

Precisely what does the writer mean by *this* in the sentence above? The term *broad reference* is fitting because the meaning of *this* covers a broad range of possibilities. Does the writer mean *this determination* or *this type of schedule* or *this handicap?* The reader may not go to the trouble of trying to understand or may try and fail to guess the intended meaning.

Broad Reference	Hamlet hid from the present, ignored the future, and took refuge in the past. He demonstrated this during the first two acts of the play.
Improved	Hamlet hid from the present, ignored the future, and took refuge in the past. He showed this tendency to procrastinate during the first two acts of the play.
Comment	The writer solved the reference problem by having *this* modify a noun phrase (*tendency to procrastinate*).
Broad Reference	Some of the classes were combined and met in the same room. This arrangement irritated the faculty, but as always the dean got his way.
Improved	Some of the classes were combined and met in the same room. This arrangement irritated the faculty, but as always the dean got his way.
Comment	It is an easy matter to place a specific noun after the pro-

noun, as we have done in the improved example. Such a change usually makes the sentence clearer.

Broad Reference	Grain was blown from the soil, and livestock perished from lack of water and pasture. This was the final blow for many of the distressed farmers.
Improved	Grain was blown from the soil, and livestock perished from lack of water and pasture. This prolonged drought was the final blow for many of the distressed farmers.
Comment	In the improved example the reader is given the specific cause of the distress. In the poor example the reader may be somewhat confused, wondering if *this* refers to the soil problem or to the livestock problem.
Broad Reference	Entering the subway, I turned to the right rather than to the left and caught the wrong train. This would not have happened if I had been paying closer attention to the signs.
Improved	Entering the subway, I turned to the right rather than to the left and caught the wrong train. This mistake would not have happened if I had been paying closer attention to the signs.
Comment	As in the previous example the writer has used *this* in a broad sense to suggest both *turning* and *catching*. The reader may have to pause several seconds to puzzle out the reference.
Broad Reference	When the United States government unloads its surpluses on the international market, it hurts the economies of other countries that we are trying to help.
Improved	The unloading of surpluses on the international market by the United States government may hurt the countries we are trying to help.
Comment	Perhaps the best way to solve the problem of broad reference is to get rid of the pronoun altogether—as the writer has done in the improved example—making the sentence not only clearer but also easier to read.

When we speak, most of us use pronouns rather loosely. Understandably this habit often carries over to writing. If you will remember that a pronoun is a word that takes the place of a noun or another pronoun and try to make your pronouns refer to specific words, your writing will be clearer and more effective.

EXERCISE 56

Read each statement carefully; then decide whether it is correct or contains an error in sentence structure. No statement contains more than one error. Indicate your decision by placing the appropriate symbol in the left-hand column next to the statement.

C   *Correct*
Frag.   *Sentence Fragment*
R.T.   *Run-Together Sentence*
C.S.   *Comma Splice*
F.R.   *Faulty Pronoun Reference*

_____ 1. Although Jack took Tom to the races, he didn't want to bet.

_____ 2. Since I wasted much of my time in high school worrying about sports and figuring out schemes to do as little work as possible.

_____ 3. If further information is needed, I shall be glad to send it to you promptly.

_____ 4. Many students do not have effective study habits, consequently, they do not make the grades that are required.

_____ 5. Ronald Cox is an experienced corporation lawyer who is also active in civic affairs. This should make him an outstanding candidate for mayor in the primary election.

_____ 6. Some students standing in line to buy their books.

_____ 7. Snow and sleet were blowing across the road, and the rush-hour traffic was beginning. This exasperated Mr. Jones.

_____ 8. After you have had a chance to read the story and to consider its merits and limitations.

_____ 9. The car still wouldn't run therefore, I checked the generator.

_____10. When you are assigned a topic for your reference paper, you should go to the library at your first opportunity; they have reference books on almost every subject imaginable.

© 1981 HBJ

_____11. The cost of the monorail system was two million dollars, it took two years to complete.

_____12. Since these poverty-stricken countries had little to offer in payment and great strain was placed on their economies.

_____13. Many careless mistakes could be found if students would proofread their themes aloud.

_____14. The salary is more than I made at my previous job.

_____15. Organic life may exist on planets other than the earth however, scientists cannot be sure of this fact.

 © 1981 HBJ

EXERCISE 57

Read each statement carefully; then decide whether it is correct or contains an error in sentence structure. No statement contains more than one error. Indicate your decision by placing the appropriate symbol in the left-hand column next to the statement.

C   *Correct*
Frag.   *Sentence Fragment*
R.T.   *Run-Together Sentence*
C.S.   *Comma Splice*
F.R.   *Faulty Pronoun Reference*

_____ 1. Men may think they can assert their authority by humiliating women, but this will not work.

_____ 2. My job does not pay very much however, I make enough to defray my expenses in college.

_____ 3. While riding home on the bus the other day, I saw something rather extraordinary.

_____ 4. Sometimes for the good but in this case for the bad.

_____ 5. Sarah was afraid to go into the deep water, the last time she went on the other side of the rope she nearly drowned.

_____ 6. Mr. Brown is a successful businessman and is highly respected in the community. This is proof that others saw his abilities as I did.

_____ 7. Although I had made fairly high grades on the entrance examinations.

_____ 8. The huge brick building was shattered and firemen stood around spraying water on the rubble.

_____ 9. Being the "baby" of the family can sometimes lead to frustrations and anxiety.

_____10. Mary told Joan that the tires on her car were too worn to survive the cross-country drive.

_____11. Late summer and early fall are bad times to visit Florida, hurricanes are quite common at this time of the year.

_____12. The speaker mumbles his words so badly that the listener can hardly understand what he says.

© 1981 HBJ

_____13. In the high school they decided to conduct an experiment and put the boys and girls in separate classes.

_____14. Hoping that we would be able to find the road back to the camp.

_____15. Ralph was the fastest skier in the group, the others were always trying to catch up to him.

 © 1981 HBJ

EXERCISE 58

Read each statement carefully; then decide whether it is correct or contains an error in sentence structure. No statement contains more than one error. Indicate your decision by placing the appropriate symbol in the left-hand column next to the statement.

C   *Correct*
Frag.   *Sentence Fragment*
R.T.   *Run-Together Sentence*
C.S.   *Comma Splice*
F.R.   *Faulty Pronoun Reference*

_____ 1. Doing a couple of hundred push-ups and touching your toes several hundred times every day will trim your waistline. But this takes a lot of willpower.

_____ 2. The debt that the next generation, our children, must face.

_____ 3. Friends can merely give you advice, they cannot solve the problems for you.

_____ 4. After practicing for six months, I decided that golf was not my sport.

_____ 5. We decided to get an early start on our trip to the lake so we agreed to meet at my house at six the next morning.

_____ 6. My parents usually made all the major decisions for me, and this was a handicap to me when I left home.

_____ 7. Which we had discovered at the edge of a grove of pine trees.

_____ 8. The pool was very crowded, therefore, we decided to play tennis rather than go swimming.

_____ 9. I am having a hard time deciding what make of camera to buy but I suppose I shall settle for a Kodak.

_____10. Roy told Dennis that he had a hole in the seat of his pants.

_____11. Just sitting under a shade tree and taking life easy.

_____12. I needed money desperately, however, I was too proud to ask my parents for a loan.

_____13. When we arrived at Dale Hallow, my sister and I put on our swimsuits and headed for the lake however, Mom and Dad decided to sit on the porch and rest after the long drive.

_____14. I can pick up clear-channel stations from a great distance on my car radio.

_____15. In some high schools they force the students to do their homework.

© 1981 HBJ

EXERCISE 59

Read each statement carefully; then decide whether it is correct or contains an error in sentence structure. No statement contains more than one error. Indicate your decision by placing the appropriate symbol in the left-hand column next to the statement.

C   *Correct*
Frag.   *Sentence Fragment*
R.T.   *Run-Together Sentence*
C.S.   *Comma Splice*
F.R.   *Faulty Pronoun Reference*

_____ 1. Some students may have a high degree of intelligence but they may not have the necessary determination for success in college.

_____ 2. The win over Southern assured our team of a berth in the regional tournament.

_____ 3. My teacher favored me and gave me odd jobs to do because I was the youngest kid in the class. This gave me more confidence.

_____ 4. Since the governor decided to call a special session of the legislature to discuss means of raising teachers' salaries.

_____ 5. Many of the voters could not understand that a "yes" vote for the bond issue would not necessitate an increase in taxes.

_____ 6. A riot broke out in the prison, and they had to call out the National Guard to restore order.

_____ 7. I was not successful in finding a part-time job consequently, I decided to apply for a loan to cover my expenses.

_____ 8. After you have had a chance to study the chapter and to find principles that are difficult for you to understand.

_____ 9. Students stayed away from classes and protested loudly, but this did not influence the college officials in altering their decision.

_____ 10. The conditions that caused the trustees of the college to decide to move the institution to a larger city.

_____11. Some pledges were beaten severely and thrown into the lake. This caused the fraternity to be put on probation.

_____12. Many voters do not have an understanding of the issues, therefore, they cannot make an intelligent choice between candidates.

_____13. The salesman gave me samples of the rustproof aluminum tubing.

_____14. Even though I am determined to make a good grade and intend to put forth extra effort.

_____15. Corn is now gathered and shucked by machine. They harvest the crops in a fraction of the time that was formerly required.

 © 1981 HBJ

EXERCISE 60

Read each statement carefully; then decide whether it is correct or contains an error in sentence structure. No statement contains more than one error. Indicate your decision by placing the appropriate symbol in the left-hand column next to the statement.

C   *Correct*
Frag.   *Sentence Fragment*
R.T.   *Run-Together Sentence*
C.S.   *Comma Splice*
F.R.   *Faulty Pronoun Reference*

_____ 1. I had too many wrong answers, therefore, I flunked the test.

_____ 2. Returned to the dorm where we played cards until midnight.

_____ 3. Warren became angry when his car wouldn't start.

_____ 4. At our college they choose ten outstanding students to participate in a national conference on education.

_____ 5. Alice sent applications to several universities for she hasn't decided where she wants to go.

_____ 6. There is a shortage of coal because of the prolonged strike, consequently, some plants had to curtail production.

_____ 7. Tom had a hard time understanding his history professor because he spoke in a low voice.

_____ 8. The entire summer working at a resort hotel in Maine.

_____ 9. Jim delivers newspapers to pay his way through college consequently, he doesn't have much leisure time.

_____ 10. The club I belong to has a softball team in the intramural league, I think we have a pretty good chance to win it.

_____ 11. Writing effectively and reading with comprehension are great assets to the college student. This will usually enable the student to succeed.

_____ 12. Entering the bus station and walking toward the ticket counter.

_____13. To become a concert pianist it is necessary to practice diligently.

_____14. Rita was among the students who made the dean's honor role she has always done well in school.

_____15. John told his brother that he made an error in figuring his income tax.

 © 1981 HBJ

EXERCISE 61

Read each statement carefully; then decide whether it is correct or contains an error in sentence structure. No statement contains more than one error. Indicate your decision by placing the appropriate symbol in the left-hand column next to the statement.

C   *Correct*
Frag.   *Sentence Fragment*
R.T.   *Run-Together Sentence*
C.S.   *Comma Splice*
F.R.   *Faulty Pronoun Reference*

_____ 1. To ask the owner of the blue automobile to move it off the grass.

_____ 2. Jane told her sister that a front tire on her car was flat.

_____ 3. Tom decided to build his own home, he is a carpenter by trade.

_____ 4. The play lasted for three hours consequently, it was late when we got back to the dorm.

_____ 5. Edna spent most of the evening in her bedroom listening to her stereo.

_____ 6. To buy the necessary office equipment and other such expenses.

_____ 7. At the university they have many activities during orientation week.

_____ 8. We are living in a violent age, I can't see how conditions can get much worse.

_____ 9. I spent most of Sunday afternoon and evening studying.

_____10. During the week Debbie goes to bed around eleven o'clock but she stays up late on the weekends.

_____11. Slipping on the ice and injuring his back.

_____12. Rudy can throw harder than any other pitcher on the baseball team, however, at times he has problems with his control.

_____13. Eating the proper diet and getting sufficient physical exercise are sometimes difficult, but this is worth the effort.

© 1981 HBJ

_____14. Rosa likes her coffee sweet however, she prefers to drink it without adding milk or cream.

_____15. On our camping trip we slept on the ground in sleeping bags.

 © 1981 HBJ

12: Sentence Structure
Faulty Parallelism

I f you lost one of several black, half-inch buttons on your coat, you would not set out to replace it with a red, two-inch button. A sense of proportion would tell you to use a button like the one you lost.

In like manner, parts of a sentence that have the same function should be in the same grammatical form. We discussed *parallelism* in the lesson on outlining, saying that topics or subtopics of the outline similar in scope should be stated in similar language. For instance, in a topic outline for a composition on "My Favorite Outdoor Sports," the main divisions were swimming, fishing, and hunting. It appears that the three sports might be of equal importance since they are expressed in parallel language. But if the series were expressed like this: "My favorite sports are swimming, to fish in rivers and lakes, and hunting," readers might have to stop and ponder before they could be sure that the sports are of similar importance. In a figurative sense the names of the sports are similar to the buttons on the coat. The sports have the same function (or thought value); therefore, they should be expressed in the same grammatical form: swimming, fishing, and hunting.

As you can see, we are dealing basically with the question of logical coordination. To repeat, similar ideas within a sentence should be expressed in the same grammatical form. Now let us examine several of the common ways that the principle of parallelism is violated in writing, leading to the sentence-structure error called *faulty parallelism.*

Two or more sentence elements that have the same function should be in the same grammatical form.

Poor	Baker was intelligent, determined, and had a dynamic personality.
Better	Baker was intelligent, determined, and dynamic.
Comment	*Intelligent* and *determined* in the preceding sentence describe Baker; both words are predicate adjectives. Having started a series of predicate adjectives, the writer should not break the series by using a verb form, as in the poor example.

Poor	Through these organizations parents become acquainted with teachers and how their child is doing in school.
Better	Through these organizations parents *become* acquainted with teachers and *learn* how their children are doing in school.
Comment	The conjunction *and* should join like things: *bread* and *butter* (two nouns); *interesting* and *enjoyable* (two adjectives); *to fish* and *to hunt* (two infinitives). In the above sentence the writer should have a verb after *and* as well as before it.

Poor	Some predictable faults of the average individual are an irresponsible attitude, the inability to see one's own faults, and everyone being basically selfish.
Better	Some predictable faults of the average individual are an irresponsible *attitude*, the *inability* to see one's own faults, and a selfish *disposition*.
Comment	In the poor example the writer started a series of noun objects, then shifted to an indefinite pronoun, breaking the parallel pattern and causing an awkward effect.

Poor	I have been accused of being rough, hardheaded, and a determined individual.
Better	I have been accused of being rough, hardheaded, and determined.
Comment	Without going into a grammatical analysis of the poor example, the student can see that *rough* and *hardheaded* are in the same class but *determined individual* is different. The revised sentence has a better rhythm, and the meaning is clearer.

Poor	A person may pursue a goal at college, at a trade school, a military career, or in industry.
Better	A person may pursue a goal at college, at a trade school, in the military service, or in industry.
Comment	Again, without going into a complicated grammatical analysis, the student can see the element in the poor example that should be changed to make the sentence parallel. The element *a military career* needs to be changed to *in the military service* to make the series of prepositions complete: *at, at, in,* or *in.*

Correlative conjunctions are used in pairs; not only _____ but (also) _____; neither _____ nor _____; either _____ or _____. When they are used in a sentence, the same part of speech (noun, verb, adjective, and so on) should come after the second conjunction as after the first.

Poor	*Either* he is right *or* wrong.
Better	He is *either* right *or* wrong.
Comment	In the poor example a pronoun, *he*, follows the first conjunction, while an adjective, *wrong*, follows the second conjunction. In the corrected version both conjunctions are followed by adjectives.

Poor	*Neither* is John too proud *nor* too busy to do the job.
Better	John is *neither* too proud *nor* too busy to do the job.
Comment	In the poor example a verb, *is*, follows the first conjunction, while an adverb, *too*, follows the second one. In the corrected example both conjunctions are followed by adverbs.

Poor	*Not only* does Sarah play a guitar *but also* she sings.
Better	Sarah *not only* plays a guitar *but also* sings.
Comment	In the poor example the first conjunction is followed by a verb, *does*, while the second is followed by a pronoun, *she*, causing faulty parallelism.

Another sentence-structure problem that is closely akin to faulty parallelism (and shall be so designated in the exercises that follow the discussion) is the needless shift of *person, tense,* or *voice* within a sentence or paragraph.

Poor	I enjoy the Christmas holidays, for you have a chance to visit your friends and relatives.
Poor	The hunters spent the afternoon trudging through the woods and spend the evening relaxing before the log fire in their cabin.
Poor	We left Peoria about noon, and Chicago was reached in three hours.

In the first example the writer shifts *person*, in the second, *tense*, in the third, *voice*. Such needless shifts in writing are awkward, detracting from the smooth flow of language. Moreover, the shifts in point of view within a sentence or paragraph may be a stumbling block to clear communication.

The point of view (person, tense, or voice) should be consistent within a sentence or paragraph.

SHIFT IN PERSON

Poor	One reason that I appreciate classical music is the enjoyment and relaxation you get from listening to it.
Better	One reason that I appreciate classical music is the enjoyment I get from listening to it.
Comment	In the poor example the writer shifts from the first to the second person.

Poor	I still remember that the heat was so intense it felt as though you were standing over a fire.
Better	The heat was so intense I felt that I was standing over a fire.
Comment	In the poor example the writer shifts from *I* to *you*—perhaps the most common shift found in writing.

SHIFT IN TENSE

Poor   The first morning at camp we swam across the lake and lie on the sandy beach most of the afternoon.

Better   The first morning at camp we swam across the lake and lay on the sandy beach most of the afternoon.

Comment   In the poor example the student changed the verb tense from the past to the present: *swam* to *lie*. A needless switch in the tense of the verb may be a problem in proofreading rather than logic, for in most instances there is no explainable reason why the writer should want to make such a change.

Poor   We parked our car at the harbor and rented one of the boats, which we use to get to Twelve Mile Island.

Better   We parked our car at the harbor and rented one of the boats, which we used to get to Twelve Mile Island.

Comment   The problem in the poor example should be obvious. The writer shifted from the past to the present tense, from *parked* and *rented* to *use*.

SHIFT IN VOICE

When the subject of the sentence does the acting, the verb is said to be in the active voice.

John drives the red automobile.

When the subject of the sentence receives the action, the verb is said to be in the passive voice.

The red automobile is driven by John.

We form the passive voice by combining a form of the verb *to be* (*be, am, is, are, was, were, being, been*) with the past participle of another verb.

The red automobile is [a form of the verb *to be*] driven [past participle of the verb *to drive*] by John.

Most of the time we speak and write in the active voice, which is the more natural form of discourse. Sometimes it is necessary to use the passive voice, but you should avoid shifting back and forth needlessly.

Poor   With greater attention, the instructions could be understood, and we would not have to ask the professor to explain the lesson outside of class.

Better   With greater attention, we could understand the instructions and not have to ask the professor to explain the lesson outside of class.

Comment   The poor example begins in the passive voice and abruptly shifts to the active. Such a shift may be avoided by placing the personal pronoun *we* near the beginning of the sentence.

Poor   The members of the fraternity decided to ask the Dean of Students for permission to hold their spring dance on campus; thus certain problems such as renting a hotel ballroom could be avoided.

Better   The members of the fraternity decided to ask the Dean of Students for permission to hold their spring dance on campus; thus they would not have to pay the high cost involved in renting a hotel ballroom.

Comment   In the poor example the writer needlessly and awkwardly shifts from the active to the passive voice in the second independent clause. In the corrected version this problem is avoided by making *they* the active subject of the second independent clause.

If you try hard to make your sentences parallel and consistent in point of view by avoiding the pitfalls and following the positive principles we have suggested, your writing should improve in style as well as in clarity.

EXERCISE 62

Read each statement carefully; then decide whether it is correct or contains an error in sentence structure. No statement contains more than one error. Indicate your decision by placing the appropriate symbol in the left-hand column next to the statement.

C   *Correct*
Frag.   *Sentence Fragment*
R.T.   *Run-Together Sentence*
C.S.   *Comma Splice*
F.R.   *Faulty Pronoun Reference*
F.P.   *Faulty Parallelism*

_____ 1. Charles and his wife greatly enjoy classical music, but this fact was concealed from their friends.

_____ 2. I wanted to go to the basketball game, however, I had to go to the library and study for a test I was having the next day.

_____ 3. Jane's mother told her that she could not go to the movie.

_____ 4. Many people in the United States distrust the so-called intellectual yet this country would be stagnant if it were not for these individuals.

_____ 5. Terry had to walk three miles along the dark, narrow road. Because he forgot to get some gas before he left Springfield.

_____ 6. Not only is John considerate but also cooperative.

_____ 7. I am attending college primarily for an education. I feel, though, that you should take part in extracurricular activities.

_____ 8. Keith was a friendly young man with an outgoing personality.

_____ 9. John and Polly went to the basketball game afterward, they stopped at the drive-in for a sandwich and Coke.

_____10. The instructor gave us our assignments, however, they were rather vague and somewhat confusing.

_____11. In some homes and stores they have the luxury of air conditioning.

_____12. A discovery that was to play a large part in changing Judy's philosophy of life.

_____13. Garvin carried newspapers, waited on tables, pitched baseball, quarterback on the football team, and took minor parts in dramatic productions.

_____14. The youngsters all seemed to enjoy the party for they all participated in the games.

_____15. Our teacher never pampered us or loaded us with busy-work. This actually helped us to develop our talents.

 © 1981 HBJ

EXERCISE 63

Read each statement carefully; then decide whether it is correct or contains an error in sentence structure. No statement contains more than one error. Indicate your decision by placing the appropriate symbol in the left-hand column next to the statement.

C   *Correct*
Frag.   *Sentence Fragment*
R.T.   *Run-Together Sentence*
C.S.   *Comma Splice*
F.R.   *Faulty Pronoun Reference*
F.P.   *Faulty Parallelism*

_____ 1. The summer gives a person a chance to get out-of-doors, to take part in your favorite sport, and to relax.

_____ 2. To my great dismay the horse that I had in the race was disqualified, he bumped another horse on the back turn.

_____ 3. Janice was a superior student; therefore, she made excellent grades in college.

_____ 4. In college a student must pay close attention because they generally cover the material only once.

_____ 5. Gil sold encyclopedias for several months however, he gave up the job because the income was too uncertain.

_____ 6. Not only would I have to pay my own train fare but also my meals and lodging.

_____ 7. Taking into consideration the pros and cons of going to college after high school.

_____ 8. I didn't receive my check from home consequently, I couldn't go to the homecoming dance.

_____ 9. In Kentucky they grow much tobacco and breed excellent thoroughbred horses.

_____10. The professor removed his roll book from his briefcase and called the names of the students.

_____11. I thoroughly enjoyed visiting Chicago, it is a city that has much to offer.

_____12. Wade is extremely proud of his "new" car. A fenderless Ford of rather ancient vintage.

© 1981 HBJ

_____13. Yesterday, after almost a week of rain, the sun finally broke through so I decided to take a walk in the park.

_____14. Eating a balanced diet and getting sufficient exercise are important for good health. It is difficult, however, if you work in a bakery, as I do.

_____15. We walked from the library to the cafeteria, and lunch was eaten as soon as we got through the long line.

 © 1981 HBJ

EXERCISE 64

Read each statement carefully; then decide whether it is correct or contains an error in sentence structure. No statement contains more than one error. Indicate your decision by placing the appropriate symbol in the left-hand column next to the statement.

C   *Correct*
Frag.   *Sentence Fragment*
R.T.   *Run-Together Sentence*
C.S.   *Comma Splice*
F.R.   *Faulty Pronoun Reference*
F.P.   *Faulty Parallelism*

_____ 1. At some colleges and universities they require all students to live in dormitories on the campus.

_____ 2. We left Bowling Green at noon, and Nashville was reached an hour later.

_____ 3. Western State beat George Washington College by ten points, however, the game was a seesaw affair until the last several minutes.

_____ 4. Because of the hot, humid weather and the exorbitant price for food and lodging.

_____ 5. The firemen were cautious in approaching the burning building.

_____ 6. Holmes generally has an optimistic and cheerful outlook on life therefore, he is a pleasant person to be around.

_____ 7. A person has to concentrate seriously on bowling, or you will probably never have a high average.

_____ 8. Ralph not only wants to be a success but also to have many friends.

_____ 9. It was raining, therefore, I drove rather than walked to school.

_____10. Rose told her best friend that she should see a doctor.

_____11. The politician used many tactics to get what he wanted: blackmail, bribery, and removed men from office.

_____12. I am sending you several books that you should find readable and stimulating.

_____13. It was necessary for Ruth to leave for college a few days earlier than she had planned therefore, we didn't have a chance to say good-by to her.

_____14. Although it was a beautiful spring day and the lake looked inviting.

_____15. Taking notes from television lectures and working them into an outline benefits high-school students. This helps them to prepare for the college method of instruction.

 © 1981 HBJ

EXERCISE 65

Read each statement carefully; then decide whether it is correct or contains an error in sentence structure. No statement contains more than one error. Indicate your decision by placing the appropriate symbol in the left-hand column next to the statement.

C   *Correct*
Frag.   *Sentence Fragment*
R.T.   *Run-Together Sentence*
C.S.   *Comma Splice*
F.R.   *Faulty Pronoun Reference*
F.P.   *Faulty Parallelism*

_____ 1. Patrick Doran thinks the book will be a success because the author simplifies a complex subject.

_____ 2. The play was panned by the critics, nevertheless, it had a long and profitable run on Broadway.

_____ 3. Arnold told his brother that his new tie was missing.

_____ 4. Farley's goal being to get ahead and to deal with his fellow men at a profitable exchange.

_____ 5. I thoroughly enjoy the summer months, for you can spend much time out-of-doors and get plenty of exercise.

_____ 6. The book was obviously a great literary work yet it was quite difficult to understand.

_____ 7. Although O'Brien was in good health and in the prime of life, he was usually depressed about one thing or another.

_____ 8. I called the department store, and they said they would be glad to exchange the sweater I had bought.

_____ 9. To help develop new fuels or a new way to power ships of all kinds.

_____10. The admission line to the movie was at least a block long so we decided to go to the dog races instead.

_____11. I greatly admire Senator Davis, for she is intelligent, articulate, and has the interest of the people at heart.

_____12. Most people seem to have a desire to help others and to see others prosper.

_____13. Doing a hundred push-ups and running two or three miles may be strenuous, but this keeps a person in good shape.

_____14. Southern Florida is an ideal place during the winter months, however, it is rather risky during the hurricane season.

_____15. Not only was Dr. Durbin a brilliant scholar but also an outstanding athlete.

 © 1981 HBJ

EXERCISE 66

Read each statement carefully; then decide whether it is correct or contains an error in sentence structure. No statement contains more than one error. Indicate your decision by placing the appropriate symbol in the left-hand column next to the statement.

C   *Correct*
Frag.   *Sentence Fragment*
R.T.   *Run-Together Sentence*
C.S.   *Comma Splice*
F.R.   *Faulty Pronoun Reference*
F.P.   *Faulty Parallelism*

_____ 1. Jean told her sister that she had to go to the grocery.

_____ 2. I gained my knowledge about cars by watching other people work on them.

_____ 3. In high school Mary hated math and seldom studied, consequently, she had to take the remedial algebra course in her first year at college.

_____ 4. My nephew is lazy, dishonest, and has a quick temper.

_____ 5. Since Marvin and his father frequently fished at Lake Hester.

_____ 6. Fred thoughtfully held the door open for the woman however, she didn't even thank him.

_____ 7. Neither is Ruth able to cook nor eager to learn.

_____ 8. Cathy studied hard for the test and was not surprised when she got one of the best grades.

_____ 9. At the first convocation we attended after we arrived on campus, they told us that we could go home on weekends.

_____10. I enjoy college much more than high school, I have more freedom to do as I please.

_____11. If a person really wants to learn to ice-skate, you must practice at least twice a week.

_____12. Writing your ideas on three-by-five cards and dividing the cards into groups is time-consuming, but this helps you to organize a composition.

© 1981 HBJ

_____13. The basketball game between Western and Eastern was broadcast last night however, I did not have time to listen to it.

_____14. May and Tom were married at noon on Saturday and left on their wedding trip immediately after the service.

_____15. Because Sue had already made up her mind that she didn't like her English instructor.

 © 1981 HBJ

13: Correct Usage

The label *correct usage* can be applied to almost any aspect of language, but as a grammatical term it has a specific meaning. In a broad sense it denotes the appropriateness of the writer's language to the occasion; in a more restricted sense *correct usage* means the rightness or wrongness of language as established by custom. You may gain a clearer understanding of this restricted sense of the term by judging which of the alternate forms in the following sentences are correct.

I think I'll *lay* down and take a nap.
I think I'll *lie* down and take a nap.

I *seen* Tom at the race track last Saturday.
I *saw* Tom at the race track last Saturday.

Jane *don't* care what anybody thinks.
Jane *doesn't* care what anybody thinks.

The outfielder made the play *easy.*
The outfielder made the play *easily.*

The child forms his letters *good.*
The child forms his letters *well.*

Me and *him* went to the game together.
He and *I* went to the game together.

The argument was between Harry and *I.*
The argument was between Harry and *me.*

As you have probably guessed, the second statement in each group is correct.

At this point, you may ask a very important question. What difference does it make if people use questionable language? Looked at from a strictly practical viewpoint, in some situations it makes little or no difference. However, in other situations it may make the difference between success or failure.

Contrary to what you may think, English teachers alone do not determine what is standard English, that is, the language to be used by the so-called well-educated group in society. Rather it is the combined professional and semiprofessional classes: medical doctors, lawyers, broadcasters, engineers, ministers, politicians, accountants, nurses, secretaries, and so forth. And you should be aware of the fact that a great deal of social pressure surrounds the use of language. It is indeed unfortunate, but sometimes people are looked down upon because they do not use proper English.

Of course, in certain occupations and social relationships nonstandard speech is acceptable. However, if you are planning a career in one of the so-called white-collar professions, you would be wise to put forth a strong effort to learn correct English.

Another consideration of *correct usage* relates to the appropriateness of the language to the occasion. To give a brief picture of how language is used in our society, we shall use a comparison that can be easily understood. The use of language has often been compared to the clothes people wear. Although we could use women's clothes in our analogy, we believe the relationship will be clearer if we use men's apparel.

Starting at the top, *formal language* might be compared to the white tie and tails a man would wear on a very formal occasion. This type of diction is used in some scholarly writing, but there is a trend away from academic prose in favor of a more down-to-earth idiom.

Next we have *semiformal language,* which might be compared to the conventional tuxedo or perhaps to the dark suit, white shirt, and appropriate necktie that a man might wear to a "dress-up" dance. This is the style you will generally be expected to use in your college writing and in your professional correspondence.

Next on the language scale comes *informal writing,* which might be compared with slacks, sport shirt, and sweater or with a colorful sport jacket worn with contrasting trousers. This is the style you might be asked to use in a composition course in which you write papers based on personal experience. Some of the marks of informal writing are the use of contractions, the clever use of slang, and the use of clichés for an ironical effect. But in most of your college writing assignments, you will be expected to use the *semiformal* style rather than the breezy, informal language you would use in a letter to a personal friend.

At the lowest end of the scale is *nonstandard* language. Using our "dress" analogy, we might compare *nonstandard* diction to the blue chambray shirt and dungarees of the working man. Here are a few examples.

> Tim *has went* to Miami Beach on his vacation.

> You *ain't got no* business going into the deep water.

> Larry *don't* care about improving his grammar.

> I *can't hardly* believe that spring is here.

> I *seen* a good movie on TV last night.

In attempting to classify language, we should not think for a moment that these distinctions are sharp and clear, for the various categories of language have more similarities than differences. Nor should you mistakenly conclude that the use of *nonstandard* language is always a drawback. However, as a college student who aspires to do well in school and perhaps in one of the so-called white-collar professions, you would be wise to eliminate nonstandard language from your speech and writing.

In the glossary that follows you will find an alphabetized list of words that are commonly misused in speech and writing. You will also find words that are frequently misspelled because they sound the same or look the same.

GLOSSARY OF USAGE

accept/except*

Accept is a verb that means "to receive with favor, willingness, or consent."

> *Correct*   John decided to *accept* the offer from General Motors rather than go to graduate school.

Except is generally used as a preposition to mean "with the exclusion or omission of."

> *Correct*   Everyone at the meeting voted for the proposal *except* David and me.

adapt/adopt

Adapt means "to fit for new use; make suitable."

> *Correct*   When I joined the Navy I had to *adapt* myself to a new way of life.

Adopt means "to take and follow as one's own, as a course of action."

> *Correct*   After John got married, he *adopted* a more conservative outlook on life.

---

*Definitions quoted by permission from Funk & Wagnalls *Standard College Dictionary*, copyright 1977 by Funk & Wagnalls, a division of Reader's Digest Books, Inc.

affect/effect

Affect is a verb that means "to influence."

> *Correct*   It is strange how the weather *affects* some people's dispositions.

Effect is a verb that means "to bring about; produce as a result; cause."

> *Correct*   The Constitutional Revision Committee was able to *effect* most of the changes it had recommended.

Effect is also a noun that means "a result."

> *Correct*   The *effect* of atomic radiation on future generations is not yet known.

Ain't is used by people from diversified backgrounds as a contraction of am not. Sometimes *ain't* is used by well-educated people to achieve a facetious or ironic effect, the user assuming that the listener or reader takes for granted that the user knows *ain't* is ungrammatical. *Ain't*, used carelessly or through ignorance in a business or social situation where the word is normally taboo, is almost certain to bring unfavorable judgment upon the user.

all right/alright

All right means "satisfactory or correct."

> *Correct*   The accountant checked my income tax return and said it was *all right*.

Alright is a deviant form of *all right*. The form alright is "a spelling not yet considered acceptable."

> *Incorrect*   The student asked his teacher if it would be *alright* to write his term paper on divorce as a modern social problem.

> *Correct*   The student asked his teacher if it would be *all right* to write his term paper on divorce as a modern social problem.

all together/altogether

All together means "all in one place."

> *Correct*   We were *all together*, sitting at the picnic table, when the rain began to fall.

Altogether means "completely, wholly."

> *Correct*   I am not *altogether* sure what you mean by that remark.

allusion/illusion

Allusion means "an indirect reference."

>*Correct*   The teacher's comment that "a student pays dearly for his educa-
>tion" was an *allusion* to a statement by Ralph Waldo Emerson.

Illusion means "a misconception."

>*Correct*   I was laboring under the *illusion* that I would get a pay raise at the
>end of the month.

almost/most

Almost means "nearly."

>*Correct*   *Almost* all the houses in my section of town are of brick construc-
>tion.

Most means "nearly all." The use of *most* in the following sentence is
considered nonstandard:

>*Incorrect*   During the summer I am at the swimming pool *most* every after-
>noon.
>
>*Correct*   During the summer I am at the swimming pool *almost* every af-
>ternoon.
>
>*Correct*   *Most* of the students live in dorms on the campus.

already/all ready

Already means "before or by this time or the time mentioned."

>*Correct*   The meeting had *already* started by the time I arrived.

All ready means "completely ready."

>*Correct*   The players were *all ready* for the second half after their rest in the
>dressing room.

amount/number

Amount is used in referring to a quantity that cannot be counted.

>*Correct*   There was a small *amount* of sugar left in the jar.

Number is generally used in referring to a quantity that can be counted.

>*Correct*   A large *number* of people gathered around the woman who had
>been hit by an automobile.

bad/badly

Bad should be used as an adjective to describe how one feels physically.

>*Incorrect*   I feel *badly*.
>*Correct*   I feel *bad*.

Badly is an adverb and should describe a type of action.

>*Incorrect*   She drives *bad*.
>*Correct*   She drives *badly*.

best/better

Best is used as "the superlative of good, well. Excelling all others; of the highest quality." *Best* is often misused in comparing two persons, objects, or things.

> *Incorrect* Karen is the *best* of the two tennis players on the court.
> *Correct* Karen is the *better* of the two tennis players on the court.

Better is the comparative of good, well. It means "superior in excellence; of higher quality." *Better* (not *best*) should be used in comparing two objects, persons, or things.

> *Correct* After listening to the two singers I decided that the first one had the *better* voice.

capital/capitol/Capitol

Capital means "the capital city or town of a country, state, etc."

> *Correct* Nashville is the state *capital* of Tennessee.
> *Correct* Washington, D.C., is the *capital* of the United States.

Capitol refers to the building in which a state legislature convenes. It is written with a small "c" unless it is the first word of a sentence.

> *Correct* The dome of the state *capitol* glistens in the sun.

Capitol (with a capital "C") refers to the official building of the U.S. Congress in Washington, D.C.

> *Correct* When our senior class visited Washington, we toured the *Capitol* and saw Congress in session.

cite/sight/site

Cite means "to quote as authority or illustration. To bring forward or refer to as proof or support."

> *Correct* The professor *cited* an example from the textbook to prove his point.

Sight means "the act or fact of seeing. That which is seen; a view."

> *Correct* The moon shimmering on the lake was a beautiful *sight*.

Site means "place or location. A plot of ground set apart for some specific use."

> *Correct* The *site* that we picked for our new home has a view overlooking the river.

complement/compliment

Complement means "that which fills up or completes a thing."

> *Correct* Her modish red hat *complements* her stylish black dress.

Compliment means "an expression of admiration, praise, or congratulation."

> *Correct*   Several people who heard the speech *complimented* Jack on his courage in taking a firm stand on the controversial subject.

continual/continuous

Continual means "renewed frequently and regularly; often repeated."

> *Correct*   The *continual* rush-hour traffic jams cause many auto accidents.

Continuous means "prolonged without break; uninterrupted."

> *Correct*   The *continuous* flow of the water over the dam provided electricity for the people in the area.

council/counsel

Council is a noun that means "an assembly of persons convened for consultation or deliberation."

> *Correct*   The city *council* meets every Thursday evening.

Counsel when used as a noun means "mutual exchange of advice, opinions, etc.; consultation." When used as a verb, counsel means "to give advice to; to advise."

> *Correct*   Brown followed the *counsel* of his lawyer and paid the fine without protest.
> *Correct*   The faculty adviser *counseled* the new student to take English and mathematics the first quarter.

desert/dessert

Desert means "a region so lacking in rainfall as to be uninhabitable."

> *Correct*   The Sahara *Desert* in Africa covers a vast area of 3,000,000 square miles.

Dessert means "a serving of pastry, ice cream, etc., as the last course of a meal."

> *Correct*   For *dessert* we had ice cream and chocolate cake.

disinterested/uninterested

Disinterested means "unbiased, impartial."

> *Correct*   In hiring a referee for the Rose Bowl classic, the officials sought a *disinterested* person who did not care which team won the game.

Uninterested means "lacking interest."

> *Correct*   Some students seem to be completely *uninterested* in their studies.

don't/doesn't

The use of *don't* for *doesn't*, though widespread, is generally considered nonstandard. It should be avoided by careful speakers and writers.

Incorrect   He *don't* live here.
Correct   He *doesn't* live here.
Incorrect   She *don't* belong to the club.
Correct   She *doesn't* belong to the club.

effect—see affect

emigrate/immigrate

Emigrate means "to move from a country."

Correct   Because of the potato famine in the British Isles, many people *emigrated* from Ireland to the United States.

Immigrate means "to move into a country."

Correct   The people who *immigrated* to the United States in the nineteenth century played an important role in the industrialization of the country.

except—see accept

fewer/less

Fewer should be used in referring to objects that can be counted.

Correct   *Fewer* players were used in the game today than last Saturday.

Less should be used in referring to material that cannot be counted.

Correct   *Less* grain was harvested today than yesterday.

good/well

Good is correctly used as an adjective, a word that modifies a noun or pronoun: *good* news; a *good* automobile; a *good* essay. It is incorrectly used as an adverb, a word that modifies a verb or an adjective.

Incorrect   Joan dances *good*.
Correct   Joan dances *well*.
Incorrect   The jockey rides *good*.
Correct   The jockey rides *well*.

Good is correctly used with the verbs of the five senses.

Correct   The music sounds *good*.
Correct   The hot chili smells *good*.
Correct   The turkey tastes *good*.
Correct   The velvet feels *good*.

Good is used *incorrectly* to describe a person's state of health.

> *Incorrect*   Mary felt *good* after taking the medicine.
> *Correct*   Mary felt *well* after taking the medicine.

Good is used correctly to describe a person's state of mind.

> *Correct*   Eleanor felt *good* after receiving a four-year scholarship.

Well is correctly used as an adverb to modify a verb, an adjective, or another adverb.

> *Incorrect*   If everything goes *good*, I am going home this weekend.
> *Correct*   If everything goes *well*, I am going home this weekend.
> *Incorrect*   Leslie performs *good* on the golf course.
> *Correct*   Leslie performs *well* on the golf course.

Well (rather than *good*) is correctly used as an adjective to describe a person's state of health.

> *Incorrect*   Tom felt *good* after he took an aspirin for his headache.
> *Correct*   Tom felt *well* after he took an aspirin for his headache.

I/me

Confusion sometimes occurs in the use of *I* and *me* when the pronoun *you* or a proper noun comes between the preposition and the second pronoun object. The correct form of the second pronoun can often be determined by reversing the words that follow the preposition and seeing and hearing if the pronoun looks and sounds correct, as we have done in the following examples.

> *Incorrect*   The final one-hundred-yard dash was between *Bill* and *I*.
> *Test*   The final one-hundred-yard dash was between (*I* or *me*) and Bill.
> *Correct*   The final one-hundred-yard dash was between *Bill* and *me*.
> *Incorrect*   Just between *you* and *I*, the contract has already been awarded.
> *Test*   Just between (*I* or *me*) and *you*, the contract has already been awarded.
> *Correct*   Just between *you* and *me*, the contract has already been awarded.

illusion—see allusion

immigrate—see emigrate

imply/infer

Imply means "to indicate or suggest without stating."

> *Correct*   I was not certain what his tone of voice *implied*.

Infer means "to derive by reasoning; conclude or accept from evidence or premises."

> *Correct* I *inferred* from all of the reading I have done on the subject that real estate is the best investment.

irregardless/regardless

Irregardless is a nonstandard usage of *regardless*.

> *Incorrect* Breakfast is served at the restaurant, *irregardless* of the time of day.
> *Correct* Breakfast is served at the restaurant, *regardless* of the time of day.
> *Incorrect* We swam in the ocean, *irregardless* of the danger of sharks.
> *Correct* We swam in the ocean, *regardless* of the danger of sharks.

its/it's

The possessive form of *it* (*its*) is written without an apostrophe.

> *Correct* The dog wagged *its* tail.

It with an apostrophe (*it's*) is a contraction of *it is*.

> *Correct* *It's* too bad that you won't be able to go home this weekend.

lay/lie

Lay means "to place." The principal parts of *lay* are: *lay* (present); *laid* (past); *laid* (past participle); *laying* (present participle).

> *Correct* I *lay* the book on the table.
> *Correct* I *laid* the book on the table.
> *Correct* I have *laid* the book on the table.
> *Correct* I am *laying* the book on the table.

Lie means "to be in or assume a position." The principal parts of *lie* are: *lie* (present); *lay* (past); *lain* (past participle); *lying* (present participle).

> *Correct* I *lie* in bed.
> *Correct* I *lay* in bed an hour after the alarm sounded.
> *Correct* I have *lain* in bed and enjoyed the sound of the rain.
> *Correct* I am *lying* in bed because I am too lazy to get up.

Lie is frequently confused with *lay* and misused in the following manner.

> *Incorrect* (Present) I *lay* in bed.
> *Incorrect* (Past) I *laid* in bed an hour after the alarm sounded.
> *Incorrect* (Past Participle) I have *laid* in bed and enjoyed the sound of the rain.
> *Incorrect* (Present Participle) I am *laying* in bed because I am too lazy to get up.

learn/teach

Learn means "to acquire knowledge of or skill in, by study."

Correct	The best time to *learn* to swim is when you are young.
Correct	It is difficult to *learn* a foreign language.

Teach means "to impart knowledge by lessons; give instructions to."

Incorrect	The teacher *learned* Johnny his lesson.
Correct	The teacher *taught* Johnny his lesson.
Incorrect	Mary asked her father to *learn* her to drive.
Correct	Mary asked her father to *teach* her to drive.

leave/let

Leave means "to allow to remain behind or in a specified place, condition, etc."

Correct You can *leave* your books here. No one will bother them.

Let means "to allow; permit."

Correct *Let* me introduce you to my friend from South America.

less—see fewer

lie—see lay

like/as if or as though

Like should be used as a preposition.

Correct Ralph runs *like* a deer.

As if or *as though* should be used as a conjunction to introduce a clause.

Correct Carl looked *as if* he had not slept for a week.

lose/loose

Lose means "to part with, as by accident or negligence, and be unable to find."

Correct It is easy to *lose* your wallet if you are not careful.

Loose means "not fastened or confined."

Correct You should cut off that *loose* button; otherwise, you may *lose* it.

most—see almost

number—see amount

principal/principle

Principal as an adjective means "first in rank, character, or importance."

Correct The *principal* speaker was Dr. Jarvis.

Principal as a noun means "one who takes a leading part or who is a leader or chief in some action."

Correct Robert T. Jacobs is the *principal* of my high school.

Principle as a noun means "a general truth or law, basic to other truths."

Correct The *principle* of relativity for most people is difficult to understand.

quiet/quite

Quiet means "making little or no noise."

Correct Let's study in the library where it is *quiet*.

Quite means "to the fullest extent; totally."

Correct I am *quite* certain I can be there by noon.

real/really

Real as an adjective means "having existence or actuality as a thing or state."

Correct The jeweler examined the ring and said the diamond was *real*.

Really as an adverb means "in reality; as a matter of fact."

Incorrect We were *real* tired when we reached the top of the mountain.
Correct We were *really* tired when we reached the top of the mountain.
Incorrect I was *real* pleased when I received my midterm grades.
Correct I was *really* pleased when I received my midterm grades.

raise/rise

Raise means "to cause to move upward or to a higher level." The principal parts of the verb are as follows: *raise* (present); *raised* (past); *raised* (past participle); *raising* (present participle).

Correct Susan decided to *raise* the window to get some fresh air.
Correct Alex *raised* the curtain to get more light in the room.
Correct Edgar has *raised* the stage curtain for every performance of the Broadway play.
Correct When I drove past the college, the janitor was *raising* the flag in front of the administration building.

Rise means "to move upward; go from a lower to a higher position." The principal parts of the verb are as follows: *rise* (present); *rose* (past); *risen* (past participle); *rising* (present participle).

Correct I *rise* every morning at seven.
Correct Jim *rose* from his chair and turned off the radio.

Correct	Charles has *risen* at the same time every morning since he started his new job.
Correct	The plane was *rising* rapidly after it took off from the airport.

regardless—see irregardless

set/sit

Set means "to put in a certain place or position; place." The principal parts of the verb are as follows: *set* (present); *set* (past); *set* (past participle); *setting* (present participle).

Correct	Before I leave the house, I *set* a pan of water on the floor for my dog.
Correct	Tom has *set* the garbage can in the alley.
Correct	The waiter was *setting* the food on the table when I came back from the restroom.

Sit means "to be in or assume a position." The principal parts of the verb are as follows: *sit* (present); *sat* (past); *sat* (past participle); *sitting* (present participle).

Correct	I like to *sit* in my favorite chair and watch TV.
Correct	Last night I *sat* in my favorite chair and watched TV.
Correct	Frequently, I have *sat* on the floor and watched TV.
Correct	Joe was *sitting* on the porch of his house reading a newspaper.

sight—see cite

site—see cite

sure/surely

Sure means "free from doubt; certain."

Correct	I am *sure* that I can pass the test if I study.

Surely means "without doubt; certainly."

Incorrect	I am *sure* glad that we took this route.
Correct	I am *surely* glad that we took this route.

teach—see learn

their/there/they're

Their is the possessive case of *they*.

Correct	They hung *their* coats in the closet.

There is an adverb that means "in, at, or about that place."

Correct   David arrived *there* before his friends.

They're is a contraction of *they are.* Contractions as a general rule should be avoided in college expository writing.

Correct   *They're* going to Chicago this weekend to do their Christmas shopping.

to/too/two

To is correctly used as the sign of the infinitive.

Correct   I like *to* hunt and *to* fish.

To is also correctly used as a preposition.

Correct   The award was given *to* Joe and me.

Too is correctly used as an adverb to mean "in addition; likewise; also. In excess quantity or degree."

Correct   Bruce, *too*, was in favor of the proposed change.
Correct   I was *too* tired to play tennis.

Two means "the sum of one and one. Anything consisting of or representing two units."

Correct   I had only *two* dollars in my wallet.
Correct   There were *two* cars parked in the driveway.

uninterested—see disinterested

weather/whether

Weather means "the general atmospheric condition."

Correct   The *weather* today is ideal for boating.

Whether means "if it be the case that."

Correct   *Whether* Tom helps me or not, I still intend to overhaul the motor.

well—see good

who/whom

In speech *who* tends to be accepted in place of *whom.* In formal writing the distinction between *who* and *whom* is generally retained. *Who* is the subject form and is in the same case as *she, he, it, they. Whom* is the object form and is in the same case as *her, him, them.*

> To *whom* am I talking?
> John knew few people on *whom* he could rely.

Never send to know for *whom* the bell tolls.
With *whom* are you going to the dance.
I was not sure to *whom* I spoke.

When in doubt as to whether to use *who* or *whom*, you may find it helpful to make a substitution test:

Problem	All the contestants (*who/whom*) the judges pick will compete in the finals on Saturday night.
Test	The judges will pick *they* or *them?*
Answer	*Them.* . . . Thus you need *whom*.
Problem	I suggest that you consult a lawyer (*who/whom*) is an expert in corporation law.
Test	*Him* is an expert? . . . or *he* is an expert?
Answer	*He.* . . . Thus you need *who*.
Problem	The horse (*who/whom*) the bettors favored won the Derby.
Test	The bettors favored *he* or *him?*
Answer	*Him.* . . . Thus you need *whom*.
Problem	(*Who/Whom*) is going to drive to Chicago this weekend?
Test	*He* or *him* is going to drive?
Answer	*He.* . . . Thus you need *who*.
Problem	I approached the man (*who/whom*) was blind.
Test	*He* or *him* is blind?
Answer	*He.* . . . Thus you need *who*.
Problem	I talked with the woman (*who/whom*) is the resident manager.
Test	*She* or *her* is the resident manager?
Answer	*She.* . . . Thus you need *who*.
Problem	Mary knew my uncle, (*who/whom*) I rarely see.
Test	I rarely see *he* or *him?*
Answer	*Him.* . . . Thus you need *whom*.
Problem	(*Who/Whom*) did you see?
Test	You did see *he* or *him?*
Answer	*Him.* . . . Thus you need *whom*.

In modern usage, *who* as a relative pronoun is usually applied only to persons, and *which* is applied only to animals or inanimate objects. Sometimes, though, *who* is used to refer to a pet or a well-known animal.

My sister's dog, *who* is a good friend of mine, greeted me as I entered the door.

Secretariat, *who* won the Belmont by thirty-one lengths, is a super horse.

EXERCISE 67

Read each sentence carefully and decide which of the italicized words in the parentheses is correct. Write your preference in the left-hand column next to the corresponding number.

_____ 1. Ralph was a likable young man (*accept/except*) that he was not too dependable.

_____ 2. When Ruth and I reached the picnic grounds, we were surprised that the others were (*all ready/already*) there.

_____ 3. The (*continual/continuous*) hum of the light fixture in the library made it difficult for me to study.

_____ 4. The band was (*altogether/all together*) at the end of the playing field waiting for the first half to end.

_____ 5. I was able to (*adapt/adopt*) my radio so I could pick up the FM stations in the area.

_____ 6. The (*desert/dessert*) is unbearably hot during the day but surprisingly cool at night.

_____ 7. The dome of the state (*capital/capitol/Capitol*) could be seen in the distance.

_____ 8. The (*cite/sight/site*) for the new city hall was accepted by the board of aldermen.

_____ 9. (*Almost/Most*) every spring we have a flood that does considerable damage.

_____10. Considering the grade he made on his final exam, Fred apparently did not pay close attention to the (*council/counsel*) he had received from his instructor.

_____11. The horror movie had no (*affect/effect*) on me.

_____12. The captain of the plane announced on the loudspeaker that everything was (*all right/alright*) after we passed through a severe thunderstorm.

_____13. David seemed embarrassed by the (*complement/compliment*) his friends paid him.

_____14. A large (*amount/number*) of cattle are taken to the stockyard on a normal market day.

_____15. Because Robert was (*disinterested/uninterested*) in school, he quit as soon as he turned sixteen.

© 1981 HBJ   **249**

_____16. (*Leave/Let*) us go to the student lounge and have a cup of coffee.

_____17. I (*implied/inferred*) from the reading I did for my term paper that there are no easy solutions to the problems of education in the United States.

_____18. A (*lose/loose*) bolt on the tie rod of the car caused the wheels to shimmy.

_____19. Tony and his wife decided to build their own house, (*irregardless/regardless*) of the time it would take.

_____20. (*Its/It's*) predicted that we will win the game by at least two touchdowns.

  © 1981 HBJ

EXERCISE 68

Read each sentence carefully and decide which of the italicized words in the parentheses is correct. Write your preference in the left-hand column next to the corresponding number.

_____ 1. Mr. Elder, the (*principal/principle*) of our high school, is a brilliant man.

_____ 2. There are (*fewer/less*) passenger trains operating now than there were ten years ago.

_____ 3. In the evening many of the guests (*set/sit*) on the porch of the hotel and enjoy the view of the ocean.

_____ 4. Dick was (*sure/surely*) disappointed when he didn't get the promotion he thought he deserved.

_____ 5. Nancy and Susan parked (*their/there/they're*) cars in front of the Student Union Building.

_____ 6. I am (*quiet/quite*) convinced that Smith is innocent.

_____ 7. Sally (*laid/lay*) on the beach an hour before she entered the water.

_____ 8. After I listened to the president on the radio, I felt (*that/like*) I should take more interest in foreign affairs.

_____ 9. The dean was generous in passing out (*complements/compliments*) to all the students who had participated in the drive.

_____10. The bad weather has a depressing (*affect/effect*) on many people.

_____11. We arrived at the political rally (*to/too/two*) late to hear the main speaker.

_____12. I felt (*all right/alright*) after I took an aspirin to relieve my headache.

_____13. Union Station in Washington, D.C., is within walking distance of the (*capital/capitol/Capitol*).

_____14. The preacher (*cited/sighted/sited*) a quotation from the Bible to conclude his sermon.

_____15. Now let us sing the song (*altogether/all together*) in a loud, clear voice.

© 1981 HBJ

_____16. Because of the inclement (*weather/whether*), the baseball game was postponed until the following evening.

_____17. In hiring a cashier, the manager of the restaurant tried to find someone (*who/whom*) he could trust.

_____18. A great (*amount/number*) of arguments could be avoided if speakers would clearly define their abstract words.

_____19. (*Almost/Most*) every summer my family takes a trip to northern Michigan.

_____20. (*Whose/Who's*) scooter is that parked in the driveway?

 © 1981 HBJ

EXERCISE 69

Read each sentence carefully and decide which of the italicized words in the parentheses is correct. Write your preference in the left-hand column next to the corresponding number.

_____ 1. Of all the candidates, I do not believe anyone is qualified for the post (*accept/except*) Allen.

_____ 2. When I entered college, I had to (*adapt/adopt*) myself to a new way of life.

_____ 3. The sailors were (*already/all ready*) for liberty by the time the ship reached Trinidad.

_____ 4. Zelda said that she was (*quiet/quite*) disappointed when she was not able to go skin diving.

_____ 5. The club holds (*its/it's*) business meeting every Wednesday night.

_____ 6. David decided to (*lay/lie*) on the bench and take a nap.

_____ 7. Inasmuch as the accident was slight, I did not feel (*as if/like*) I should call the police.

_____ 8. For (*desert/dessert*) we had chocolate cake and vanilla ice cream.

_____ 9. The judge was a (*disinterested/uninterested*) person from another county who would be unbiased in trying the case.

_____10. The (*continual/continuous*) use of heroin will cause narcotic addiction.

_____11. (*Leave/Let*) me take this opportunity to thank all those who participated in the heart fund drive.

_____12. The rattle was caused by a (*lose/loose*) shock absorber.

_____13. The playground instructor (*counseled/counciled*) the two boys after they had a fight on the baseball diamond.

_____14. There are (*fewer/less*) students at the university this fall semester than last year.

_____15. The most difficult (*principal/principle*) for me to understand was Einstein's theory of relativity.

_____16. The jury (*implied/inferred*) from the evidence presented that the defendant was guilty.

© 1981 HBJ

_____17. The historic building severely damaged by the tornado will be restored, (*irregardless/regardless*) of the expense.

_____18. Mark and Edward wrote letters to the dean enclosing (*there/their/they're*) high-school transcripts.

_____19. I go to the YMCA (*almost/most*) every afternoon and work out in the gym.

_____20. Milton was not (*altogether/all together*) certain that he would go home for the weekend.

 © 1981 HBJ

EXERCISE 70

Read each sentence carefully and decide which of the italicized words in the parentheses is correct. Write your preference in the left-hand column next to the corresponding number.

_____ 1. By the time we reached Nashville, the sun had (*already/all ready*) disappeared behind the horizon.

_____ 2. Rose was not (*affected/effected*) by the advice of her parents.

_____ 3. I am (*to/too/two*) tired to go to the movies.

_____ 4. Gruber (*raised/rose*) from his chair and turned off the television.

_____ 5. A large (*amount/number*) of people attend the Kentucky Derby.

_____ 6. Larry said that he did not feel qualified to (*accept/except*) the nomination.

_____ 7. The (*weather/whether*) is quite warm for this time of the year.

_____ 8. Sally said she felt (*all right/alright*) after her long bout with the flu.

_____ 9. Before I left the office I (*sat/set*) the cover on my typewriter.

_____ 10. We should pick the person (*who/whom*) is best qualified for the job.

_____ 11. (*Whose/Who's*) the man in the dark blue suit?

_____ 12. Albany is the state (*capital/capitol/Capitol*) of New York.

_____ 13. The (*cite/sight/site*) for the new post office was decided upon by the government officials.

_____ 14. The jury (*implied/inferred*) from the conflicting evidence that the defendant was not guilty.

_____ 15. Edna's chic red hat (*complements/compliments*) her stylish black dress.

_____ 16. The dog wagged (*its/it's*) tail when I entered the yard to read the gas meter.

_____ 17. The (*continual/continuous*) interruption of the television

© 1981 HBJ

movie for commercials made me lose interest in the story.

_____18. The lifeguard was (*laying/lying*) on the beach when he heard someone scream for help.

_____19. When the headache persisted, Harry felt (*as if/like*) he should see a doctor.

_____20. Harper was elected to the student (*council/counsel*) in spite of his radical ideas.

 © 1981 HBJ

EXERCISE 71

Read each sentence carefully and decide which of the italicized words in the parentheses is correct. Write your preference in the left-hand column next to the corresponding number.

_____ 1. Your answer is (*all right/alright*), but you might add a few more details.

_____ 2. For (*desert/dessert*) we had vanilla ice cream garnished with fruit salad.

_____ 3. (*Leave/Let*) us rent a boat and row over to the island.

_____ 4. There were (*fewer/less*) spectators at the game this Saturday than last.

_____ 5. Although Gordon has a pleasing personality, he usually will not (*accept/except*) responsibility.

_____ 6. I am not (*all together/altogether*) convinced that Stan is capable of holding the office.

_____ 7. The members of the student senate expressed (*there/their/they're*) views on the proposed plan to beautify the campus.

_____ 8. The teacher (*who/whom*) I liked best was Dr. Graham.

_____ 9. The game had (*all ready/already*) started by the time we reached the stadium.

_____ 10. We were able to find a (*quiet/quite*) motel away from the main highway.

_____ 11. The doctor didn't seem (*to/too/two*) pleased with my father's condition.

_____ 12. David (*sat/set*) a pan of water on the stove to heat for coffee.

_____ 13. It appears doubtful (*weather/whether*) a compromise can be reached between the two factions.

_____ 14. Although my pastor is broad-minded and tolerant, he will not compromise his (*principals/principles*) on certain issues.

_____ 15. It seems that the rainy weather (*affects/effects*) my disposition.

© 1981 HBJ

_____16. It is easy to (*lose/loose*) control of an automobile if one of the tires is punctured.

_____17. (*Who's/Whose*) going to volunteer to wash the dishes?

_____18. A large (*amount/number*) of people were assembled in the stadium to watch the football game.

_____19. The umpire was (*disinterested/uninterested*) in which team won the game.

_____20. Montgomery is the state (*capital/capitol/Capitol*) of Alabama.

 © 1981 HBJ

EXERCISE 72

Read each sentence carefully and decide which of the italicized words in the parentheses is correct. Write your preference in the left-hand column next to the corresponding number.

_____ 1. The teacher's tone of voice (*implied/inferred*) that she was disappointed with the test.

_____ 2. The salesman told Frank that the dark gray slacks would (*complement/compliment*) the sports coat.

_____ 3. We decided to take the trip to Europe, (*irregardless/regardless*) of the expense.

_____ 4. Flying over the South Pole is a (*cite/site/sight*) I shall never forget.

_____ 5. The cat arched (*its/it's*) back when the dog came near the fence.

_____ 6. There were (*fewer/less*) people at the dance this year than last.

_____ 7. The (*continual/continuous*) interruption of the televised movie by commercials was very annoying.

_____ 8. Marvin was disappointed because he was not elected to the student (*counsel/council*).

_____ 9. In going from Nigeria to France our plane flew across the Sahara (*Desert/Dessert*).

_____ 10. I like all of my classes (*accept/except*) history.

_____ 11. Air pollution (*affects/effects*) the health of many people.

_____ 12. My father said it was (*all right/alright*) to use the family car on my spring vacation.

_____ 13. Mary could (*already/all ready*) speak Spanish before she moved to Mexico.

_____ 14. The horses were (*all together/altogether*) in the paddock before the race.

_____ 15. Some apples were (*laying/lying*) on the ground under the tree.

_____ 16. The (*principal/principle*) of my high school had been an All-American tackle at Notre Dame.

_____17. A large (*amount/number*) of people attended the gradua-
tion exercise.

_____18. Last night I was (*to/too/two*) tired to study.

_____19. Dr. Able is the surgeon (*who/whom*) operated on me.

_____20. (*Their/There/They're*) a number of reasons why I prefer to
attend a college in my home town.

 © 1981 HBJ

14: Agreement

SUBJECT WITH VERB

A common grammatical mistake—even among professional writers—is faulty subject-verb agreement. Many such errors result from careless proofreading. Under the pressure of meeting a deadline or for some less excusable reason, a writer may erroneously make a verb agree with the nearest noun, which may be a modifier of the simple subject. The following examples will illustrate this problem.

> The poor attitude of many students (is/are) responsible for the high number of failures.

A careful reading of the sentence will indicate that *attitude* (not *students*) is the simple subject, requiring the singular verb *is* to agree with the singular noun *attitude*.

> Two sets of plans for building the house (was/were) submitted to the Jones family.

The writer might easily be led into making a mistake in agreement by relating *was* to *house* rather than correctly matching the plural verb *were* with the plural subject *sets*.

> The noises that drift from the street below (is/are) frustrating when I am trying to study.

The verb is separated from its subject by a long modifier, understandably causing the writer to associate *is* with *street* rather than *are* with *noises*.

INDEFINITE PRONOUNS

In formal writing (the type of writing that one does in college and most professions as distinguished from informal writing and speech), the writer is obliged to follow definite rules of grammar. One of these rules is to use a singular verb with indefinite pronouns even though the pronoun may suggest more than one entity. You should check your writing carefully to make sure you have not violated this principle. What form of the verb should you use in the following examples?

> Every one of the professors (has/have) at least five years of experience in teaching on the college level.

> Nobody in the class (was/were) willing to serve on the committee.

> We decided that each of us (was/were) obliged to pay an equal amount for the broken window.

You should use the singular verbs (*has, was, was*) to agree with the indefinite pronouns (*one, nobody, each*) even though they suggest more than one person. Besides the indefinite pronouns in the examples, the following also require singular verbs for correct grammatical agreement: *anyone, either, everybody, neither, no one, somebody.*

In general, how the sentence looks or sounds will tell you if it is right or wrong. If you read the sentence "Joe and Mary is sure to get the leading parts in the play," your innate sense of grammar should tell you that it is wrong. The sentence neither looks right nor sounds right. Thus you should conclude that *are* is needed to agree with the compound subject "Joe and Mary."

However, with indefinite pronouns you cannot depend on your sense of sight or sound as a reliable guide, for the forms commonly used in speech are not always acceptable in formal writing. Therefore, you will have to apply established rules of subject-verb agreement to achieve the correctness that is expected of a competent writer. An understanding of the rules that follow should enable you to eliminate errors in subject-verb agreement.

COMPOUND SUBJECTS

1. In most cases when the subjects (nouns or pronouns) are joined by *and*, a plural verb is needed.

> Tom and his brother *were* home for the holidays.

> The president and the secretary of state *were* having a meeting in the Oval Office.

2. When two or more singular subjects refer to the same person or thing, a singular rather than a plural verb is required.

> My math teacher and friend *was* responsible for my becoming an engineer.

> A poet and philosopher *is* a rare person in today's society.

3. If either or both of the compound subjects are preceded by *each* or *every*, a singular verb is required.

Every dog and cat in the neighborhood *was* yelping at the moon.

Each boy and girl *was* given a free ticket to the zoo.

4. If the compound subjects are thought of as belonging together, a singular verb is needed. If they are thought of as being separate, a plural verb is needed.

Ham and eggs *is* my favorite dish.

Ham and eggs *are* on the top shelf of the refrigerator.

5. If singular compound subjects are joined by *or* or *nor*, a singular verb is required.

Either democracy or communism *is* the form of government that will ultimately prevail.

Fowler or Hill *is* bound to receive the appointment to the student council.

6. If singular and plural subjects are joined by *or* or *nor*, the verb agrees in number with the nearest subject.

Neither Larry nor his classmates *were* satisfied with the way the test was given.

Neither his classmates nor Larry *was* satisfied with the way the test was given.

COLLECTIVE NOUNS

A collective noun refers to a whole composed of individuals or things, for example, *jury, contents, family, band, congregation, team, committee, group, herd.* As a general rule, collective nouns take singular verbs: *jury was, family goes, band plays, congregation sings, team runs, committee meets, group participates.* Sometimes, though, a writer may want to stress the individuals or things within the group and use a plural rather than a singular verb.

To emphasize the group:

The jury *was* instructed by the judge.

The band *was* assembled at the end of the playing field.

To emphasize the individuals within the group:

The jury *have* left the courtroom for their hotel.

The family *were* seated around the table enjoying their Thanksgiving dinner.

The band, carrying their instruments, *have* moved to the end of the playing field.

SEPARATED SUBJECTS

Careful writers draw a distinction between compound subjects and separated subjects, which are sometimes called parenthetical elements. As previously stated, compound subjects joined by *and* require a plural verb: Tom and his brother *were* home for the holidays. However, if *his brother* had been preceded by *along with, as well as, together with,* a singular verb would be needed.

> Elaine, as well as her sister, *belongs* to the Girl Scouts.

> The president, along with his cabinet members, *is* standing in front of the White House.

> The governor, in addition to his assistants, *was* present at the news conference.

In order to make the subject-verb agreement more logical, it is best to set off the less important element with commas. This punctuation will indicate to the reader that the two or more subjects are not of equal importance. That is, you want to emphasize the subject that is not set off by commas by making the verb agree with that subject.

DELAYED SUBJECTS

Frequently, writers begin sentences with *There is* or *There are.* This construction can easily lead to faulty subject-verb agreement by confusing *there* with the subject of the sentence. When *There* is the first word, the simple subject is removed from its usual place (before the verb), often promoting faulty subject-verb agreement. If you use *there is* or *there are,* you should double-check to make sure that you have used the correct form of the verb.

> There are [*not* is] a cow and two horses in the pasture.

> There have [*not* has] never been any charges brought against him during his term in office.

NOUNS THAT ARE PLURAL IN FORM BUT SINGULAR IN MEANING

Should you write *A thousand dollars is a lot of money* or *A thousand dollars are a lot of money?* Even though *dollars* is plural, you should use a singular verb. Many other words in English are plural in form but singular in meaning, requiring a singular rather than a plural verb: *economics, ethics, mathematics, measles, mumps, news, physics, politics,* and so on.

> Economics *is* the study of business and commerce.

> Mathematics *is* my favorite subject.

> Measles *is* the only childhood disease I haven't had.

> The news *is* basically good.

SINGULAR OR PLURAL VERBS USED WITH RELATIVE PRONOUNS

Relative pronouns—such as *that, what, whatever, which, who, whom, whoever*—usually refer to the nearest noun (not necessarily the subject of the sentence). Consequently, a relative pronoun is singular or plural according to the number (singular or plural) of the word to which it refers. This relationship determines the subject-verb agreement pattern, that is, whether the relative pronoun takes a singular or plural verb. Let us consider these examples:

> Brucker is one of those people who (is/are) always helping someone else.
>
> *Correct*   Brucker is one of those people who *are* always helping someone else.
>
> *Comment*   The relative pronoun "who" refers to "people," making "who" plural and requiring the plural verb "are."

> Jones and Smith are like the fellow who (throws/throw) the baby out with the bathwater.
>
> *Correct*   Jones and Smith are like the fellow who *throws* the baby out with the bathwater.
>
> *Comment*   The relative pronoun "who" refers to "fellow," making "who" singular and requiring the singular verb "throws."

EXERCISE 73

Consider the subject-verb relationship in each of the following sentences. Decide which form of the verb is correct, and indicate your choice by writing the verb in the column to the left of the number.

_____ 1. Each boy and girl in the class (*was/were*) given a special project to develop.

_____ 2. Tom, as well as his brother, (*is/are*) a top-notch student.

_____ 3. There (*is/are*) to be at least fifteen horses in the featured race.

_____ 4. The team (*goes/go*) through many calisthenics to get into condition for the game.

_____ 5. The congregation (*worships/worship*) at the same time every Sunday.

_____ 6. The suits in the display window (*is/are*) priced at $150 each.

_____ 7. Anyone who is interested in rare books (*is/are*) encouraged to visit the museum this week.

_____ 8. The horse and buggy (*is/are*) a thing of the past.

_____ 9. (*Do/Does*) either of the candidates in the primary have a chance in the general election?

_____ 10. My former shipmate and close friend (*visit/visits*) me every summer.

_____ 11. There (*is/are*) in the opinion of the experts many factors that could affect the election.

_____ 12. The parties that were sponsored by the club (*was/were*) always a big success.

_____ 13. The chapter on pronouns (*is/are*) difficult to understand.

_____ 14. Economics (*hold/holds*) an interest even for students who are not business majors.

_____ 15. Anyone who is recommended by the teachers (*is/are*) eligible for the award.

_____ 16. A hundred dollars (*is/are*) all I need to go on the senior trip.

_____17. The fire chief, in addition to his assistant, (*come/comes*) to every major fire.

_____18. Everyone who (*donate/donates*) old newspapers and magazines is given a certificate.

_____19. Each of the boys in the fraternities (*was/were*) encouraged to donate blood.

_____20. My friend is like most fishermen who (*brags/brag*) about the big fish that got away.

 © 1981 HBJ

EXERCISE 74

Consider the subject-verb relationship in each of the following sentences. Decide which form of the verb is correct, and indicate your choice by writing the verb in the column to the left of the number.

_____ 1. Neither Bill nor his friends (*was/were*) satisfied with the new regulation.

_____ 2. The chief justice of the Supreme Court, in addition to the associate justices, (*was/were*) present for the dedication ceremony.

_____ 3. Neither the students nor the teacher (*like/likes*) to stay after school.

_____ 4. The group of actors (*extends/extend*) an invitation to the audience to visit them backstage.

_____ 5. Walter is one of those men who (*is/are*) never satisfied with working conditions.

_____ 6. An honest novel that will dramatize the conflicts of teen-agers (*is/are*) badly needed.

_____ 7. The governor, along with her assistants, (*was/were*) present for the opening of the convention.

_____ 8. Gin and tonic (*is/are*) a refreshing drink.

_____ 9. The team (*praises/praise*) its coach at every opportunity.

_____10. The ringing of the bells (*indicates/indicate*) the start of a new year.

_____11. A hundred dollars (*are/is*) all I need to make a down payment on the car.

_____12. The counting of the votes (*take/takes*) all afternoon and evening.

_____13. There (*is/are*) the keys to the house hanging on a hook.

_____14. The leader of the rebel forces (*was/were*) thrown into jail.

_____15. Each of the group leaders (*decides/decide*) the schedule for any given day.

_____16. Helen and Barbara are like the girl who (*appears/appear*) in the magazine advertisement.

© 1981 HBJ

_____ 17. Neither of the players (*have/has*) a legitimate excuse for missing the bus.

_____ 18. The head coach, together with his assistants, (*was/were*) disgusted with the referee.

_____ 19. The recommendations of the chairperson (*were/was*) presented to the members.

_____ 20. (*Do/Does*) every man and woman on the committee favor the proposal in its present form?

 © 1981 HBJ

PRONOUN WITH ANTECEDENT

The rules governing pronoun agreement follow the same principles as subject-verb agreement. Stated in capsule form, the pronoun must agree with its antecedent in person, gender, and number. What do these terms mean?

ANTECEDENT—the word or words to which the pronoun refers

John told his boss that *he* disagreed with the procedure.
(*John* is the antecedent of *he*).

PERSON—any one of the three relationships underlying discourse

	Singular	Plural
1st (person speaking)	my	our
2nd (person spoken to)	your	your
3rd (person spoken about)	his, her, its	their

GENDER—the sex (or lack of sex) of a person, other animal, or thing

Masculine gender   John put *his* coat on the rack.
Feminine gender   Mary put *her* coat on the rack.
Neuter gender   The tree cast *its* shadow on the ground.

NUMBER—whether the pronoun refers to one or more entities

Singular   Joyce went to see *her* adviser.
Plural   Joe and Harry went to see *their* adviser.

INDEFINITE PRONOUNS

One of the most common mistakes in pronoun reference stems from using the plural pronoun (for example, *their* instead of *his*) to refer to indefinite pronouns that are singular in grammatical form but may imply more than one entity. In formal writing, a singular pronoun in the appropriate gender refers to the following indefinite pronouns:

one	someone	everybody	neither
anyone	somebody	each	no one
anybody	everyone	either	nobody

Everybody gave the speaker *his* undivided attention.

Neither of the girls could do *her* best work under pressure.

Nobody would volunteer *his* time for the unpleasant job of collecting the money.

Either of the boys may jeopardize *his* future in college sports by accepting the invitation from the alumni.

Everyone agreed that *he* would give ten percent of *his* December salary to the charity drive.

Each of the girls has *her* own ideas about the Christmas decorations.

Note that in the preceding examples the masculine pronoun is used when the gender could be either masculine or feminine or both: Everybody gave the speaker *his* undivided attention.

In recent years, there has been a trend away from using the masculine pronoun to refer to both male and female. Many writers prefer to use both the masculine and feminine pronouns: *he* and *she; his* and *her.* However, the older form is still widely used. One way to solve the problem is to use a plural noun that could refer to both genders and use the plural pronouns *them* or *their* or *they* in reference:

> All the people gave the speaker *their* undivided attention.

> The club members would not donate *their* time for the unpleasant job of collecting the money.

> All of the office workers agreed that *they* would give ten percent of their December salary to the charity drive.

COLLECTIVE NOUNS

Collective nouns (*jury, council, committee, herd, band*) usually take singular verbs and pronouns, except when the writer wants to stress the individuals within the group. The verb used with the collective noun determines the number and gender of the pronoun.

> The jury *gives its* (or *give their*) decision to the judge.

> The council *is* determined to enact *its* (or *are—their*) proposal.
> The committee *pleads its* (or *plead their*) case before the director.

> The herd *is* stopping by the water hole to quench *its* (or *are—their*) thirst.

> The band *takes its* (or *take their*) place at the end of the field.

In proofreading your composition, you should make sure that the verb and pronoun used with a collective noun are of the same number—singular or plural.

COMPOUND SUBJECTS

The same rules that govern subject-verb agreement are applicable to pronouns that refer to compound subjects. If the subjects are joined by *and* (Earl *and* Frank), the plural form of the pronoun is generally used.

> Earl and Frank brought *their* records to the dance.

> Marie and Sally straightened *their* rooms before going to dinner.

If singular compound subjects are joined by *or* or *nor*, a singular pronoun is generally required.

> Neither Earl nor Frank would admit that *he* was wrong.

> Marie or Sally will be asked to present *her* plans for the dance.

If singular and plural compound subjects are joined by *or* or *nor*, the pronoun should agree with the nearest noun.

> Neither management or the workers *expect* to have all *their* wishes satisfied.

> Neither the workers or management *expects* to have all *its* wishes satisfied.

RELATIVE PRONOUNS

The number (singular or plural) of the relative pronoun is determined by the noun to which the pronoun refers, often the object of a phrase modifying the subject of the sentence.

> Jones is one of those individuals *who* never meet *their* obligations.
>
> *Comment*   The relative pronoun *who* refers to *individuals*, making it plural in number and requiring *their* rather than *his* for correct pronoun agreement.

> Many people are like the man *who* thinks *he* can get something for nothing.
>
> *Comment*   The relative pronoun *who* refers to *man*, making it singular in number and requiring *he* rather than *they* for correct pronoun agreement.

EXERCISE 75

Consider the pronoun-antecedent relationship in each of the following sentences. Decide which form of the pronoun enclosed in parentheses is correct, and indicate your preference by writing the pronoun in the left-hand column next to the number.

_____ 1. Neither the leading man nor the supporting actors will express (*his opinion/their opinions*) about the success of the movie.

_____ 2. Alice Jackson is one of those women who are always expressing (*her opinion/their opinions*).

_____ 3. One of the women left (*her/their*) purse in the dining room.

_____ 4. Neither the students nor the teacher would express (*his/their*) views about the story.

_____ 5. Bruce is one of those policemen who give (*his/their*) superiors a difficult time.

_____ 6. The taxi driver was one of those men who could not keep (*his mouth/their mouths*) shut.

_____ 7. The congregation sings (*its/their*) hymns in unison.

_____ 8. Everyone in the apartment building was depressed when (*he/they*) received the rent increase notice in (*his/their*) mail box.

_____ 9. Any recruit who is caught smoking in (*his/their*) bunk will be restricted.

_____10. Every girl in the senior class was told to report to the gym to have (*her/their*) picture taken.

_____11. Was it the players or the coach who could not control (*his temper/their tempers*)?

_____12. Ruth was one of those good neighbors who mind (*her/their*) own business.

_____13. The jury retired to (*its/their*) quarters to reach a verdict.

_____14. Each of the girl scouts has decided to spend (*her/their*) weekend at the camp.

_____15. Every man who is hired by the construction company is expected to furnish (*his/their*) own tools.

© 1981 HBJ

_____ 16. The chief of the Indians expressed (*his/their*) welcome in tribal language.

_____ 17. Not one of the men is going to place (*his/their*) signature on the petition.

_____ 18. The Advertising Club picks (*its/their*) officers from the older members.

_____ 19. Neither the clerks nor the supervisor could express (*his/their*) views to the president of the company.

_____ 20. Tim is like every Broadway actor who (*thinks his/think their*) voice is divine.

© 1981 HBJ

EXERCISE 76

Consider the pronoun-antecedent relationship in each of the following sentences. Decide which form of the pronoun enclosed in parentheses is correct, and indicate your preference by writing the pronoun in the left-hand column next to the number.

_____ 1. The jury reaches a verdict after (*its/their*) deliberations.

_____ 2. Glenn is one of those men who (*knows his/know their*) own mind.

_____ 3. The lab assistants or the professor puts (*his/their*) stamp of approval on the students' work.

_____ 4. The troop of boy scouts was making (*its/their*) way through the forest.

_____ 5. Everyone in the contest felt that (*his/their*) painting should take the first prize.

_____ 6. Neither of the doctors would divulge (*his/their*) diagnosis to the patient.

_____ 7. The salesman is one of those men who usually (*gets his/get their*) way.

_____ 8. Amy is one of those mothers who (*puts her/put their*) children's interests before everything else.

_____ 9. The members of the student council agree that (*its/their*) decisions would not be binding on the student body.

_____ 10. Someone left (*his/their*) overcoat in the bedroom.

_____ 11. Every person in the dormitory is expected to clean (*his/their*) own bedroom.

_____ 12. None of the women plans to quit (*her/their*) job after (*she gets/they get*) married.

_____ 13. Any student who loses the key to (*his/their*) locker can get another one.

_____ 14. The entertainment committee submits (*its/their*) recommendations to the president of the club.

_____ 15. Owen is one of those fellows who (*thinks he knows/think they know*) everything.

_____ 16. No progress can be made as long as everyone is clamoring to express (*his/their*) own opinion.

© 1981 HBJ

_____17. A student should spend several hours studying each day if (*he expects/they expect*) to excel in school.

_____18. The group of teen-agers (*spends its/spend their*) time helping the mentally retarded.

_____19. The members of the board of aldermen or the mayor will give (*his/their*) attention to the matter.

_____20. Jim Baker is one of those men who (*is/are*) satisfied with (*his/their*) job.

 © 1981 HBJ

EXERCISE 77

Consider the subject-verb or pronoun-antecedent relationship in each of the following sentences. Decide which form of the verb or pronoun enclosed in parentheses is correct, and indicate your preference by writing it in the left-hand column next to the number.

_____ 1. Either John or Charles is likely to have (*his/their*) poster accepted for publication.

_____ 2. A person who has strong determination may very well reach (*his/their*) goal.

_____ 3. Neither of the professors (*has/have*) a doctorate.

_____ 4. The herd of cattle (*graze/grazes*) in the open field.

_____ 5. Sally is one of those girls who (*are/is*) always willing to serve on a committee.

_____ 6. Every boy and girl in the class (*was/were*) asked to comment on the short story.

_____ 7. Mathematics in high schools and colleges (*is/are*) becoming more popular each year.

_____ 8. The members of the congregation or the pastor (*spends his/spend their*) time helping the needy.

_____ 9. Neither O'Brien nor his colleagues (*feels/feel*) an obligation to take the initiative.

_____10. Each of the contestants is asked to specify (*his/their*) area of interest.

_____11. The professors or the dean (*spends her/spends their*) time advising the students.

_____12. At their annual banquet the members of the band (*gives/give*) warm praise to their director.

_____13. The student senate (*holds/hold*) (*its/their*) meeting every Tuesday evening.

_____14. Every man and woman at the meeting (*was/were*) given a chance to comment on the proposal.

_____15. The association of medical technicians has (*its/their*) headquarters in New York.

_____16. There (*is/are*) in the city many people who would prefer to live in the country.

© 1981 HBJ

_____17. The tennis team has (*its/their*) picture in the yearbook under spring sports.

_____18. Neither of the engineers was free to express (*his/their*) opinion on the design of the building.

_____19. Robert is one of those lucky individuals who (*does/do*) (*his/their*) own typing.

_____20. Every boy and girl at the camp (*was/were*) given a strength test.

   © 1981 HBJ

EXERCISE 78

Consider the subject-verb or pronoun-antecedent relationship in each of the following sentences. Decide which form of the verb or pronoun enclosed in parentheses is correct and indicate your preference by writing it in the left-hand column next to the number.

_____ 1. The secretary of state, as well as his assistants, gave (*his/their*) attention to the problem.

_____ 2. Tom and his brother are like the fellow in the song who never (*has/have*) time for school.

_____ 3. The chief complaint of the hotel employees (*was/were*) the bad food.

_____ 4. The group of tourists spent (*its/their*) morning at the zoo.

_____ 5. Neither the students nor the teacher (*was/were*) impressed by the president's speech.

_____ 6. The band has (*its/their*) annual banquet during the last week of school.

_____ 7. Two solutions for solving the financial problem (*was/were*) submitted to the legislature.

_____ 8. His regular salary and his commission (*comes/come*) to three hundred dollars per week.

_____ 9. The board of aldermen had (*its/their*) number increased by three.

_____ 10. The patrolmen or the sergeant did not give (*his/their*) full cooperation to the captain of the district.

_____ 11. Every boy and girl in the class (*was/were*) asked to bring in a toy for the children at the hospital.

_____ 12. The members of the New York Stock Exchange (*watches/watch*) the market closely.

_____ 13. The members of the band or the leader (*makes/make*) the traveling arrangements.

_____ 14. Neither of the women would sign (*her/their*) name to the petition.

_____ 15. There (*is/are*) in the paddock the seven horses that will run in the race.

© 1981 HBJ

_____16. Every policeman and fireman in the city (*was/were*) asked to join the union.

_____17. His supporters and Senator Hume (*has/have*) no explanation for the crushing defeat.

_____18. Nobody would admit that (*he/they*) made a mistake.

_____19. Tony is one of those children who (*chews/chew*) gum as if it were beefsteak.

_____20. Everyone in the firm agreed that (*he/they*) would attend the picnic.

 © 1981 HBJ

15: Punctuation

PERIODS

Periods are used at the end of declarative, imperative, and mildly exclamatory sentences. Moreover, a period (not a question mark) comes at the end of an indirect question.

Declarative	January has been a horrible month.
Imperative	Please shut the door.
Mildly Exclamatory	What a magnificent sunset.
Indirect Question	He asked me what road to take.

ELLIPSIS POINTS

Three spaced periods (. . .), known as ellipsis points, are used to indicate an omission in a quoted passage. If one or more complete sentences are omitted or if the omission comes at the beginning or end of a sentence, four periods are used—the ellipsis points and the regular period.

The material quoted below is from *Gulliver's Travels* by Jonathan Swift. Note that four periods are used at the end of the passage because the last sentences of the paragraph were not quoted. Three periods are used at the beginning of the paragraph since only a part of a sentence has been omitted there.

> . . . I came back out of my house, having occasion for fresh air. The Emperor was already descended from the tower, and advancing on horseback towards me, which had like to have cost him dear; for the beast, though

very well trained, yet wholly unused to such a sight, which appeared as if a mountain moved before him, reared on his hinder feet; but that prince, who is an excellent horseman, kept his seat, till his attendants ran in, and held the bridle, while his master had time to mount. . . .

Quoted passages of five lines or more (either typed or written in longhand) are not enclosed by quotation marks. Instead, they are set off from the preceding material and block indented; that is, they are indented from the left-hand margin about twice as much as a regular paragraph. If the composition is typed, the quoted passage should be single-spaced. Quoted passages enclosed in quotation marks—that is, those of fewer than five lines—are neither single-spaced nor set off from the preceding material.

ABBREVIATIONS

Periods are used after most abbreviations. Only one period is used when an abbreviation falls at the end of a sentence.

Names	J. B. Smith, James T. Dugan
Degrees	B.A., M.A., Ph.D.
Months	Jan., Feb., Mar.
States	Ind., Ky., Ill., Ala., N.J.
Titles	Rev., Dr., Mr., Mrs., Ms.
Others	Ave. (Avenue), St. (Street), St. (Saint)
	A.D. (in the year of the Lord), B.C. (before Christ)
	e.g. (*exempli gratia*—for example)
	etc. (*et cetera*—and so forth)
	i.e. (*id est*—that is)
	A.M. or a.m. (before noon), P.M. or p.m. (after noon)

The abbreviated names of most governmental agencies, call letters of television or radio stations, and many other common abbreviations are not followed by periods.

Government Agencies		*Others*
CIA	NATO	Btu (British thermal unit)
FBI	UNESCO	cc (cubic centimeter)
NASA	UN	K (carat)
TVA	WHO	MS (manuscript)

Radio or Television Stations		
WBLS	CBS-TV	MSS (manuscripts)
WLW	PBS	rpm (revolutions per minute)
WCBS	WLW-TV	UHF (ultrahigh frequency)
WKTU		VHF (very high frequency)

QUESTION MARKS

A question mark is placed at the end of a direct question.

How much money do you have in the bank?

A period (not a question mark) comes at the end of an indirect question.

> Don asked me if I would help fix his car.

A question mark is sometimes used after an aside question interjected into a statement.

> Everyone who wants to be paid—can there be anyone who doesn't?—should muster at the drill hall.

A question mark should follow a brief question at the end of a declarative sentence.

> The Joneses have definitely decided to move to Boston, haven't they?

When a question mark and quotation marks fall together, the question mark goes outside the quotes if the complete statement is a direct question. If only the quoted matter is a question, the question mark goes inside the quotation mark.

> Did Professor Clark say, "Who would like to try out for the play"?

> Professor Clark walked into the classroom and asked, "Who would like to try out for the play?"

> "What time does the audition begin?" Helen asked.

A question mark is used to express uncertainty as to dates or other factual data.

> The castle was destroyed in 1156 (?).

The use of a question mark after a word or phrase to achieve a humorous or ironic effect is considered poor practice.

> His funny (?) stories were more effective than any sleeping pills.

EXCLAMATION POINTS

The exclamation point is used after emphatic interjections and statements expressing very strong emotion.

> Extra! Extra! Extra! Read all about it!

> Help! Help! I'm drowning!

The comma or period—rather than the exclamation point—should be used after mild interjections and temperate exclamatory statements.

> Oh, I would just as soon not go to the dance.

> What a beautiful sunset.

Where the exclamation point and quotation marks fall together, the exclamation point goes inside or outside the quotation marks, depending upon whether the entire statement or only the quoted words are considered exclamatory.

"Get out of those bunks!" yelled the master-at-arms.

"Give me liberty—or give me death!"

COLONS

The colon is used at the end of a complete statement that introduces an enumeration or a long quotation. The words *as follows* or *the following* often precede the colon. A colon is unnecessary, however, between a verb and its object or complement.

Wrong: My favorite colors are: red, white, and blue.
Right: My favorite colors are red, white, and blue.
Right: I have three favorite colors: red, white, and blue.

Wrong: On my vacation I visited: New York, Boston, Philadelphia, and Washington.
Right: On my vacation I visited the following cities: New York, Boston, Philadelphia, and Washington.

In factual writing (not fiction), a colon is usually placed at the end of a *complete* statement that precedes a direct quotation.

Emerson made this statement: "The President pays dearly for his White House."

A colon is sometimes used between two main clauses if the second one is intended to explain the first clause.

I have decided to become a competent writer: I have made up my mind to learn the basic principles of English composition.

The explanatory word or words that follow the colon may be an incomplete sentence or a list.

I have finally decided where to go on my vacation: Puerto Rico.

Three cars were parked in the driveway: a Ford, a Dodge, and a Chevrolet.

The colon is also used in the following situations:

After the formal salutation in a letter   Dear Sir:
                                            Dear Mr. Brown:

Between the hour and minutes in noting time   5:30 P.M.
                                                1:20 P.M.

In Biblical references   Mark 8:13-21
                           Luke 10:42

When a colon and quotation marks fall together, the colon goes outside the quotation marks.

"Sweet are the uses of adversity": famous words by William Shakespeare.

EXERCISE 79

Read the following statements carefully and insert the omitted punctuation. In some instances the wrong punctuation marks are used. Delete the erroneous mark by drawing a circle around it, and if punctuation is required at all, write the correct form above or next to the circle.

1. My favorite cities are: St. Louis, New Orleans, and Boston.

2. Radio station W.S.M. is located in Nashville.

3. When will the next train leave for Chicago.

4. Did he say, "You can leave after you finish your theme?"

5. "Get out of that tree," the mother shouted to her son!

6. Susan had an appointment with the dentist at 10 30 A.M.

7. The team is going to the tournament, isn't it.

8. Dr Vogel gave an informative lecture on the need for conservation.

9. Melvin asked me if I would lend him a car?

10. The chief Biblical virtues are: faith, hope, and charity.

11. Harold asked, "What time does the dance begin"?

12. Did he actually say, "Don't you think I'm qualified?"

13. Dr Kirk has her Ph D from the University of Alabama.

14. The following is one of my favorite Biblical quotations. "Every kingdom divided against itself is brought to desolation."

15. Who has the answers to the problems.

16. "Are you going to the Indianapolis 500 this year," he asked casually?

17. He shouted in a loud voice, "Get out of here"!

18. The spring quarter begins Mar 15 and ends May 25.

19. The sergeant gave the following orders to the privates. "Prepare the barracks for Saturday morning inspection."

20. Barbara asked me if I would type her term paper?

© 1981 HBJ

EXERCISE 80

Read the following statements carefully and insert the omitted punctuation. In some instances the wrong punctuation marks are used. Delete any erroneous mark by drawing a circle around it, and if punctuation is required at all, write the correct form above or next to the circle.

1. This semester we read the following essays; "Self-Reliance," "Culture and Anarchy," and "Literature and the Modern World."

2. Ralph asked me if I would lend him my typewriter?

3. The F.B.I. was called in to investigate the bank robbery.

4. "Knock off the loud talk," the scoutmaster shouted!

5. We arrived in Miami at 8—45 P.M.

6. "Who is going to take up the collection," the minister asked?

7. The cab did not stop for the red light

8. Did the instructor ask, "Who is going to visit the museum?"

9. The following students are being considered for the award. Cooke, Johnson, and Bishop.

10. "Oh, my aching back," the coach shouted loudly!

11. Peter Foster has an M A degree in English from Vanderbilt University.

12. This is the highway to Indianapolis, isn't it.

13. Gruber was employed by N.A.S.A. at Huntsville, Alabama.

14. The following students are excused from physical education. Rush, Eiler, and O'Hearn.

15. Classes will resume Jan 3 at 8 00 A.M.

16. "Rise and shine," Amanda shouted as she entered Tom's bedroom!

17. The radio announcer gave the following information. "The main highway is closed because of high water."

18. "Who would like to go to the Wooden Indian for a cup of coffee," Don asked his friends?

19. The short story was written by D H Lawrence

20. The following words are coordinate conjunctions; and, but, for, nor, or.

EXERCISE 81

Read the following statements carefully and insert the omitted punctuation. In some instances the wrong punctuation marks are used. Delete the erroneous mark by drawing a circle around it, and if punctuation is required at all, write the correct form above or next to the circle.

1. You wanted the morning class, didn't you.

2. After we arrived at the camp, we went down to the lake and took a swim

3. The following students made the honor role. Deane, Kruer, and Sawyer.

4. "Fresh strawberries," the peddler shouted as he moved down the street!

5. Barbara O'Brien has an M A in political science from the University of Tennessee.

6. What time does the bus leave for St. Louis.

7. The best design for the new library was submitted by J T Morton.

8. The contract contained the following stipulation. The builder was to pay the fire insurance while the house was being constructed.

9. "Stop that horsing around," the coach shouted to the football players!

10. What is the difference between mass and energy," the professor asked the student?

11. The F.B.I. has agents in every large city in the United States.

12. Any student who wishes to write a term paper on Einstein—I wonder how many eager beavers are in the class—may do so.

13. The superjet for Dallas and Los Angeles leaves at 3 30 P.M.

14. Linda asked me if I would drive her to the lake?

15. "Who is going to rake the leaves," the father asked his children?

16. The following notice was posted on the bulletin board; You may sign up for part-time jobs at the placement office.

© 1981 HBJ

17. "Grab the life preserver," the captain shouted to the sailor who had fallen overboard!

18. Dr Stoddard earned her Ph D at the University of Maryland.

19. Did the professor ask, "Who is going to report on Emerson?"

20. I visited several cities on my quick trip through the South. Nashville, Decatur, Birmingham, Mobile, and New Orleans.

© 1981 HBJ

COMMAS AND SEMICOLONS

COMMAS AND SEMICOLONS TO SET OFF INDEPENDENT CLAUSES

Commas—and sometimes semicolons—are used before coordinate conjunctions (*and, but, for, nor, or*) that join independent clauses in a compound sentence.

> The high school was located near the airport, and the loud drone of the planes was a distraction to the students and teachers.

If one or both of the independent clauses are unusually long or contain commas, a semicolon may be used at the end of the first independent clause.

> During the day, there was much activity along the main street; but at night, except for an occasional pedestrian, the sidewalks were deserted.

Semicolons are used to separate independent clauses if the second clause is introduced by one of the adverbial conjunctions: *so, yet, still, also, besides, then, thus, hence, accordingly, consequently, however, therefore, otherwise, moreover, furthermore, nevertheless.* (Some texts on writing classify *so* and *yet* as coordinate conjunctions. In matters of punctuation in this book, they will be treated as adverbial conjunctions.) A semicolon is also used to separate independent clauses that are not joined by a conjunction.

> The frigid temperature kept most of the students indoors; however, the football team assembled on the field for its usual practice.

> The south wing of the dormitory was completed in August; the new field house should be ready by next fall.

COMMAS TO SET OFF ITEMS IN A SERIES

Commas are generally used to separate sentence elements in a series.

> The teacher insisted that we listen closely, write the instructions in a notebook, and follow them precisely when we wrote the reference paper.

Note that a comma is inserted before the coordinate conjunction, *and,* that precedes the last element in the series. Following convention, newspaper and magazine writers omit the comma before the last element; however, the *United States Government Printing Office Style Manual* requires the final comma. Students in college English courses are usually instructed to insert the comma before the last element in a series.

For the sake of variety—or for some more specific reason—writers sometimes omit the conjunction before the last element in a series.

> At Kentucky Lake we spent most of the day boating, fishing, swimming.

The semicolon (rather than the comma) is sometimes used to separate items in a series if they are unusually long or internally punctuated.

Several solutions have been suggested to alleviate the problem: bringing water in by tank truck; drilling for additional wells, which seems impractical; and asking the people to use water only when absolutely necessary.

EXERCISE 82

Read the following statements carefully and insert the punctuation that is needed. To the left of the statement, indicate by number the principle you applied.

1. Comma or Semicolon Between Independent Clauses
2. Commas or Semicolons Between Items in a Series
3. Correct

_____ 1. In the late spring I have to cut the grass every week however, in the middle and late summer I cut it every other week.

_____ 2. My favorite vegetables are green beans asparagus and tomatoes.

_____ 3. Our examination was based on ten essays from the anthology and three novels read during the semester.

_____ 4. The fire chief his assistant and the head of the arson squad carefully examined the gutted building.

_____ 5. We left Boston at noon three hours later we arrived at Kennebunk Beach.

_____ 6. I had an interview with the manager filled out an application and received my medical examination all in the same day.

_____ 7. The English Department was composed of three professors, four assistant professors, and six instructors.

_____ 8. The chapter on the reference paper explained the necessity of an outline the use of quote and summary cards and the correct use of the bibliography.

_____ 9. I returned to my hotel took a shower and dressed for dinner.

_____10. Our plane touched down at O'Hare for fifteen minutes then it took off for Los Angeles.

© 1981 HBJ

_____ 11. The doctor told the patient to stay in bed drink plenty of liquids and cut down on smoking.

_____ 12. Freud, Adler, and Jung are famous names in the field of psychiatry.

_____ 13. Faith hope and charity are stressed throughout the New Testament.

_____ 14. I stopped by the service station and had my car checked then I took off for St. Louis.

_____ 15. I passed through Pontiac Bloomington and Springfield on my way to Macomb, Illinois.

 © 1981 HBJ

EXERCISE 83

Read the following statements carefully and insert any punctuation that is needed. To the left of the statement, indicate by number the principle you applied.

1. Comma or Semicolon Between Independent Clauses
2. Commas or Semicolons Between Items in a Series
3. Correct

_____ 1. We decided to spend our vacation at a resort on Lake Michigan however, we were not able to get reservations until the first week in August.

_____ 2. I had to fill out an application take a battery of aptitude tests and convince the personnel manager that I was ambitious.

_____ 3. Susie stopped by the supermarket and bought some cold cuts, rolls, and potato chips for the picnic.

_____ 4. Vernon Charley and Joel were assigned to the same room in the dormitory.

_____ 5. Around daybreak we set out for Springfield two hours later we reached our destination.

_____ 6. The adviser told Mary Lou that she should study at least three hours each day that she should not go home on weekends and that she should not hesitate to discuss her academic problems with her teachers.

_____ 7. The paint on the house was chipping and peeling but the owners could not afford to have it repainted.

_____ 8. I moved into the dorm on Friday however, classes did not begin until the following Monday.

_____ 9. When Mark finished his last class, he hurried to the student union found several of his friends and talked them into playing cards.

_____ 10. The president, provost, and dean were the principal speakers at the freshman convocation.

_____ 11. We spent the first two days of our vacation swimming and lolling on the beach however, the third day we decided to drive to Miami and do some shopping.

_____ 12. The bus for Springfield St. Louis and Kansas City left on time.

_____ 13. We spent most of our vacation walking around the French Quarter.

_____ 14. Frank did not make the honor role therefore, he had to take the final examination.

_____ 15. We decided to take a ride on the Staten Island Ferry and look at the Statue of Liberty in the distance.

 © 1981 HBJ

COMMAS AFTER INTRODUCTORY ELEMENTS

A comma is generally inserted after introductory elements (clauses or phrases) unless the introductory element is short and the meaning is clear without the comma.

> *Comma Needed* Taking all the factors into consideration, I decided to sell my car and use public transportation.
>
> *Comma Not Needed* From the top of the hill I could see the Golden Gate Bridge.

COMMAS AND DEPENDENT CLAUSES

If a dependent clause appears at the beginning of a sentence, a comma is placed after the clause. However, if the dependent clause forms the second part of the sentence, a comma is not placed before the clause.

> *Comma Needed* Since the Fourth of July was only two days away, the stores were doing a thriving business in fireworks.
>
> *Comma Not Needed* The stores were doing a thriving business in fireworks since the Fourth of July was only two days away.

COMMAS TO SET OFF INTERRUPTERS

Commas are used to set off interrupters within a sentence.

> I am certain, however, that I will be able to attend the next meeting.

> We are, of course, delighted that you will be able to come to the party.

COMMAS BETWEEN COORDINATE ADJECTIVES

A comma is inserted between coordinate (equal value) adjectives when the conjunction is omitted.

> The calm, clear water of the river looked inviting.

To determine whether or not the adjectives are coordinate, read the sentence with a conjunction between the words in question. If the construction sounds right (for example, "the calm *and* clear water"), the writer can be reasonably sure that the adjectives are coordinate and a comma is needed. On the other hand, if the construction sounds awkward (for example, "the little *and* old lady"), the writer can conclude that the adjectives *little* and *old* are not coordinate and a comma is not required.

> The teacher had a difficult time controlling the anxious, restless teen-agers.

> The scorching midday sun made us move under the trees.

COMMAS TO PREVENT MISREADING

A comma is frequently needed for the sake of clarity or to prevent misreading although no formal rule applies. The writer, however, is not only justified but obliged to use the comma for such purposes, the main purpose of all punctuation being to ensure clarity.

> After all, the field trips will help as much as their classroom work.

> High above, the mountain looked as if it were holding up the sky.

COMMAS TO SET OFF DATES AND PLACES

Commas are used to set off a year when it is part of a date within a sentence.

> Helen was born on October 16, 1954, in Albany, New York.

> The Emancipation Proclamation was signed on September 22, 1862, by President Lincoln.

Commas are used to set off the name of a state when it follows the name of a city.

> Miami, Florida, is a favorite tourist mecca—especially during the winter months.

> Pasadena, California, is the home of the famous Rose Bowl football classic.

EXERCISE 84

Read the following statements carefully and insert any punctuation that is needed. To the left of the statement, indicate by number the principle you applied.

1. Commas After Introductory Elements
2. Commas to Set Off Interrupters
3. Commas Between Coordinate Adjectives
4. Commas to Prevent Misreading
5. Commas to Set Off Dates and Places
6. Correct

_____ 1. Because the bridge has been washed out by the flood we had to take a different route.

_____ 2. It is difficult therefore to find a parking space during business hours.

_____ 3. For many a trip to Europe is no longer a wistful dream.

_____ 4. Las Vegas, Nevada is a place that attracts many visitors.

_____ 5. The high dropout rate in college is an appalling reflection on our educational system.

_____ 6. The customs official spoke to us in an impatient sarcastic voice.

_____ 7. Many people however had to stand to see the last game of the World Series.

_____ 8. Having reached the campus sooner than expected we took a quick tour of the buildings.

_____ 9. Outside the temperature hovered around zero.

_____ 10. June 15, 1958 is my birth date.

_____ 11. Although the problems were extremely complex the professor did an effective job of explaining them.

_____ 12. The unruly boisterous crowd congregated in front of the United States embassy.

_____ 13. His warm sense of humor and interest in other people made Conrad a popular candidate for alderman.

_____ 14. You will of course develop a large stomach if you eat too much and exercise too little.

_____15. High above the peak of the mountain was covered with snow.

_____16. A big brown dog growled at us as we parked in front of the house.

_____17. December 7, 1941 is a day that will live in infamy.

_____18. When the guide had finished his spiel we returned to the bus for the trip back to the city.

_____19. His vivid spontaneous imagination frequently caused Henry to embellish the truth.

_____20. The little white rabbit scurried about in the cage.

 © 1981 HBJ

EXERCISE 85

Read the following statements carefully and insert any punctuation that is needed. To the left of the statement, indicate by number the principle you applied.

1. Commas After Introductory Elements
2. Commas to Set Off Interrupters
3. Commas Between Coordinate Adjectives
4. Commas to Prevent Misreading
5. Commas to Set Off Dates and Places
6. Correct

_____ 1. Having received notice that I was hired I was eager to start work the following Monday.

_____ 2. When I returned my roommate's typewriter was lying on my bed.

_____ 3. The smiling affable headwaiter greeted us as we entered the restaurant.

_____ 4. Mobile, Alabama is located on the Gulf of Mexico.

_____ 5. No matter how hard I tried though I was never able to bowl a two-hundred game.

_____ 6. The little gray squirrel scampered for the tree when I came near.

_____ 7. Above the squad of soldiers plodded across the bridge.

_____ 8. If I do not get a promotion by the end of the year I am going to look for another job.

_____ 9. The restive high-spirited horse kicked the back of his stall.

_____ 10. Careful proofreading is of course absolutely necessary.

_____ 11. The happy little boy held the kitten in his arms.

_____ 12. Nashville, Tennessee is the home of the Grand Ole Opry.

_____ 13. Although I didn't have enough money for my first year's tuition I was able to secure a loan from the government.

_____ 14. Outside the mailman and the milkman discussed the weather.

_____ 15. Brownsville, Texas is a border town located on the Rio Grande River.

_____ 16. The inquisitive appreciative audience listened to the scientist as he explained the purpose of the booster.

_____ 17. Having completed all his research Fred was ready to begin writing the first draft of his term paper.

_____ 18. Roger's old Model-T Ford drew attention wherever it went.

_____ 19. Outside the temperature was twenty degrees higher than in my apartment.

_____ 20. The narrow streets of course make driving difficult.

© 1981 HBJ

RESTRICTIVE AND NONRESTRICTIVE MODIFIERS

Restrictive (essential) modifiers are *not* set off by commas, but nonrestrictive (unnecessary) modifiers *are* set off by commas. A restrictive modifier is essential to convey the main idea of a sentence.

The man *who is standing near the door* is my uncle.

"Who is standing near the door" is a necessary part of the sentence. If the clause were deleted, the meaning of the sentence would be changed. Thus restrictive modifiers are not set off by commas:

A book on golf *that concentrates on the fundamentals* is badly needed.

A man *with progressive ideas* is badly needed in the office of the mayor.

A nonrestrictive modifier, although giving additional information, is not necessary to the main idea of the sentence. Nonrestrictive (nonessential) modifiers are usually set off by commas.

My Uncle George, *who used to be a stockbroker,* now lives in Florida.

George Gallup, *whose opinion polls are highly regarded,* is an expert on political affairs.

O. Henry, *whose real name was William Sydney Porter,* wrote many fascinating stories with surprise endings.

EXERCISE 86

The sentences below contain modifiers that are either restrictive (essential) or nonrestrictive (nonessential). Insert the needed punctuation if the modifier is nonrestrictive. To the left, indicate the classification by writing *R* for restrictive or *N* for nonrestrictive.

_____ 1. Arnold Kemper who is a deacon at my church was chosen to direct the Heart Fund Drive.

_____ 2. A carburetor that can give greater gas mileage is sorely needed.

_____ 3. The stockyard that you pass right before you enter town is owned by the farm cooperative.

_____ 4. Jesse Owens who was the son of a poor Alabama sharecropper is considered one of the greatest Olympic runners of all time.

_____ 5. The teacher whom I greatly admire was presented the award for outstanding service.

_____ 6. Dr. Sellers who was a captain in the Air Force before he entered medical school performed the delicate operation on my father.

_____ 7. Rio de Janeiro which is the former capital of Brazil has one of the most beautiful harbors in the world.

_____ 8. George Farley whom I consider a good friend presented my petition in the probate court.

_____ 9. The man who is now being introduced by the master of ceremonies will probably win the contest.

_____10. The Louisiana Purchase which doubled the size of the United States was acquired from France for fifteen million dollars.

_____11. The man who is wearing a grey suit owns one of the largest farms in the county.

© 1981 HBJ

_____ 12. The chairman of the board who used to be president of a bank brought the meeting to order.

_____ 13. Many plays that appear on Broadway close after a short run.

_____ 14. Our physics teacher who formerly worked for NASA explained how the space capsule is constructed.

_____ 15. The class president who happens to be one of my best friends moderated the discussion.

_____ 16. Mechanics who can repair all types of automobiles are hard to find.

_____ 17. The gossip column which is usually amusing was read first by most of the students.

_____ 18. The elderly woman who is sitting next to the president of the university is the former dean of women.

_____ 19. Captain James Cook who was a brilliant mapmaker discovered Australia.

_____ 20. The person who bowls a three hundred game is given $300 and a diamond pin.

 © 1981 HBJ

EXERCISE 87

The sentences below contain modifiers that are either restrictive (essential) or nonrestrictive (nonessential). Insert the needed punctuation if the modifier is nonrestrictive. To the left, indicate the classification by writing *R* for restrictive or *N* for nonrestrictive.

_____ 1. The director of the fund drive who had the same job last year gave an impressive talk at the banquet.

_____ 2. The man in the blue sports shirt and gray slacks is favored to win the tournament.

_____ 3. The Army-Navy game which always creates a great deal of interest will be played this year in Philadelphia.

_____ 4. The lawyer appointed by the court will defend the man accused of murder.

_____ 5. Jackie Robinson who was born on a farm in Georgia was the first black man to play baseball in the major leagues.

_____ 6. The students who do not live on campus have no curfew.

_____ 7. The parakeet that I gave my friend loves to look at himself in a mirror.

_____ 8. The chief of police who was formerly a captain in the Army has done a splendid job in reorganizing the department.

_____ 9. The camera that my parents gave me for Christmas was broken at the New Year's Eve party.

_____ 10. The Panama Canal which is now controlled by the Panamanian government connects the Atlantic and Pacific Oceans.

_____ 11. The North Atlantic Treaty Organization which now has its headquarters in Brussels was formed in 1949 to deter Soviet aggression.

© 1981 HBJ

_____12. Short stories that have little or no plot are disliked by most readers.

_____13. The manager of the boat club who as usual was dressed in sports shirt and summer slacks is a good friend of mine.

_____14. The undersecretary of state who was formerly a college professor is an expert on Russian economics.

_____15. The FBI agent who was assigned to the bank robbery interviewed the teller and the manager.

_____16. The trucks that have "Explosives" written across the back are loaded with dynamite.

_____17. Napoleon Bonaparte who was once a great military hero was banished to a desolate island in the Atlantic Ocean.

_____18. The town that looms on the horizon is Centerville.

_____19. Louis Pasteur who is known as the father of bacteriology made several great scientific discoveries.

_____20. The bishop who officiated at the ground-breaking ceremony gave an inspiring speech.

© 1981 HBJ

OTHER USES OF COMMAS

Elements out of position   Commas are used to set off elements that are not in their usual position in the sentence.

The game, I am afraid, will be postponed because of wet ground.

Conjunctions of two or more syllables   A comma is generally placed after conjunctions of two or more syllables that come at the beginning of a sentence or an independent clause.

However, I am convinced that Bradley was to blame for the accident.

I am convinced that Bradley was to blame for the accident; however, he will not be prosecuted.

Interrupters   Commas are used to set off interrupters within a sentence.

I believe, on the other hand, that Smith should be given another chance.

Appositives   Commas are used to set off appositives. An appositive is a word or phrase placed beside another word or phrase to define or amplify it.

The fantail, the aftermost part of the ship, was hardly visible because of the high waves.

Direct address   Commas are used to set off names or titles used in direct address.

Harry, call me soon as you reach Cincinnati.

I feel confident, Senator, that the subsidy bill will eventually be enacted.

Mild interjections   A comma is used after mild interjections.

No, I would rather not go to the play.

Yes, I will be there at eight in the morning.

Alas, I don't know.

EXERCISE 88

Read the following sentences carefully and insert the punctuation that is needed. In the left-hand column, indicate by number the rule you applied.

1. Elements Out of Position
2. Interrupters
3. Appositives
4. Direct Address
5. Mild Interjections

_____ 1. The use of satire poking fun at cherished institutions is prevalent in the plays of George Bernard Shaw.

_____ 2. I am confident Mr. Gilpin that this car will give you excellent service.

_____ 3. Using an outline I learned after much trial and error is the best way to write a composition.

_____ 4. I believe therefore that the city and county should be administered as a single unit.

_____ 5. Dorothy I wonder if I could borrow your typewriter?

_____ 6. Henry Manning the United States congressman from this district gave the principal address.

_____ 7. The new constitution the governor stressed will eliminate many antiquated practices.

_____ 8. I shall of course be glad to help you in every way I can.

_____ 9. Milton how about going bowling with me?

_____10. Yes I am very much in favor of coeducation.

_____11. This winter if I am still living I am going to rent an apartment that has central heating.

_____12. I hold fast therefore to my opinion that the dismissal of the board chairman was not justified.

_____13. Penicillin an antibiotic drug has saved countless lives since it first appeared.

© 1981 HBJ

———— 14. No I won't be able to go home this weekend because of the gas shortage.

———— 15. Dean Sales a former English professor emphasized the importance of an effective writing style for success in college.

 © 1981 HBJ

EXERCISE 89

Read the following sentences carefully and insert the punctuation that is needed. In the left-hand column, indicate by number the rule you applied.

1. Elements Out of Position
2. Interrupters
3. Appositives
4. Direct Address
5. Mild Interjections

_____ 1. Yes I am convinced that Henry would make a good counselor.

_____ 2. I am therefore going to have to get a job this summer and save some money.

_____ 3. Edgar do you think that wage and price controls would halt inflation?

_____ 4. The booster the part of the rocket that puts the space capsule in orbit was fabricated at Huntsville, Alabama.

_____ 5. No I am not at all satisfied with my new car.

_____ 6. The most serious threat to democracy I believe is the materialistic philosophy of the general population.

_____ 7. I would have to pay for instance $400 for a new transmission.

_____ 8. Bill are you going to Houston this weekend?

_____ 9. Yes I will be glad to serve on the committee.

_____ 10. Ted O'Brien a very capable and conscientious lawyer was chosen as president of the bar association.

_____ 11. No I am sure that I have never met your sister.

_____ 12. The road to Memphis I was happy to learn is a four-lane interstate highway all the way.

_____ 13. The tornado however did not touch down in the area predicted by the weather bureau.

© 1981 HBJ

_____ 14. Bob Morris the master of ceremonies at the banquet has a sparkling personality and a warm sense of humor.

_____ 15. I am fairly certain Mr. Lester that I can report for work next Monday.

 © 1981 HBJ

QUOTATION MARKS

Double quotation marks ("...") are used to enclose the exact words of another writer or of a speaker in dialogue.

> In the preface to *A Dictionary of the English Language*, Samuel Johnson describes how he approached this mammoth project: "Having therefore no assistance but from general grammar, I applied myself to the perusal of our writers. . . ."

The use of double quotation marks is the usual way of indicating the exact words of another writer or the speech of a character in a story. However, a second technique, used for longer quotes, is considered standard procedure in writing reference papers. If the quotation is five lines or more, the material is block indented and single-spaced; no quotation marks are used. Paragraphs are indented three spaces rather than the customary five.

In the preface to *A Dictionary of the English Language*, Samuel Johnson describes how he approached this mammoth project:

> Having therefore no assistance but from general grammar, I applied myself to the perusal of our writers; and noting whatever might be of use to ascertain or illustrate any word or phrase, accumulated in time the materials of a dictionary, which, by degrees, I reduced to method, establishing to myself, in the progress of the work, such rules as experience and analogy suggested to me. . . .

In using quotation marks to enclose the exact words of the speaker in dialogue, most professional writers begin a new paragraph for new each speaker.

> "Cold," the old man answered blowing on his chapped hands. "That wind's like a knife. You better give me a cup of hot chocolate to warm me up."
>
> Carl smiled and drew a glass of beer and set it on the bar in front of him.
>
> A sly look appeared on the old man's face. "Say, Carl, you made a mistake. I wanted hot chocolate. Well, as long as you got it drawn I won't let it go to waste."
>
> "I'm certainly sorry," Carl apologized. "I could have sworn that was hot chocolate."

Double quotation marks are also used to enclose the following:

titles of short stories

> "Counterparts" from *Dubliners* by James Joyce is one of my favorite short stories.

poems not published as a separate volume

> "Woman's Constancy" is one of John Donne's earlier poems.

articles from magazines

> "The Danger of Education in America," an article in this week's *Newsweek*, is worth reading.

The introductory chapter, "The Substance of Shakespearean Tragedy," from *Shakespearean Tragedy* by A. C. Bradley, is profound without being pedantic.

Single quotation marks ('. . .') are used to enclose a quotation within a quotation.

John crumbled up the newspaper and vehemently threw it on the floor. "Shakespeare was right," he shouted. " 'It is a tale told by an idiot. Full of sound and fury. Signifying nothing.' "

These are famous lines by Whittier: "For of all sad words of tongue or pen,/The saddest are these: 'It might have been.' "

Note that periods and commas go inside single and/or double quotation marks. Colons and semicolons, however, go outside the quotation marks.

In the words of Alexander Pope, "A little learning is a dangerous thing": superficial learning is sometimes worse than no learning at all.

Dr. Kesler concluded, "Thus you can see the close connection between psychology and literature"; then he walked out of the classroom.

The question mark goes inside or outside the quotation marks, depending on whether the entire statement or only the quoted material is a question. If only the quoted part of the sentence is a question, the question mark goes inside the quotation marks. If the entire statement is a question, the question mark goes outside the quotation marks.

Ms. Byrd asked, "How many of you plan to go on the trip?"

Did Ms. Byrd say, "Only the seniors can go on the trip"?

EXERCISE 90

Correct the following statements by inserting the needed punctuation that was omitted. In some cases, there may be marks that should be deleted. Circle such marks before you write in the correct punctuation.

1. The minister used the following text for his sermon: "Do not be afraid, little flock, for it has pleased your Father to give you the kingdom".

2. "The wind cuts like a knife," the old man said. You better give me a cup of coffee to warm me up.

3. "Do you want lettuce and tomato on your hamburger" the waitress asked as she took my order?

4. Senator Keith replied, "Today we hear so many complaints about corruption in government. But I would like to remind you of a remark by William Penn: 'Let men be good, and government cannot be bad' ".

5. From Hero to Celebrity is one of the most interesting chapters in *The Image* by Daniel Boorstin.

6. Iago said to Roderigo, "How poor are they that have not patience".

7. Whitman's famous poem O Captain! My Captain! was written to lament the death of Lincoln.

8. Larry told his father, "I would rather get a job as a mechanic than go to college.

9. William Cullen Bryant wrote the first draft of his famous poem Thanatopsis when he was only seventeen years old.

10. Professor King said, "The test will be put off until the following week;" so I won't have to study this weekend.

11. I recently read an article in *Newsweek* titled The Shame of the Cities that made me shudder.

12. The governor concluded his speech with these words: "The time is

© 1981 HBJ

long overdue that the average citizen should have a voice in govern-ment".

13. "A walk through the woods on an autumn day, David said to his friend, "is one of my favorite pastimes."

14. Dr. Hicks asked the class, "How many of you have previously written a reference paper"?

15. William Butler Yeats' poem That the Night Come gives a word picture of a seriously disturbed woman.

 © 1981 HBJ

EXERCISE 91

Correct the following statements by inserting the needed punctuation that was omitted. In some cases, there may be marks that should be deleted. Circle such marks before you write in the correct punctuation.

1. "Do you believe, Barbara asked, "the favorite will win the race"?

2. Haircut is one of Ring Lardner's famous short stories.

3. Larson asked, "Where do I sign up for a loan"?

4. "I am convinced", the mayor said, "that the snow removal plan will be effective".

5. The director of the play said to the leading lady, "I agree with Benjamin Franklin. 'If you have a wax head, you shouldn't walk in the sun".

6. Dr. Cain said, "Classroom attendance is not compulsory;" so I intend to spend some of my class time in the library.

7. "The most important thing for a complete recovery", the doctor said, is plenty of rest and relaxation".

8. The poem Chicago by Carl Sandburg is frequently quoted.

9. "I have no intention of buying a new car, Rita said. "The one I have now has only 30,000 miles on it".

10. The Blue Hotel, a short story by Stephen Crane, is widely anthologized.

11. "What time does the featured movie start," Charles asked the ticket seller?

12. "I'm definitely against the use of atomic energy", Lobb said in a belligerent tone.

13. "How do you get on the interstate for Nashville," the driver asked me as she stopped for a traffic light?

© 1981 HBJ

14. Dr. Schmidt said, "The term papers have to be in by Monday;" so I have to spend the weekend finishing my final draft.

15. Adventure is one of the best short stories from *Winesburg, Ohio,* by Sherwood Anderson.

  © 1981 HBJ

APOSTROPHES

The apostrophe (') is used with nouns or pronouns to indicate possession. Singular nouns that do not end in *s* form their possessive by adding *'s*.

boy	boy's
girl	girl's
mouse	mouse's

Singular nouns that end in *s* form their possessives by adding either an apostrophe after the *s* or an apostrophe and an *s*. If the additional *s* makes an awkward pronunciation, use only the apostrophe.

Xerxes' army	Lois's hat
Moses' followers	James's boat
Keats' poems	

Plural nouns that do not end in *s* form their possessives by adding an apostrophe and an *s*.

men's	teeth's
women's	mice's
oxen's	

Plural nouns that end in *s* form their possessives by adding only the apostrophe.

babies'	boys'
fathers'	dogs'
soldiers'	brothers'
schoolgirls'	horses'

The possessive case of hyphenated words is formed by adding the apostrophe and *s* to the final word.

my brother-in-law's car

If joint possession is to be shown, only the last noun is in the possessive case.

John and Robert's boat
(They own the boat together.)

Helen's and Joan's books
(They own the books separately.)

Apostrophes are not used with personal possessive pronouns (*his, hers, ours, theirs, yours, its*) or the relative interrogative pronoun (*whose*).

His coat is on the bed.
That painting is *hers.*
The boat at the end of the dock is *ours.*
Does this book happen to be *yours?*
Whose car is parked in front of the house?

Possessives and contractions are frequently confused. Often people write *who's* for *whose, you're* for *your, it's* for *its.* The forms with apostrophes are contractions of a pronoun and a verb.

who's	who is
you're	you are
they're	they are
it's	it is

The words without apostrophes (*whose, your, its*) show possession.

Who's coming to the party? *They're* sure they can be there.
Whose record player is that? *Their* reaction was predictable.

You're the one I've been looking for. *It's* too late to catch the train.
Your car has a flat tire. *Its* sudden bark frightened me.

The possessive of indefinite pronouns is formed by adding an apostrophe and *s* to the singular.

anybody's business	one's personality
anyone's opinion	nobody's concern
everybody's belief	someone's mistake

Apostrophes are used to mark the omission of letters in contracted words or of figures in dates.

cannot	can't	I have	I've
I am	I'm	has not	hasn't
I will	I'll	is not	isn't
it is	it's	1949	'49

Apostrophes are used in dialectal speech to mark the omission of one or more letters in a word.

I'm *goin'* downtown.
'Is mother is *callin'* *'im.*

An apostrophe and *s* are used to form the plural of letters, figures, and words used as words.

Be sure to dot your *i*'s and cross your *t*'s.
His *6*'s look like *8*'s.
He has ten *and*'s in the first two sentences.

The apostrophe and *s* are used with some idiomatic expressions.

This *month's* quota is larger than the previous *month's.*
An *hour's* walk brought us to the lake.
I reached my *wits'* end before he told me the answer.

EXERCISE 92

Circle the form that is misused. Write the correct form in the blank space to the left of the number.

_____ 1. The boys bicycle was stolen.

_____ 2. Tim and Bob's motor scooters were parked in front of the fraternity house.

_____ 3. The horses stalls are cleaned every morning.

_____ 4. My sister's-in-law baby has the mumps.

_____ 5. Helen's and Tom's house caught on fire.

_____ 6. Somebodys car is blocking the driveway.

_____ 7. Jerry's 4s look like 7s.

_____ 8. Jean and Larry's coats were lying on the bed.

_____ 9. The dog wagged it's tail.

_____ 10. Ones sense of humor is a good index of his intelligence.

_____ 11. Who's car is parked in the driveway?

_____ 12. Womens rights should not be violated.

_____ 13. You're shoes will be ready tomorrow afternoon.

_____ 14. The devastating flood of 37 covered most of the city.

_____ 15. Its such a beautiful day that I think I'll take a walk in the park.

_____ 16. Nobodys opinion was ignored by the teacher.

_____ 17. They're apartment is beautifully furnished.

_____ 18. My brother's-in-law car was stolen last night.

_____ 19. The books lying on the divan are her's.

_____ 20. My sisters husbands all work at the same factory.

© 1981 HBJ

EXERCISE 93

Circle the form that is misused. Write the correct form in the blank space to the left of the number.

_____ 1. The dogs collars all had licenses attached.

_____ 2. Ones future depends to a large extent upon chance.

_____ 3. Who's poem won the literary award this year?

_____ 4. Mary's and Tom's trailer was hitched to the car and ready to go.

_____ 5. Try to remember that Elliott's name has two ls and two ts.

_____ 6. Its a shame that John can't get any of his stories published.

_____ 7. My mother's-in-law fried chicken is hard to beat.

_____ 8. Someones books were left in the classroom.

_____ 9. Moses criticism of the Hebrew people was severe.

_____ 10. The boys attitude was an example to all his friends.

_____ 11. Who's motor scooter is parked in the driveway?

_____ 12. In December of 41 Pearl Harbor was attacked by Japan.

_____ 13. Everybodys opinion was welcomed by the teacher.

_____ 14. Mike and Pat's sleeping bags were soaked by the sudden downpour.

_____ 15. My sister-in-laws degree is from the University of Chicago.

_____ 16. The boys hats were all the same.

_____ 17. The gambler at Las Vegas threw five 7s in a row.

_____ 18. Its a misdemeanor to hunt without a license.

_____ 19. I cant believe that Lois would do such a thing.

_____ 20. Saturday afternoon I'm goin to the races.

© 1981 HBJ

PARENTHESES

Punctuation marks called parentheses ( ) are used within a sentence to enclose a qualifying comment or an explanation that may add meaning but that is unessential to the grammatical structure of the sentence. Moreover, a complete sentence or several sentences may be considered parenthetical. In such a case, parentheses are placed before the first word and after the final period, as in the second example below. A comma may be used after a parenthesis—but not before it.

> The United Nations (established after the battles of the Second World War had ended) was organized to prevent future wars.

> From daybreak to sundown the planes took off and landed on the aircraft carrier. (More will be said about this operation later.)

Parentheses are used to enclose letters or numbers that precede a listing.

> The government agency was set up for several reasons: (1) to provide food and housing for the needy; (2) to find jobs for the unemployed; and (3) to give free medical care to those who cannot afford it.

Parentheses are sometimes used to clarify an ambiguous pronoun reference.

> John told his father that his (John's) car had been wrecked.

Parentheses are used to enclose cross references.

> The cost of living rose by one percent in the month of June. (See Appendix A.)

In some formal business transactions, parentheses are used to restate numbers and amounts that are spelled out in the document.

> The undersigned promises to pay four hundred dollars ($400) within six months of the date of this note.

Parentheses are used to set off compound appositives that might be confusing if commas were used. (An appositive is a noun construction that restates another noun construction.)

> Three naval vessels (an aircraft carrier and two destroyers) were moored to the dock.

Parentheses are used to enclose the original publication date of a literary work.

> *The Sun Also Rises* (1926) was Ernest Hemingway's first published novel.

Parentheses and a question mark are used to indicate doubt or uncertainty.

> Chaucer was born in 1340 (?) and died in 1400.

Avoid using this device when the information is readily available. Also avoid using it to achieve an ironical or humorous effect.

Parentheses are used to enclose the birth and/or death years of individuals.

F. Scott Fitzgerald (1896–1940)

Kurt Vonnegut, Jr. (b. 1922)

Confucius (551?–479 B.C.)

BRACKETS

Brackets [ ] do not appear on the keyboard of many standard typewriters; if necessary, they can be made with the slant and the underscore keys or written in longhand. They are used to enclose explanatory material or editorial comments within a passage, especially a quoted passage.

"Amen I say to you, no prophet [this certainly applied to Jesus] is acceptable in his own country."

Brackets are used to enclose the Latin word *sic* (which means *thus*) to indicate that the preceding word or phrase is written exactly as it appeared in the original text.

The students should be seperated [*sic*] according to their abilities.

ITALICS

In typewritten or longhand papers, italics that would occur in print are indicated by underlining. In such a manuscript, the following items should be underlined.

Names of magazines and newspapers	The New York Times
	Newsweek
	Saturday Evening Post
Titles of books, motion pictures, works of art, names of ships and planes	The Old Man and the Sea
	El Cid
	The Thinker
	Queen Mary
	Spirit of St. Louis
Titles of plays and other literary works published separately	J.B.
	Othello
	Paradise Lost
Foreign words that are not considered standard English	After his scathing editorial in the Torch, he was persona non grata among his teachers.
	Sirloin steak was the pièce de résistance of the meal.

Underline to call particular attention to the word or letter or figure being named. (Sometimes quotes are used.)

What does <u>dubiously</u> mean?

I could not tell if the last figure was <u>5</u> or <u>7</u>.

Shorter literary works (short stories, essays, and poems) that are published in a volume or anthology are enclosed by quotation marks rather than underlined.

"The Boarding House" from <u>Dubliners</u> by James Joyce

"Birth of Christ" from <u>The Life of the Virgin Mary</u> by Rainer Maria Rilke

DASHES

The dash (two unspaced hyphens if written on a typewriter) is a flexible and useful punctuation mark if used correctly. When used haphazardly, it connotes carelessness and ignorance and implies that the writer lacks even a rudimentary understanding of punctuation.

The dash is used to indicate an abrupt break in the continuity of a sentence.

On my first trip to Trinidad—I'll tell you about that later.

He told us they discovered gold—who could believe such a story?—on their first expedition.

A dash is used to emphasize a word or phrase at the end of a sentence.

Thomas Wolfe admitted that he had only one goal in life—fame.

Roosevelt had one consuming ambition—to be president of the United States.

The dash is sometimes used in place of a colon before a listing or summary in less formal writing.

He had the qualities of a great leader—courage, humility, and fairness.

The ability to hold the attention of the class, the imagination to allow for individual differences, the restraint and humor to control his emotions—these are some of the qualities of an effective teacher.

The dash is used to set off abrupt parenthetical elements.

I would like to tell you—if I may be so presumptuous—what is wrong with our educational system.

HYPHEN

A hyphen is used at the end of a line to divide a word into syllables.

ac-com-mo-date
de-pen-dent
en-vi-ron-ment

Most careful writers will not divide words so as to begin the second line with a vowel.

The hyphen is used to join two or more words that form a phrase serving as an adjective before a noun.

> a never-to-be-forgotten experience
> a hard-to-face decision
> a tailor-made suit

The hyphen is used in spelling out compound numbers.

> twenty-one
> ninety-nine

EXERCISE 94

Circle the punctuation that is misused and insert whatever punctuation is needed.

1. Recently, I read an interesting article in "Newsweek" on higher education in America.

2. My weekend in Cincinnati, believe it or not, provided me with an idea for a short story.

3. Tom told Milton that he, Tom, should have studied for the examination.

4. I was not their (*sic*) when the accident happened.

5. Some astute critics consider "Moby Dick" to be the greatest American novel.

6. The increase in urban population has been astonishing. See diagram attached.

7. The medical team, two doctors and four nurses, visited the primitive villages.

8. Chicago is called the Windy City. (The "wind" is sometimes referred to as the "hawk").

9. I took my first trip to Europe on the "Queen Mary."

10. At present I have one main problem, lack of money.

11. The Indiana University Press has recently published a biography of Emerson entitled "The Disciple of Plato."

12. I agree to repay five hundred dollars—$500—on or before June 21.

13. When I visited Trinidad . . . but who would believe such a story?

14. Our language teacher uses the Spanish word "saludos" as a greeting when she enters the classroom.

15. "Look at the birds of the air. (This is a famous quotation from the New Testament.) They neither sow nor reap nor gather into barns, yet your Heavenly Father feeds them."

© 1981 HBJ

16. The check for twenty-five dollars—$25—was returned because of insufficient funds.
17. The profits for the month of January showed an increase of 10 percent over last year. See chart attached.
18. "The Starry Night," a famous painting by Vincent van Gogh, was on display in the museum.
19. This summer I'm going . . . oh, who cares where I'm going?
20. "The New York Times" is one of the best newspapers published in the United States.

 © 1981 HBJ

EXERCISE 95

Circle the punctuation that is misused and insert whatever punctuation is needed.

1. From Christmas to Easter seemed like an eternity. (I shall write more about my stay in Alaska later).

2. Postal rates have gone up steadily in recent years. See chart attached.

3. I could not tell whether the last figure was a 6 or a 9.

4. Some critics feel that "The Sound and the Fury" is Faulkner's greatest novel.

5. "For everyone who exalts himself shall be humbled. (This Biblical quotation is taken from the parable of the Pharisee and the Publican.) And he who humbles himself shall be exalted."

6. When I was in high school . . . but who cares about that?

7. I agree to pay John Hayden forty thousand dollars—$40,000—on or before June 15, 1984.

8. Four police officers, two patrolmen, a sergeant, and a captain, were at the scene of the fatal accident.

9. During the month of December the stock market rose steadily. See chart attached.

10. My roommate had a reproduction of Cézanne's "Card Players" hanging over his bed.

11. I thought The Dead was the best short story in James Joyce's book "Dubliners."

12. "Neither a borrower nor a lender be. (These lines are taken from *Hamlet*.) For loan oft loses both self and friend."

13. Today I recieved (*sic*) $500 in cash from the undersigned.

14. Howard wore a tailor-made suit.

© 1981 HBJ

15. In my opinion "All the King's Men" by Robert Penn Warren is an excellent novel.

16. The miners had only one thought on their minds . . . gold.

17. Mary told Nora that she would take her [Nora's] books back to the library.

18. "Mr. Johnson was the principle (*sic*) speaker at the banquet."

19. I wrote a check for seventy five dollars.

20. A large statue of "The Thinker" is located in front of the Administration Building.

 © 1981 HBJ

EXERCISE 96

GENERAL REVIEW OF PUNCTUATION

The sentences that follow are either correct or contain one or more punctuation errors. Circle any punctuation that is incorrect and insert new punctuation as needed. If the sentence is correct put a C to the left of the number.

_____ 1. Our ship left Trinidad on Monday three days later it arrived in Boston.

_____ 2. Do you think the company will give a bonus this year.

_____ 3. The man who is wearing the wide-brimmed hat is a member of the entertainment committee.

_____ 4. Don Jarett our drama coach graduated from Northwestern University.

_____ 5. In my opinion the movie "The Sun Also Rises" was much better than the novel on which it was based.

_____ 6. For many the time to make definite plans for an occupation is while they are in high school.

_____ 7. Bruce Grant our playground instructor is a medical student at Vanderbilt.

_____ 8. The baseball equipment, bats, balls, gloves, and catcher's mask, was stored in the gear locker.

_____ 9. The dialogue in Ben Anderson's novel "Soon After Dawn" is unrealistic.

_____10. In my opinion "The New York Times" is the best newspaper in the United States.

_____11. The student who does the most push-ups will be given a prize.

_____12. Amy and Karen's horses won prizes in the jumping contest.

_____13. For many years the Grand Ole Opry has been broadcast from Nashville over radio station W.S.M.

_____14. Alvin asked me if I had finished my practice set?

_____15. "The vices of the rich (This statement is typical of Alexander Hamilton.) are more congenial to good government than the vices of the poor."

_____16. The man in charge of the state park who used to be a master sergeant in the Army directed us to our cabin.

_____17. Ann's and Bert's boat was anchored at the head of the island.

_____18. We were assigned a short story entitled A Simple Heart by Gustave Flaubert.

_____19. The restless dissatisfied crowd lined up in front of the soup kitchen.

_____20. What does sophistication mean in this instance?

_____21. Senator Hume who is chairman of the Rules Committee gave an inspiring talk at the convocation.

_____22. I finished my term paper and gave it to my roommate to proofread.

_____23. This year the class of 50 had their 30th-anniversary banquet.

_____24. The bus for Nashville leaves at 9 30 P.M.

_____25. Carl asked me if I would help him with his math?

_____26. "If I am elected," the candidate promised, "I will do everything to bring more industry to the city".

_____27. Outside the crowd waited to get a look at the movie stars.

_____28. Its too bad that Senator Hicks won't be able to attend the graduation exercises.

_____29. Who do you think will win the World Series.

 © 1981 HBJ

_____ 30. Norman's sleek shiny automobile was greatly admired by the attendants at the parking lot.

_____ 31. No I don't think I'll be able to go to the lecture tomorrow.

_____ 32. I walked down to the corner and entered the drugstore.

_____ 33. The chapter entitled Stereotypes from Walter Lippmann's book *Public Opinion* has been frequently quoted.

_____ 34. When my plane was shot down over Germany . . . but you've heard that story before.

_____ 35. For several hours we sat on the bank of the creek and waited for the fish to bite on our lines.

_____ 36. "The Red and the Black," Stendhal's famous novel, does not tell you how to win at roulette.

_____ 37. My brothers wives get along very well with my mother.

_____ 38. "What is your goal in life," the counselor asked the high-school student?

_____ 39. I am quite sure Dr. Brown that I will have my thesis ready by Monday of next week.

_____ 40. The students themes were carefully checked by the English instructor.

_____ 41. "Stop that messing around," the lifeguard shouted to the boy on the diving board!

_____ 42. The man who is standing next to the president is in charge of the Secret Service detail.

_____ 43. The first thing we discussed at the meeting was finances then we made plans for our annual picnic.

_____ 44. "Who would like to pull a rabbit out of this hat," the magician asked the audience.

_____ 45. Ones determination is often an important factor in success.

© 1981 HBJ

_____46. I was fascinated by Dali's famous painting "The Persistence of Memory."

_____47. "The tour of the United Nations buildings, Joel said, "was the highlight of our senior trip.

_____48. New Orleans I believe is the second largest port in the United States.

_____49. The young woman who is talking with the dean is the president of the senior class.

_____50. This year the Christmas vacation will begin on Dec 21.

 © 1981 HBJ

EXERCISE 97

GENERAL REVIEW OF PUNCTUATION

The sentences that follow are either correct or contain one or more punctuation errors. Circle any punctuation that is incorrect and insert new punctuation as needed. If the sentence is correct put a *C* to the left of the number.

_____ 1. Having reached the end of the trail we decided to return to camp.

_____ 2. My mother's-in-law house was damaged by the storm.

_____ 3. Did Helen say, "I'll meet you at the student union?"

_____ 4. Oh I would just as soon eat in the cafeteria as go to a restaurant in town.

_____ 5. I promise to pay five hundred dollars—$500—on or before the date agreed.

_____ 6. The woman who just entered the library is my English instructor.

_____ 7. N.A.S.A has its headquarters in Houston, Texas.

_____ 8. Although I studied all weekend for the exam I made barely a passing grade.

_____ 9. The budget for the next fiscal period is three million dollars. See schedule attached.

_____ 10. Moses decision to turn to the left rather than to the right after he crossed the Red Sea has had profound historical repercussions.

_____ 11. The mayor of my town who was formerly the director of safety is a graduate of Notre Dame.

_____ 12. "How far is it to Rock Island," the motorist asked the attendant when he drove into the service station.

_____ 13. I was glad however that I didn't lose my temper.

_____ 14. Whose going to drive to Chicago this weekend.

_____ 15. J P Morgan was one of the leading American financiers of the late nineteenth and early twentieth centuries.

_____ 16. I walked along the river and watched the barges pass up and down.

_____ 17. I hereby promise to pay the First National Bank of Mount Vernon five thousand dollars—$5,000—on or before January 1, 1984.

_____ 18. Harry what is your honest opinion of the movie?

_____ 19. J. D. Salinger's novel "Franny and Zooey" was published after "The Catcher in the Rye."

_____ 20. My trip to Europe was a never to be forgotten experience.

_____ 21. The flood had washed out the bridge so we had to take a roundabout route.

_____ 22. Bruce told Don that he, Don, had been chosen to represent the company.

_____ 23. A good index of ones intelligence is his reading interests.

_____ 24. "What band instrument do you play?" the musical director asked me.

_____ 25. Who do you think will win the tournament this year.

_____ 26. If I ever get the chance . . . but what's the use of complaining.

_____ 27. "Let's walk down to the square and take in a movie", Ted suggested to his girl friend.

_____ 28. Homer's boat I believe is the fastest on the river.

_____ 29. The following student nurses are assigned to Ward C. Agnes Grant, Eileen Montez, and Kevin O'Brien.

_____ 30. When I returned the car was parked in the driveway.

_____ 31. Thomas Mann's novel "Confessions of Felix Krull, Confidence Man" has an intriguing plot.

_____32. Betty's and Bob's house is located on a cliff overlooking the River.

_____33. Dr. Lindsey said, "I will not accept any term papers after Monday;" therefore, I will have to spend the weekend finishing mine.

_____34. The tennis courts were soaked by the downpour but the scorching sun dried them within a few hours.

_____35. My father's-in-law truck is ideal for camping trips.

_____36. After all the extra time I spent practicing helped me to win the tennis tournament.

_____37. The FBI received the following note: "I knowed (sic) the bank robber when he worked on my farm."

_____38. I put on my foul-weather clothes and went topside to stand watch.

_____39. Our train pulled into Union Station at 8 45 P.M.

_____40. Can you tell me Dr. Morton the grade I made on the last test?

_____41. This is the highway to Springfield, isn't it.

_____42. I graduated from high school started to work at the factory and bought a new car all in the same week.

_____43. The student who makes the highest grade on the test is bound to get an A.

_____44. Did Carol say, "I will meet you at the library?"

_____45. Our baseball coach who is also the assistant basketball coach was a catcher with the Chicago Cubs.

_____46. Whistler's famous painting "Arrangement in Grey and Black" is on display in the Louvre Museum in Paris.

_____47. I agree to pay the Shady Glenn Tree Service seventy-five dollars—$75—to remove one damaged oak tree from my property at 3511 Orion Road, Cincinnati, Ohio.

© 1981 HBJ

_____48. I bought a new power mower that cuts the front and back yards in less than an hour.

_____49. The dog wagged it's tail as I approached.

_____50. My favorite sports are: baseball, tennis, and golf.

 © 1981 HBJ

EXERCISE 98

GENERAL REVIEW OF PUNCTUATION

The sentences that follow are either correct or contain one or more punctuation errors. Circle any punctuation that is incorrect and insert new punctuation as needed. If the sentence is correct put a *C* to the left of the number.

_____ 1. "Fantastic Voyage" is perhaps the most unusual movie I have ever seen.

_____ 2. "Who do you think will win an Oscar this year for the best actress," our drama teacher asked me?

_____ 3. Barbara walked into the living room and turned on the television set.

_____ 4. State Senator Henderson who has a law degree from Harvard would not commit herself on the controversial housing bill.

_____ 5. Ones interest in science is often developed at an early age.

_____ 6. My sisters husbands came from different parts of the country.

_____ 7. Larry's nasty irascible disposition made him unpopular with most of the students in the class.

_____ 8. I scraped the ice from the window therefore, I was able to see well enough to drive.

_____ 9. Recently the F.B.I. moved its regional offices to the new Federal Building.

_____10. "My visit to the White House," Gary said, was the high point of my trip to Washington.

_____11. The boys bicycle was lying under a tree near the baseball diamond.

_____12. "Only those are fit to live (Teddy Roosevelt certainly practiced what he preached.) who do not fear to die."

_____13. The woman who just entered the auditorium is the dean of students.

_____14. For some time is a monster that must be killed.

_____15. The office supplies, pencils, erasers, notebooks, and typewriter ribbons, were stored in the file cabinet.

_____16. Theodore Dreiser's first novel, "Sister Carrie," raised a furor because of its realism.

_____17. Yes I agree that the street should be repaved.

_____18. Ann and Maggie's blouses took prizes in the sewing contest.

_____19. The man who is wearing the ten-gallon hat is the manager of the circus.

_____20. "What is your excuse for being late," the manager asked the clerk?

_____21. The plane for Miami leaves at 7 30 P.M.

_____22. Norma's and David's camping trailer was stored in their garage.

_____23. The manager of the restaurant who used to be a mess sergeant in the Army told me that business had fallen off in recent months.

_____24. "The New Yorker" is a very sophisticated magazine.

_____25. We arrived at Yankee Stadium about an hour before the game and watched the batting practice.

_____26. Over inflation of tires by a couple of pounds I have been told will increase gas mileage.

_____27. Bill asked me to loan him my tennis racket?

_____28. Its too early in the campaign to make a definite prediction.

_____29. The seething pulsating crowd jammed the bus station.

  © 1981 HBJ

_____ 30. The theme of Camus' novel "The Stranger" is quite subtle.

_____ 31. Who do you think will win the Nobel Prize in literature this year.

_____ 32. This year the Thanksgiving dance will be held on Nov 15.

_____ 33. I read in the alumni news bulletin that the class of 71 is going to have a reunion.

_____ 34. The angry restless mob shouted insults at the president.

_____ 35. Benjamin stopped at the red light and looked in the rear-view mirror.

_____ 36. You can be assured Ms. Mastin that such a mistake will never happen again.

_____ 37. Most of the action in F. Scott Fitzgerald's novel "The Great Gatsby" happens on Long Island.

_____ 38. After I finished reading the newspaper, I forced myself to wash the dishes.

_____ 39. Terry asked me if I would help him with his math?

_____ 40. The state trooper gave me the following directions. Continue on this road until you come to the first traffic light and then turn left.

_____ 41. Inside the fireplace provided warmth for the hunters.

_____ 42. We left Indianapolis at noon four hours later we arrived in Chicago.

_____ 43. The boys black leather jackets all have the same insignia painted on the backs.

_____ 44. "I intend to prove," the district attorney stated, "that the accused is guilty of arson".

_____ 45. Edgar Allan Poe was born in Boston, Massachusetts in 1809.

_____ 46. My math teacher who was a captain in the Air Force during the Second World War has a unique way of putting across his material.

_____47. "The St. Louis Post-Dispatch" is one of the outstanding newspapers in the United States.

_____48. The truck driver who goes through the year without having an accident will be given an award.

_____49. Do you think that Becht has a chance to be elected.

_____50. On July 4, 1776 the Declaration of Independence was signed in Philadelphia.

 © 1981 HBJ

EXERCISE 99

GENERAL REVIEW OF PUNCTUATION

The sentences that follow are either correct or contain one or more punctuation errors. Circle the punctuation that is incorrect and insert new punctuation as needed. If the sentence is correct put a *C* to the left of the number.

_____ 1. I have decided however to have my car painted rather than to buy a new one.

_____ 2. When John Wells talked to the lawyer, he—John Wells—was very angry.

_____ 3. The man who just entered the cafeteria is the dean of the law school.

_____ 4. I think The Chrysanthemums is one of John Steinbeck's better short stories.

_____ 5. The birds nests are high in the tree.

_____ 6. My first class is at 8 30 in the morning.

_____ 7. Did Randy say, "I will wait for you in the student union building?"

_____ 8. "For thy sweet love remembered such wealth brings (These are the last two lines of Shakespeare's 29th sonnet.) That then I scorn to change my state with kings."

_____ 9. My history teacher who also sponsors the drama club recently had an article on the Boston Massacre published in a national magazine.

_____ 10. I entered the hotel and asked the desk clerk if he had a room available.

_____ 11. Yes! I am going to write a protest letter to my congressman.

_____ 12. Some of Ring Lardner's short stories first appeared in "The Saturday Evening Post" magazine.

_____ 13. Yesterday we had our first snowfall however, the snow melted as soon as the flakes touched the ground.

_____ 14. "How long did it take you to drive to St. Louis," Marvin asked?

_____ 15. I climbed to the top of the hill and gazed at the sunset.

_____ 16. After all the discipline my parents taught me helped me to stay out of trouble.

_____ 17. My father's-in-law boat was damaged by the storm.

_____ 18. The smash-up happened at the intersection of 22nd and Jefferson Streets. See diagram attached.

_____ 19. Having reached the raft we sprang out of the water and stretched out in the sun.

_____ 20. Somebodys car is blocking the driveway.

_____ 21. This is the last day for dropping a class, isn't it.

_____ 22. "How do you spend your leisure time," the personnel director asked me when I applied for a job?

_____ 23. Stephen Crane's poem War Is Kind is a striking example of poetic irony.

_____ 24. Since I don't have an automobile I had to take the bus to Detroit.

_____ 25. Your trip I can well imagine must have been exciting.

_____ 26. Oh I would just as soon stay home and watch television.

_____ 27. Sinclair Lewis's novel "Elmer Gantry" was made into a movie starring Burt Lancaster.

_____ 28. Jim told Henry that he—Jim—had made a mistake.

_____ 29. My wifes companionship is one of the reasons I never regret being married.

_____ 30. The woman who just rang up the sale on the cash register is the manager of the store.

_____ 31. Peggy have you decided to go to school this summer.

   © 1981 HBJ

_____ 32. The doctor said, "You will have to lose at least twenty pounds;" consequently, I can no longer eat potatoes.

_____ 33. Alton asked me if I would loan him my jack so that he could change his flat tire?

_____ 34. The dancers costumes glittered as the spotlight flooded the stage.

_____ 35. Our governor who was formerly a state senator spoke on the importance of passing the constitutional amendment.

_____ 36. I entered the loan company and asked to see the manager.

_____ 37. The main highway was closed for repairs therefore, we had to take the detour through Shelbyville.

_____ 38. I hereby promise to pay the Liberty National Bank one thousand dollars—$1,000—plus 14% interest one year from the date of this note.

_____ 39. The following personnel have been made supervisors. Arthur Mondun, Elizabeth North, and Michael Quinn.

_____ 40. "The New York Times Magazine" is published as a supplement to the Sunday edition of "The New York Times."

_____ 41. Since my grade on the placement exam was low I had to take the course in remedial English.

_____ 42. When I returned the power mower was still in the middle of the yard.

_____ 43. Did Ann say, "I am going to go home?"

_____ 44. Joan told Sally that she, Sally, had been chosen to represent the parts department.

_____ 45. Who was the first man to reach the summit of Mount Everest?

_____46. "Let's bet two dollars on the number-seven horse", Mary suggested to her boyfriend.

_____47. The driver who goes a year without having an accident will be given an award.

_____48. The cost of living has increased steadily since the end of the Second World War. See graph attached.

_____49. Thomas Wolfe's novel "You Can't Go Home Again" was published two years after his death.

_____50. The spring semester begins on Feb 7.

© 1981 HBJ

16: Spelling

One of the most serious writing problems for many people is the inability to spell correctly and confidently. The fear of making a "stupid" mistake in spelling and exposing their "ignorance" often makes it difficult for poor spellers to put their ideas on paper. Thus, although many of these individuals may speak effectively, they tend to dread the thought of writing. The writer who is a poor speller may want to use a particular word in a sentence but, unsure of the correct spelling, may settle on a substitute that proves to be imprecise and awkward in the context. Therefore, it is to your great advantage to be an accurate and confident speller, for this will enable you to relax and let your ideas flow smoothly.

Poor spelling may be a serious handicap for reasons other than the mental block it may cause. An otherwise acceptable (maybe even superior) piece of writing may be downgraded by your teacher because of misspelled words. Employers, too, often place much emphasis on correct spelling when they screen applicants for certain jobs. For instance, if you are applying for a secretarial job you may be expected to be a faultless speller, or if you aspire to become a business executive, accurate spelling should prove helpful. What we have said about the field of business applies to most jobs and professions. Whether you become a nurse, lawyer, teacher, accountant, physician, member of the armed forces, social worker, or engineer, you will have to do some amount of writing. The ability to spell correctly will be important to your success.

At present, though, you are perhaps most concerned about your writing in college. You may have already discovered that many college instructors look on incorrect spelling as a sign of incompetence. So if you are a poor speller you should make a determined effort to overcome this handicap. Most people (unless they have a rare disability) can improve their spelling if they make the necessary effort.

You may be a better speller than you think. If you kept a record of the words that you frequently misspell, you would probably discover that they are fewer in number than you imagined. Moreover, if you study your spelling mistakes you may be surprised to discover that most of them are among the words that are listed at the end of this chapter. With determination you can master these troublesome words in a short time, especially if you apply the spelling aids that are given in the following paragraphs.

Spell one syllable at a time

Many people complain that English is not a phonetic language; some words are not spelled as they are pronounced. Thus, they are difficult to spell. There is some truth in this statement. For instance, many English words are harder to spell than, say, Spanish words. In Spanish you do not have the silent "e" or unpronounced consonants or indistinct vowel sounds. However, if you study English closely you will find that most words in the language are spelled as they are pronounced. Therefore, if you pronounce words clearly and spell one syllable at a time you will avoid many spelling errors. The several words that follow this paragraph are examples of words that are spelled as they are pronounced. In these examples and throughout this lesson, the abbreviation *Pro.* indicates how to pronounce the word, and *Spell* indicates how to spell it.

arguing
   Pro. (ar′ gu ing)
   Spell (ar gu ing)

benefited
   Pro. (ben′ e fit ed)
   Spell (ben e fit ed)

dependent
   Pro. (de pen′ dent)
   Spell (de pen dent)

destroy
   Pro. (de stroy′)
   Spell (de stroy)

independent
   Pro. (in de pen′ dent)
   Spell (in de pen dent)

partner
   Pro. (part′ ner)
   Spell (part ner)

Pay close attention to words that have double consonants, one of which is not pronounced.

Many words in the English language have double consonants, one of which is not pronounced. This peculiarity causes countless spelling mistakes. As you study the word list at the end of this chapter, note the words that fall into this class and pay close attention to how the pronunciation differs from the correct spelling. A few of these words are listed below:

abbreviate
Pro. (a bre' ve at)
Spell (ab bre vi ate)

accommodate
Pro. (a com' o dat)
Spell (ac com mo date)

appetite
Pro. (ap' e tit)
Spell (ap pe tite)

immediately
Pro. (i me' di at ly)
Spell (im me di ate ly)

occurrence
Pro. (o kur' ens)
Spell (oc cur rence)

written
Pro. (rit' n)
Spell (writ ten)

Pay close attention to indistinct vowel sounds that may cause you to misspell a word.

Another reason English is a hard language to spell is that its vowel sounds are frequently indistinct. Other languages, such as Spanish, do not present this problem. The Spanish letter *a* is always pronounced as the letter *a* in the English "father"; the other vowel sounds in Spanish are also regular. Such is not the case in English, a fact that sometimes causes serious spelling problems, even among intelligent and well-educated native speakers of English. As you study the list of words frequently misspelled, note the words that might cause you trouble because they contain a vowel sound that could be represented by one letter as well as another, such as the examples given below:

describe
Pro. (de scrib')
Spell (de scribe)

experience
Pro. (eks per' e ens)
Spell (ex per i ence)

grammar
Pro. (gram' er)
Spell (gram mar)

pursue
Pro. (per su')
Spell (pur sue)

separate
Pro. (sep' e rat)
Spell (sep a rate)

sergeant
Pro. (sar' gent)
Spell (ser geant)

To overcome this difficulty, focus your attention on the trouble spot in the word. It might also help to overpronounce the vowel sound for the sake of correct spelling, using the long sounds of the vowels. These sounds are the same as the letters of the alphabet: a, e, i, o, u. For instance, you might say sep-a-rate rather than sep-ă-rate, as the word is actually pronounced.

Pronounce words clearly and distinctly

Some words are misspelled because the speller does not pronounce them correctly. For instance, if you say "nowdays" instead of "nowadays," you may follow the incorrect pronunciation when spelling and leave out the middle syllable, "a." The word is spelled as it is correctly pronounced: "now-a-days." The same is true of *experiment;* the word is pronounced "ex-per-i-ment" as it is spelled, not "ex-per-ment." If you realize that careless speech can cause a spelling problem and therefore attempt to improve your pronunciation, you may become not only a better speller but a better speaker. Look over the word list at the end of this section and see if you can find words that you might misspell because of faulty pronunciation.

Pay close attention to words that are not spelled as they are pronounced

The words listed below are taken from the list at the end of this chapter. They are not spelled as they are pronounced. As you study the longer list, see if you can find other words that are spelled differently than they are pronounced.

achievement
Pro. (a chev' ment)
Spell (a chieve ment)

acquainted
Pro. (a kwant' ed)
Spell (ac quaint ed)

adequate
Pro. (ad' e kwit)
Spell (ad e quate)

amateur
Pro. (am' a tur)
Spell (am a teur)

analyze
Pro. (an' a liz)
Spell (an a lyze)

awkward
Pro. (ok' ward)
Spell (awk ward)

brilliant
Pro. (bril' yant)
Spell (bril liant)

conquer
Pro. (con' ker)
Spell (con quer)

conscientious
Pro. (con she en' shus)
Spell (con sci en tious)

courage
Pro. (kur' ij)
Spell (cour age)

deficiency
Pro. (de fish' en se)
Spell (de fici en cy)

efficient
Pro. (e fish' ent)
Spell (ef fici ent)

genius
Pro. (gen' yus)
Spell (gen ius)

leisure
Pro. (le' zher)
Spell (lei sure)

occurred
Pro. (o kur')
Spell (oc curred)

permission
Pro. (per mish' un)
Spell (per mis sion)

psychology
Pro. (si kol' o je)
Spell (psy chol o gy)

rhythm
Pro. (rith' m)
Spell (rhyth m)

sufficient
Pro. (su fish' ent)
Spell (suf fici ent)

thorough
Pro. (thor' o)
Spell (thor ough)

STANDARDIZED SPELLING RULES

Spelling rules are confusing to some students yet an invaluable help to others. Try to use them. If you find them baffling, forget them and concentrate on the individual words. Unless you understand the complete rule, you are probably better off not trying to apply it.

Composition textbooks contain many rules and their exceptions, but the four rules that follow are usually accepted as basic. They can be relied on in most instances.

Double the final consonant

If a word of one syllable (like *run*) or a word of more than one syllable that is accented on the last syllable (like *prefer*) ends in a single consonant preceded by a single vowel, you should double the final consonant when adding a suffix beginning with a vowel.

Words of one syllable

bag	bagged	dim	dimmed
can	canning	grin	grinning

Words accented on the last syllable

omit	omitted	admit	admitted
control	controlling	submit	submitting

Words not accented on the last syllable

benefit	benefited	profit	profiting
happen	happened		

Words that end in silent *e*

If a word ends in silent *e*, drop the *e* when a suffix beginning with a vowel is added—for example, *have–having*. If a word ends in silent *e*, retain the *e* when a suffix beginning with a consonant is added—for example, *hope–hopeful*.

Suffix begins with a vowel

abide	abiding
acquire	acquired
come	coming
dine	dined
divide	dividing
leave	leaving
glare	glared

Suffix begins with a consonant

acquire	acquirement
lone	lonely
pale	paleness
profane	profanely
rare	rarely
pure	purely
purpose	purposeful

Words that might be spelled with *ei* or *ie*

When the two letters come after the letter *c*, the *i* is preceded by the *e*.

ceiling	deceive
conceit	perceive
conceive	receipt
deceit	receive

When they follow a letter other than *c*, the sound of the syllable can usually be relied upon. If the sound is long *ee* as in piece, *i* generally comes before *e*.

achieve   niece
belief   piece
believe   priest
brief   relieve
chief   shriek

(Exceptions: either, neither, seize, leisure, financier)

When the sound is long *a* as in *sleigh*, *e* usually comes before *i* as in the following words:

eight   sleigh
neighbor   vein
reign   weight

Words ending in *y*

In words ending in *y* preceded by a consonant, change the *y* to *i* when adding a suffix; for example, *mercy–merciful*. If the suffix begins with *i*, the *y* is retained; for example, *copy–copyist*. If the final *y* is preceded by a vowel, the *y* is retained before the suffix.

y preceded by a consonant

baby   babies   happy   happiness
copy   copies   lovely   loveliness
try   tries   modify   modifier

Suffix begins with *i*

copy   copyist

y preceded by a vowel

attorney   attorneys
chimney   chimneys
enjoy   enjoys
obey   obeyed
valley   valleys

As stated before, spelling is a serious writing problem for those people whose fear of misspelling words impedes the smooth flow of thought. Therefore, when writing a first draft, you should not worry too much about spelling. If you have doubts about the spelling of a word, write it out in syllables the way it sounds. For instance, if you want to write "His diet was deficient in vitamin D" but are not sure how to spell *deficient*, write the word as it sounds (de-fish-ent), and correct it according to a dictionary after you finish writing your first draft. Excessive worry over spelling can lead to a mental block or cause you to water down your writing by using an alternate word that you can spell for the word you really need.

In giving this advice we do not mean to understate the indispensability of the dictionary as a tool in correct spelling. As you proofread your writing, if there is the slightest doubt that a word may be misspelled, look it up in your dictionary. It may well be that more than half of the misspelled words found in writing can be traced to careless proofreading.

Perhaps the best way to proofread is to use a ruler or blank piece of paper to cover the material below the line that you are reading. You will be surprised how easy it is to spot misspelled words if you proofread in this manner. It is at this point that you should become a slave to the dictionary. If you suspect that a word is misspelled, look it up in your dictionary to be on the safe side.

No doubt you have noted that in the examples that show words divided as they are pronounced, we have placed an accent mark on the syllable that is stressed. We shall follow the same procedure for the words that are listed at the end of this section. These accent marks are provided especially for the benefit of students whose native language is not English and who may not know which syllable is accented.

In concluding this chapter we wish to emphasize one spelling suggestion in particular: BECOME SYLLABLE CONSCIOUS. Once you get the hang of dividing words into syllables you can analyze words you find difficult to spell and discover the trouble spot. With interest and determination you can become a first-rate speller and a competent writer.

WORD LIST

1. abbreviate
   Pro. (a bre ve' at)
   Spell (ab bre vi ate)
2. accidentally
   Pro. (ak si den' ta le)
   Spell (ac ci den tal ly)
3. accommodate
   Pro. (a com' o dat)
   Spell (ac com mo date)
4. accompanied
   Pro. (a com' pa ned)
   Spell (ac com pa nied)
5. accumulate
   Pro. (a cum' u lat)
   Spell (ac cum u late)
6. achievement
   Pro. (a chev' ment)
   Spell (a chieve ment)
7. acquainted
   Pro. (a kwant' ed)
   Spell (ac quaint ed)
8. acquire
   Pro. (a kwir')
   Spell (ac quire)
9. address
   Pro. (a dres')
   Spell (ad dress)

10. adequate
    Pro. (ad' e kwit)
    Spell (ad e quate)
11. advice
    Pro. (ad vis')
    Spell (ad vice)
12. aggravate
    Pro. (ag' ra vat)
    Spell (ag gra vate)
13. all right
    Pro. (al rit')
    Spell (all right)
14. amateur
    Pro. (am' a tur)
    Spell (am a teur)
15. analyze
    Pro. (an' a liz)
    Spell (an a lyze)
16. apparent
    Pro. (a par' ent)
    Spell (ap par ent)
17. appearance
    Pro. (a per' ans)
    Spell (ap pear ance)
18. appetite
    Pro. (ap' e tit)
    Spell (ap pe tite)

19. approaching
    Pro. (a proch' ing)
    Spell (ap proach ing)
20. appropriate
    Pro. (a pro' pri it)
    Spell (ap pro pri ate)
21. approximately
    Pro. (a prok' si mit le)
    Spell (ap prox i mate ly)
22. arguing
    Pro. (ar' gu ing)
    Spell (ar gu ing)
23. argument
    Pro. (ar' gu ment)
    Spell (ar gu ment)
24. arrangement
    Pro. (a rang' ment)
    Spell (ar range ment)
25. article
    Pro. (ar' ti kul)
    Spell (ar ti cle)
26. athletic
    Pro. (ath let' ik)
    Spell (ath let ic)
27. awkward
    Pro. (ok' ward)
    Spell (awk ward)

28. balance
    Pro. (bal' ans)
    Spell (bal ance)
29. beginning
    Pro. (be gin' ing)
    Spell (be gin ning)
30. belief
    Pro. (be lef')
    Spell (be lief)
31. believe
    Pro. (be lev')
    Spell (be lieve)
32. beneficial
    Pro. (ben e fish' al)
    Spell (ben e fici al)
33. benefited
    Pro. (ben' e fit ed)
    Spell (ben e fit ed)
34. breathe
    Pro. (breth)
    Spell (breathe)
35. brilliant
    Pro. (bril' yant)
    Spell (bril liant)
36. buried
    Pro. (ber' ed)
    Spell (bur ied)
37. business
    Pro. (biz' nes)
    Spell (bus i ness)
38. calculate
    Pro. (kal' ku lat)
    Spell (cal cu late)
39. carrying
    Pro. (car' e ing)
    Spell (car ry ing)
40. changeable
    Pro. (chan' ja bul)
    Spell (chan gea ble)
41. collaborate
    Pro. (co lab' o rat)
    Spell (col lab o rate)
42. committee
    Pro. (co mit' e)
    Spell (com mit tee)
43. competition
    Pro. (com pe tish' un)
    Spell (com pe titi on)
44. conceive
    Pro. (con sev')
    Spell (con ceive)
45. conquer
    Pro. (con' ker)
    Spell (con quer)
46. conscientious
    Pro. (con she en' shus)
    Spell (con sci en tious)

47. conscious
    Pro. (con' shus)
    Spell (con scious)
48. continually
    Pro. (con tin' u a le)
    Spell (con tin u al ly)
49. controversial
    Pro. (con tro ver' shul)
    Spell (con tro ver sial)
50. controversy
    Pro. (con' tro ver se)
    Spell (con tro ver sy)
51. convenience
    Pro. (con ven' yuns)
    Spell (con ven ience)
52. copies
    Pro. (cop' es)
    Spell (cop ies)
53. courage
    Pro. (kur' ij)
    Spell (cour age)
54. course
    Pro. (kors)
    Spell (course)
55. courteous
    Pro. (kur' te us)
    Spell (cour te ous)
56. courtesy
    Pro. (kur' te se)
    Spell (cour te sy)
57. criticism
    Pro. (crit' i cis m)
    Spell (crit i cis m)
58. criticized
    Pro. (crit' i sized)
    Spell (crit i cized)
59. damage
    Pro. (dam' ij)
    Spell (dam age)
60. decision
    Pro. (de sizh' un)
    Spell (de cisi on)
61. deficiency
    Pro. (de fish' en se)
    Spell (de fici en cy)
62. define
    Pro. (de fin')
    Spell (de fine)
63. definitely
    Pro. (def' i nit le)
    Spell (def i nite ly)
64. definition
    Pro. (def i nish' on)
    Spell (def i niti on)
65. dependent
    Pro. (de pen' dent)
    Spell (de pen dent)

66. describe
    Pro. (de skrib')
    Spell (de scribe)
67. description
    Pro. (de scrip' shun)
    Spell (de scrip tion)
68. desirable
    Pro. (de zir' a bul)
    Spell (de sir a ble)
69. despair
    Pro. (de sper')
    Spell (de spair)
70. desperate
    Pro. (des' per it)
    Spell (des per ate)
71. destroy
    Pro. (de stroy')
    Spell (de stroy)
72. deteriorated
    Pro. (de ter' e o rat ed)
    Spell (de ter i o rat ed)
73. develop
    Pro. (de vel' up)
    Spell (de vel op)
74. different
    Pro. (dif' er unt)
    Spell (dif fer ent)
75. dining
    Pro. (din' ing)
    Spell (din ing)
76. disappeared
    Pro. (dis a pird')
    Spell (dis ap peared)
77. disappointed
    Pro. (dis' a point ed)
    Spell (dis ap point ed)
78. disastrous
    Pro. (dis as' trus)
    Spell (dis as trous)
79. discipline
    Pro. (dis' i plin)
    Spell (dis ci pline)
80. diseases
    Pro. (di zez' es)
    Spell (di seas es)
81. dissatisfied
    Pro. (dis sat' is fid)
    Spell (dis sat is fied)
82. division
    Pro. (di vizh' on)
    Spell (di visi on)
83. effect
    Pro. (e fect')
    Spell (ef fect)
84. efficiency
    Pro. (e fish' un ce)
    Spell (ef fici en cy)

85. efficient
   Pro. (e fish' unt)
   Spell (ef fici ent)
86. effort
   Pro. (ef' ert)
   Spell (ef fort)
87. embarrass
   Pro. (em bar' as)
   Spell (em bar rass)
88. emotional
   Pro. (e mo' shun al)
   Spell (e mo tion al)
89. emphasize
   Pro. (em' fa siz)
   Spell (em pha size)
90. enthusiastic
   Pro. (in thoo ze as' tik)
   Spell (en thu si as tic)
91. environment
   Pro. (en vi' ron ment)
   Spell (en vi ron ment)
92. equipped
   Pro. (e kwipt')
   Spell (e quipped)
93. especially
   Pro. (es pesh' a le)
   Spell (es peci al ly)
94. exaggerate
   Pro. (eg zaj ' er at)
   Spell (ex ag ger ate)
95. excellent
   Pro. (ek' se lunt)
   Spell (ex cel lent)
96. excitement
   Pro. (ek sit' ment)
   Spell (ex cite ment)
97. executive
   Pro. (eg zek' u tiv)
   Spell (e xec u tive)
98. exhausted
   Pro. (eg zost' ed)
   Spell (ex haust ed)
99. existence
   Pro. (eg zis' tens)
   Spell (ex is tence)
100. existent
   Pro. (eg zis' tent)
   Spell (ex is tent)
101. experience
   Pro. (eks per' e uns)
   Spell (ex per i ence)
102. explanation
   Pro. (eks pla na' shun)
   Spell (ex pla na tion)
103. familiar
   Pro. (fa mil' yer)
   Spell (fa mil iar)

104. fascinate
   Pro. (fas' i nat)
   Spell (fas ci nate)
105. feature
   Pro. (fe' chur)
   Spell (fea ture)
106. finally
   Pro. (fi' na le)
   Spell (fi nal ly)
107. foreign
   Pro. (for' in)
   Spell (for eign)
108. formally
   Pro. (for' ma le)
   Spell (for mal ly)
109. formerly
   Pro. (for' mer le)
   Spell (for mer ly)
110. forty
   Pro. (for' te)
   Spell (for ty)
111. fourth
   Pro. (forth)
   Spell (fourth)
112. friend
   Pro. (frend)
   Spell (friend)
113. generally
   Pro. (gen' er a le)
   Spell (gen er al ly)
114. genius
   Pro. (gen' yus)
   Spell (gen ius)
115. government
   Pro. (gov' ern ment)
   Spell (gov ern ment)
116. grammar
   Pro. (gram' er)
   Spell (gram mar)
117. guarantee
   Pro. (gar' an te)
   Spell (guar an tee)
118. guard
   Pro. (gard)
   Spell (guard)
119. height
   Pro. (hit)
   Spell (height)
120. hindrance
   Pro. (hin' drans)
   Spell (hin drance)
121. hurriedly
   Pro. (hur' id le)
   Spell (hur ried ly)
122. hypocrisy
   Pro. (hi pok' ri se)
   Spell (hy poc ri sy)

123. imagination
   Pro. (i maj' i na shun)
   Spell (i mag i na tion)
124. immediately
   Pro. (i me' de ut le)
   Spell (im me di ate ly)
125. incidentally
   Pro. (in si dent' a le)
   Spell (in ci dent al ly)
126. independent
   Pro. (in de pen' dent)
   Spell (in de pen dent)
127. influence
   Pro. (in' floo ens)
   Spell (in flu ence)
128. initiative
   Pro. (i nish' u tiv)
   Spell (i nit i a tive)
129. intelligence
   Pro. (in tel' i juns)
   Spell (in tel li gence)
130. interfere
   Pro. (in ter fer')
   Spell (in ter fere)
131. interpreted
   Pro. (in ter' pre ted)
   Spell (in ter pre ted)
132. interrupted
   Pro. (in te rup' ted)
   Spell (in ter rup ted)
133. irresistible
   Pro. (ir e zis' ti bul)
   Spell (ir re sis ti ble)
134. judgment
   Pro. (juj' ment)
   Spell (judg ment)
135. juvenile
   Pro. (joo' ve nil)
   Spell (ju ve nile)
136. knowledge
   Pro. (nol' ej)
   Spell (know ledge)
137. laboratory
   Pro. (lab' o ra to re)
   Spell (lab o ra to ry)
138. laid
   Pro. (lad)
   Spell (laid)
139. led
   Pro. (led)
   Spell (led)
140. leisure
   Pro. (le' zher)
   Spell (lei sure)
141. lightning
   Pro. (lit' ning)
   Spell (light ning)

142. livelihood
Pro. (liv′ le hood)
Spell (live li hood)
143. loneliness
Pro. (lon′ le ness)
Spell (lone li ness)
144. lose
Pro. (looz)
Spell (lose)
145. losing
Pro. (looz′ ing)
Spell (los ing)
146. luxury
Pro. (lug′ zhoo re)
Spell (lux u ry)
147. maintenance
Pro. (man′ te nans)
Spell (main te nance)
148. marriage
Pro. (mar′ ij)
Spell (mar riage)
149. mathematics
Pro. (math e mat′ iks)
Spell (math e mat ics)
150. mechanic
Pro. (me kan′ ik)
Spell (me chan ic)
151. meant
Pro. (ment)
Spell (meant)
152. medicine
Pro. (med′ i sin)
Spell (med i cine)
153. mediocre
Pro. (me de o′ ker)
Spell (me di o cre)
154. mere
Pro. (mer)
Spell (mere)
155. miniature
Pro. (min′ e a tur)
Spell (min i a ture)
156. minute
Pro. (min′ it)
Spell (min ute)
157. mysterious
Pro. (mis ter′ e us)
Spell (mys ter i ous)
158. naturally
Pro. (nach′ u ra le)
Spell (nat u ral ly)
159. necessary
Pro. (nes′ e sar e)
Spell (nec es sar y)
160. nevertheless
Pro. (nev er the les′)
Spell (nev er the less)

161. nickel
Pro. (nik′ el)
Spell (nick el)
162. niece
Pro. (nes)
Spell (niece)
163. ninety
Pro. (nin′ te)
Spell (nine ty)
164. ninth
Pro. (ninth)
Spell (ninth)
165. noisily
Pro. (nois′ i le)
Spell (nois i ly)
166. noticeable
Pro. (no′ tis a bul)
Spell (no tice a ble)
167. nowadays
Pro. (now′ a daz)
Spell (now a days)
168. occasion
Pro. (o ka′ zhun)
Spell (oc ca sion)
169. occasionally
Pro. (o ka′ zhun a le)
Spell (oc ca sion al ly)
170. occurred
Pro. (o kurd′)
Spell (oc curred)
171. occurrence
Pro. (o kur′ ens)
Spell (oc cur rence)
172. occurring
Pro. (o kur′ ing)
Spell (oc cur ring)
173. omission
Pro. (o mish′ un)
Spell (o missi on)
174. omitted
Pro. (o mit′ ed)
Spell (o mit ted)
175. operate
Pro. (op′ er at)
Spell (op er ate)
176. opinion
Pro. (o pin′ yun)
Spell (o pin ion)
177. opportunity
Pro. (op or tu ′ ni te)
Spell (op por tu ni ty)
178. original
Pro. (o rij′ i nal)
Spell (o rig i nal)
179. paid
Pro. (pad)
Spell (paid)

180. paragraph
Pro. (par′ a graf)
Spell (par a graph)
181. parallel
Pro. (par′ a lel)
Spell (par al lel)
182. paralyzed
Pro. (par′ a lizd)
Spell (par a lyzed)
183. parliament
Pro. (par′ li ment)
Spell (par li a ment)
184. particular
Pro. (par tik′ u ler)
Spell (par tic u lar)
185. partner
Pro. (part′ ner)
Spell (part ner)
186. pastime
Pro. (pas′ tim)
Spell (pas time)
187. peculiar
Pro. (pe kyul′ yer)
Spell (pe cul iar)
188. performance
Pro. (per for ′ muns)
Spell (per for mance)
189. perhaps
Pro. (per haps′)
Spell (per haps)
190. permission
Pro. (per mish′ un)
Spell (per mis sion)
191. persistent
Pro. (per sis′ tent)
Spell (per sis tent)
192. personal
Pro. (per′ son al)
Spell (per son al)
193. personnel
Pro. (per so nel′)
Spell (per son nel)
194. persuade
Pro. (per swad′)
Spell (per suade)
195. physically
Pro. (fiz′ i ka le)
Spell (phys i cal ly)
196. piece
Pro. (pes)
Spell (piece)
197. pleasant
Pro. (plez′ unt)
Spell (pleas ant)
198. possession
Pro. (po zesh′ un)
Spell (pos sessi on)

199. possible
Pro. (pos' i bul)
Spell (pos si ble)

200. practical
Pro. (prak' ti kal)
Spell (prac ti cal)

201. precede
Pro. (pre sed')
Spell (pre cede)

202. precision
Pro. (pre sizh' un)
Spell (pre cisi on)

203. preference
Pro. (pref' er ens)
Spell (pref er ence)

204. preferred
Pro. (pre furd')
Spell (pre ferred)

205. prejudice
Pro. (prej' u dis)
Spell (prej u dice)

206. prepare
Pro. (pre par')
Spell (pre pare)

207. prevalent
Pro. (prev' a lent)
Spell (prev a lent)

208. principal
Pro. (prin' ci pul)
Spell (prin ci pal)

209. principle
Pro. (prin' ci pul)
Spell (prin ci ple)

210. privilege
Pro. (priv' i lej)
Spell (priv i lege)

211. probably
Pro. (prob' a ble)
Spell (prob a bly)

212. procedure
Pro. (pro ce' jur)
Spell (pro ce dure)

213. proceed
Pro. (pro sed')
Spell (pro ceed)

214. profession
Pro. (pro fesh' un)
Spell (pro fessi on)

215. professor
Pro. (pro fes' er)
Spell (pro fes sor)

216. propeller
Pro. (pro pel' er)
Spell (pro pel ler)

217. psychology
Pro. (si kol' o ji)
Spell (psy chol o gy)

218. pursue
Pro. (pur su')
Spell (pur sue)

219. quantity
Pro. (kwon' ti te)
Spell (quan ti ty)

220. quiet
Pro. (kwi' et)
Spell (qui et)

221. quite
Pro. (kwit)
Spell (quite)

222. quitting
Pro. (kwit' ing)
Spell (quit ting)

223. realize
Pro. (re' a liz)
Spell (re a lize)

224. really
Pro. (re' a le)
Spell (re al ly)

225. receive
Pro. (re sev')
Spell (re ceive)

226. receiving
Pro. (re sev' ing)
Spell (re ceiv ing)

227. recognize
Pro. (rec' og niz)
Spell (rec og nize)

228. recommend
Pro. (rec' o mend)
Spell (rec om mend)

229. referring
Pro. (re fer' ing)
Spell (re fer ring)

230. relieve
Pro. (re lev')
Spell (re lieve)

231. religious
Pro. (re lij' us)
Spell (re lig ious)

232. repetition
Pro. (rep e tish' on)
Spell (rep e titi on)

233. resource
Pro. (re' sors)
Spell (re source)

234. restaurant
Pro. (res' to rant)
Spell (res tau rant)

235. rhythm
Pro. (rith' m)
Spell (rhyth m)

236. ridicule
Pro. (rid' i kyul)
Spell (rid i cule)

237. ridiculous
Pro. (ri dik' u lus)
Spell (ri dic u lous)

238. sacrifice
Pro. (sac' ri fis)
Spell (sac ri fice)

239. safety
Pro. (saf' te)
Spell (safe ty)

240. scarcely
Pro. (skars' le)
Spell (scarce ly)

241. schedule
Pro. (skej' yul)
Spell (sched ule)

242. science
Pro. (si' ens)
Spell (sci ence)

243. secretary
Pro. (sec' re tar e)
Spell (sec re tar y)

244. seize
Pro. (sez)
Spell (seize)

245. sense
Pro. (sens)
Spell (sense)

246. separate
Pro. (sep' a rat)
Spell (sep a rate)

247. separation
Pro. (sep a ra' shun)
Spell (sep a ra tion)

248. sergeant
Pro. (sar' junt)
Spell (ser geant)

249. severely
Pro. (se ver' le)
Spell (se vere ly)

250. shining
Pro. (shin' ing)
Spell (shin ing)

251. similar
Pro. (sim' i ler)
Spell (sim i lar)

252. sincerely
Pro. (sin ser' le)
Spell (sin cere ly)

253. sophomore
Pro. (sof' o mor)
Spell (soph o more)

254. source
Pro. (sors)
Spell (source)

255. specific
Pro. (spe sif' ik)
Spell (spe cif ic)

256. stomach
 Pro. (stum' ak)
 Spell (stom ach)
257. stopped
 Pro. (stopt)
 Spell (stopped)
258. strength
 Pro. (strength)
 Spell (strength)
259. stretched
 Pro. (strecht)
 Spell (stretched)
260. studying
 Pro. (stud' e ing)
 Spell (stud y ing)
261. succeed
 Pro. (suk sed')
 Spell (suc ceed)
262. successful
 Pro. (suk ses' ful)
 Spell (suc cess ful)
263. succession
 Pro. (suk sesh' un)
 Spell (suc cessi on)
264. sufficient
 Pro. (su fish' ent)
 Spell (suf fici ent)
265. summary
 Pro. (sum' a re)
 Spell (sum ma ry)
266. suppress
 Pro. (su pres')
 Spell (sup press)
267. surely
 Pro. (shoor' le)
 Spell (sure ly)
268. surprise
 Pro. (sur priz')
 Spell (sur prise)
269. suspicion
 Pro. (sus pish' un)
 Spell (sus pici on)
270. technique
 Pro. (tek nek')
 Spell (tech nique)

271. than
 Pro. (than)
 Spell (than)
272. their
 Pro. (ther)
 Spell (their)
273. then
 Pro. (then)
 Spell (then)
274. there
 Pro. (ther)
 Spell (there)
275. they're
 Pro. (ther)
 Spell (they're)
276. thorough
 Pro. (thur' o)
 Spell (thor ough)
277. though
 Pro. (tho)
 Spell (though)
278. thought
 Pro. (thot)
 Spell (thought)
279. through
 Pro. (throo)
 Spell (through)
280. truly
 Pro. (tru' le)
 Spell (tru ly)
281. undoubtedly
 Pro. (un dou' ted le)
 Spell (un doubt ed ly)
282. unnecessary
 Pro. (un nes' e sar e)
 Spell (un nec es sar y)
283. until
 Pro. (un til')
 Spell (un til)
284. usually
 Pro. (u' zhoo a le)
 Spell (u su al ly)
285. varieties
 Pro. (va ri' e tez)
 Spell (va ri e ties)

286. vegetable
 Pro. (vej' ta bul)
 Spell (veg e ta ble)
287. vigorous
 Pro. (vig' er us)
 Spell (vig or ous)
288. village
 Pro. (vil' ij)
 Spell (vil lage)
289. wander
 Pro. (won' der)
 Spell (wan der)
290. weather
 Pro. (weth' er)
 Spell (weath er)
291. whether
 Pro. (weth' er)
 Spell (wheth er)
292. whole
 Pro. (hol)
 Spell (whole)
293. wholly
 Pro. (hol' le)
 Spell (whol ly)
294. who's
 Pro. (hooz)
 Spell (who's)
295. whose
 Pro. (hooz)
 Spell (whose)
296. wonder
 Pro. (wun' der)
 Spell (won der)
297. worrying
 Pro. (wur' e ing)
 Spell (wor ry ing)
298. write
 Pro. (rit)
 Spell (write)
299. writing
 Pro. (rit' ing)
 Spell (writ ing)
300. written
 Pro. (rit' n)
 Spell (writ ten)

A 0
B 1
C 2
D 3
E 4
F 5
G 6
H 7
I 8
J 9